Historic Graves

of Maryland and the District of Columbia

Edited Under the Auspices of
The Maryland Society of the
Colonial Dames of America

by

Helen W. Ridgely

HERITAGE BOOKS
2010

HERITAGE BOOKS
AN IMPRINT OF HERITAGE BOOKS, INC.

Books, CDs, and more—Worldwide

For our listing of thousands of titles see our website
at
www.HeritageBooks.com

A Facsimile Reprint
Published 2010 by
HERITAGE BOOKS, INC.
Publishing Division
100 Railroad Ave. #104
Westminster, Maryland 21157

Copyright © 1908 The Grafton Press

— Publisher's Notice —
In reprints such as this, it is often not possible to remove blemishes from the original. We feel the contents of this book warrant its reissue despite these blemishes and hope you will agree and read it with pleasure.

International Standard Book Numbers
Paperbound: 978-1-58549-209-1
Clothbound: 978-0-7884-8521-3

HISTORIC GRAVES OF MARYLAND AND THE DISTRICT OF COLUMBIA

SLAB FROM THE FRANCIS SOURTON TOMB
Poplar Hill Church, St. Mary's County

FOREWORD

IN the history of the early settlements along the Chesapeake and its tributaries, there is found a continuity of English customs adapted to new conditions; and during the sixty years that elapsed between the arrival of the first colonists and the historic period of church building in Maryland, manorial customs in modes of sepulture prevailed. In fact, the burial of the dead on the home plantation—or near the chapel of the Lord of the Manor, as we have reason to believe was the habit among the Catholics—continued even after the enactment of laws for the building of churches or the walling in of churchyards.

Some of the most interesting monuments of bygone days have been found on out-of-the-way farms, and even where monuments are wanting, tradition often indicates the spot where some manor lord or Colonial Governor lies buried. The various stones, tablets and traditions, still remaining serve to revive much of Maryland's primitive social life. Had it not been for the vandalism of some and the ignorance of others, much more might be found to supply missing links in county records, or to fill the gaps in carelessly kept parish registers.

The facts collected in this book are the result of an investigation set on foot by the Maryland Society of the Colonial Dames of America, with a view to promote a more general knowledge of such things, and to quicken an interest in the preservation of our ancient monuments and places of burial. Isolated stones have been found in fields, by the roadside and beneath dwellings, also in use as doorsteps or as flagstones with the inscriptions turned under. By the efforts of a committee known as the Memorial Committee some of these have been removed to the nearest churchyard, where they stand a better chance of remaining unmolested, while others have been restored, railed in or otherwise protected.

During the process of investigation, unsuspected nooks and corners of interest, left undisturbed by the march of progress, have been discovered, and it is in these sequestered neighborhoods that the work of the Memorial Committee has aroused the keenest interest and met with the most cordial response. By the assistance of both men and women recruits, thickets have been penetrated, traditionary graveyards traced, shattered tablets fitted together and inscriptions copied or verified.

The gravestone of the earliest date yet found in Maryland lies in Anne Arundel county, that section of the Province which in 1649–50 saw the arrival of the Puritans. Near it is a memorial to Christopher Birkhead, who died in 1676. For more than two hundred years these stones lay at "Birkhead's Meadows." In 1888 they were removed to St. James Parish Churchyard, and their scanty history shows a custom in Maryland—namely, that of burying the dead in private grounds—which has been the cause why so few graves from remote times have been preserved. In fact, the seventeenth-century tombs are limited to thirty-one; though some persons claim that a stone, inserted of late years in the wall of the dwelling at Bohemia Manor, once marked the burial place of Augustine Herman. He speaks of it in his will as his "Monument Stone," and on it describes himself "Bohemian, The First Founder and seater of Bohemea Manner, Anno. 1661." It was doubtless prepared in his lifetime. He died about the year 1686. The seventeenth-century inscriptions will appear among those of the counties where they belong, but a few of the worthies, whose names they commemorate, must find more particular mention here.

Foreword

The sudden departure of Christopher Rousby in 1684, for other worlds, opens to us a chapter revealing the jealousy that existed between the King's collectors of customs and those of the Lord Proprietary. Rousby's tomb, which records also the death of his brother John, in 1685, lies on the St. Mary's side of the Patuxent—across the river from the historic seat of the family, "Rousby Hall." Maj. Thomas Truman, another figure on the background of the past, also calls to mind incidents of dramatic significance. Impeached in 1676 for the "barbarous murder" of five Indians, he was subsequently released, and restored to posts of honor under his Lordship's government. He died in 1684, within a year of his change of fortune. Near him were buried his wife Mary, his brother Nathaniel, Commissioner of the Peace in 1675-76, his brother James and members of his family whose deaths occurred during the following century. After the Rousby and Truman tragedies, it sounds tame to mention persons holding positions as Councillor, Deputy Governor, General of the Military Forces of the Province, or Keeper of the Great Seal. Col. William Burgess, who died in 1686, and Col. Nicholas Greenberry, who died in 1697, divided, and in some cases shared, these honors between them.

In the private burying ground at Wye House, Talbot county, the only one where the dead of two centuries repose side by side with their descendants of the present generation, Col. Philemon Lloyd, a well-known dignitary, was buried in 1685, and his wife, a namesake of the unfortunate Queen Henrietta Maria, in 1697. The inscription on her tomb is fragmentary. This was erected by Richard Bennett, her son by a former marriage, who died in 1749 and was buried at Bennett's Point. The stones at "Wye" show many a well executed escutcheon; only "the boast of heraldry" is usually accompanied by the inevitable skull and cross bones.

George Robins, another seventeenth-century character,

settled in Talbot county in 1670. The tract of one thousand acres which came to him under the name of "Job's Content" descended to posterity as "Peach Blossom." On this place now owned by strangers is to be found a promiscuous heap, where young trees and bushes have thriven in spite of the rival claims of marble, brick and stone. A broken arch supporting the mass on one side, has served the same purpose as a bit of wreck on a sandy beach, catching and holding whatever time and tide waft in its direction. Under this drift of the centuries George Robins lies, and strewed about are fragments of his descendants' tombs.

A stone that stands as a monument to the filial piety of a certain Mary Dawson is that of Thomas Impey, and is to be found on the farm of the late James Hazlett in the Bay Hundred district, Talbot county.

The few examples given above furnish an epitome of what is to follow. They call our attention to the people of Maryland, who acted their part in unsettled times or figured with distinction in positions of authority; or better still, who stood as the exponents of family affection. Also with them lay the germ of patriotism that developed at the time of the Revolution, adding to our history the names of heroes, statesmen and divines.

HELEN W. RIDGELY.

"HAMPTON,"
Baltimore, Maryland.

Members of the Memorial Committee of the Maryland Society of the Colonial Dames of America

Mrs. Matthew Atkinson.
Mrs. Robert Atkinson.
Mrs. James Bateman.
Mrs. Belknap.
Mrs. Eugene Blackford.
*Mrs. A. H. Blackiston.
Miss Ida Brent.
Mrs. Tracy Browne.
Mrs. Roberdeau Buchanan.
Mrs. Charles B. Calvert.
*Mrs. Duncan Campbell.
Miss Campbell.
Miss Mary C. Carter.
Mrs. Thomas C. Chatard.
Mrs. Burton Crane, née Smith.
Miss Daves.
Miss Mary Davis.
Miss Ella Loraine Dorsey.
Miss Isabel Earle.
Mrs. Alex. Early.
Mrs. Charles Gibson.
*Mrs. Wm. H. Gill.
Mrs. W. Goldsborough.
Mrs. Monte Griffith.
Mrs. George W. S. Hall.
Mrs. Wm. T. Hamilton.
Mrs. K. Kearney Henry.
*Mrs. O. Horsey (Hon. Member).
Mrs. Robert Hinckley.
Mrs. Harry P. Huse.
Mrs. J. J. Jackson.

Mrs. Plowden Jenkins.
Mrs. J. Kinear.
*Miss Virginia King.
Mrs. Frederick von Kapff.
Miss Margaret Leakin.
Miss Elizabeth Ligon.
Mrs. John M. Littig.
Mrs. Lloyd Lowndes.
Mrs. Gustav Lurman.
Miss Sallie G. Mackall.
Miss Florence Mackubin.
Mrs. John R. Magruder.
*Mrs. John Mullan.
Mrs. W. C. Nicholas.
Mrs. Owen Norris.
Miss Juliana T. Paca.
Miss Mary S. W. Pearre.
Mrs. Wm. S. Powell.
Miss Anna M. Polk.
Mrs. John Ridgely of Hampton.
*Mrs. John Ritchie.
Miss Louisa Robinson.
Mrs. Henry Rogers.
Mrs. C. Lyon Rogers.
Mrs. Albert L. Sioussat.
Miss V. McBlair Smith.
Miss Mary E. Steuart.
Miss Henrietta Steuart.
Miss Mary Tilghman.
Miss Charlotte Thompson.

* Deceased.

CONTENTS

CHAPTER I 1

Historic St. Anne's, Annapolis. The City cemetery. Facts and fancies about the tombs at "Greenberry's Point." The graveyards at "Whitehall," "Brampton," "Bellefield," "Mt. Stewart" and "Belvior;" a notable group. The Quaker burying ground at West River. Anecdote about a privateer turned pirate. A seventeenth-century worthy buried at "Java" supposed to be of the same family as the author of the "Junius Letters." All Hallows' churchyard. The owner of the brig Peggy Stewart and the historic South River Club. Herring Creek churchyard and the oldest tomb in Maryland. St. Margaret's Westminster and other churchyards.

CHAPTER II 27

St. Mary's county and one of the earliest of the Jesuit missions. Historic homesteads. All Faith churchyard. St. Joseph's churchyard, also the graveyards of St. Aloysius, the Sacred Heart, St. John's, St. Francis and St. Nicholas where repose the Roman Catholic dead. Chaptico churchyard and its traditions. The "Three Notched Road," "Trent Hall," and some seventeenth-century worthies. Charlotte Hall and the Dent Memorial. The "Plains," "Cornfield Harbor," "Fresh Pond Neck," "Porto Bello," "Ellenborough," "Deep Falls." The ancient but now defunct "City of St. Maries." The first burial place on record in 1658.

CHAPTER III 50

Calvert county, a peninsular with historic coves and creeks. The refuge of a deposed commander of a county. An epitaph from Whitechurch, England, a connecting link with the Old World. A Popish priest tried after death, showing the celebrated act of Toleration in abeyance. Ancestors of the first Governor of the State. "Hallowing Point" and something about ferries. Christ Church, its early promoters and its monuments. Middleham chapel, its ancient bell and its graveyard. The lady who married two husbands, but died at the age of 75, having lived half that time a widow. Port Tobacco, Charles county. One of the oldest stations of the

xii   Contents

Jesuits. "Rose Hill" and the Gustavus Browns. "Paynton Manor" and the Stones. "Equality" and the Hansons. St. Mary's Roman Catholic church and extracts from the church register of Upper and Lower Zacaiah and Mattawoman congregations. Indian arrow heads. The Smallwood monument. A list of those interested in the repairs of old Durham church in 1792. The Piccawaxen churchyard. Another Jesuit mission and St Peter's cemetery. "Marshall Hall," "Pamonky."

CHAPTER IV   74

A jaunt through Prince George's county. Old St. Barnabas, its memorial windows and its churchyard. "Covington's Fields." "Ranelagh." "Belair." St. Thomas' church near Croome and the home of Maryland's first bishop. The Waring genealogy on an eighteenth-century tomb. "Brookfield." "Brookfield Manor." Tribute to a young wife. St. Paul's churchyard. The undertaker Joy and his horses "Brightly" and "Sprightly." Magounskin and the Greenfield tombs. Wanton destruction at "White's Landing." The "Burnt House" farm. Oldfield's chapel. The old gentleman with the plaited beard. The glebe of Trinity parish and the old graveyard. "Birmingham," "Montpelier," "Oakland" and other estates of the Snowden family. The Calverts of Riversdale.

CHAPTER V   92

The venerable age of Baltimore county. Harford county an offshoot. The site of a defunct town on the Bush river. A name on an ancient tomb unlocking some of the local history of the past. How Spesutia church got its name. Those buried in its churchyard. "Pretty Betty Martin, tip-toe fine." Vandalism. Churchyards of different religious sects. "Priest Neal's Mass House" and a Jesuit burying ground. Aquila Deaver and Lafayette. Abingdon and the first Methodist college for higher education in the world. "My Lady's Manor" and the Manor church and churchyard. Old St. John's and the defunct town of Joppa. Patapsco Hundred and the first St. Paul's churchyard. The historic name of Jones perpetuated for more than two hundred years in "Jones' Falls."

CHAPTER VI 116

The Garrison Forest church and churchyard. A man who "enjoyed the respect and esteem of a select acquaintance." "Saters" the oldest baptist meetinghouse and its graveyard. Druid Hill Park and the graves of its original owners. Family burying grounds of the Hunts, the Howards, the Talbotts, the Merrymans, the Harrymans, the Nisbets, the Cockeys, the

Contents xiii

Jessups, the Roystons, the Peerces, the Ridgelys, the Taylors, the Stansburys and the Hillens. St. John's churchyard, Worthington Valley. The Worthington tombs and others. Howard county: some of the Ellicott and Dorsey graves. Historic Christ church. The Rt. Rev. Thomas Claggett again. "Doughoregan," the old manor house in Carroll county where lived Charles Carroll of Carrollton, the last surviving signer of the Declaration of Independence.

CHAPTER VII 159

All Saints parish churchyard. Frederick. A memorial to Thos. Johnson the first governor of the State of Maryland. Linganore cemetery and traditions of Asbury. "Pleasant Fields." Mt. Olivet cemetery and Francis Scott Key. The Roman Catholic Cemetery and Chief Justice Taney. The priests' cemetery at Emmittsburg. The burying ground of the Elder family at "Pleasant Valley" mission. Washington county and the founder of Hagerstown. St. John's graveyard and that of the Lutherans. Riverview cemetery and more vandalism. Mountain View cemetery and the old Lutheran churchyard, Sharpsburg. "Fountain Rock." "Rockland." The "Vale." Alleghany county, and a "soldier of the Revolution."

CHAPTER VIII 171

Old traditions preserved by the Monocacy Cemetery Society of Montgomery county. The Rock Creek mission, the "Nancy Carroll" chapel and an interesting graveyard. Some of the old family graveyards of Montgomery county in which we find the names of Crabb, Griffith, Johns, Bowie, Davis, Dorsey, Magruder, Cooke, Hempstone, Trundle and others.

CHAPTER IX 184

Kent Island and Col. Wm. Claiborne. The first churchyard on Broad creek. Bennett's Point and its graves. "Bolingly," Queenstown. "The Hermitage" and its quaint epitaphs. Public cemetery at Centreville. Old family servants in the Earle lot. "Readbourne." St. Luke's, Church Hill. A revolutionary worthy and his political creed. "Meadow and Vale." "Ripley." "Cloverfields." St. Paul's churchyard and its beautiful oaks. Tablet in Emmanuel church to a "good Woman." Public cemetery near Chestertown. The "Whitehouse" farm. Shrewsbury church and churchyard. Quaint inscriptions. Gap in tombstone records left by the removal to Philadelphia of the Cadwalader tomb. Graves at Hillsborough, Caroline county. Nathan Trifett, a centenarian. The Roman Catholic cemetery.

xiv   Contents

CHAPTER X 205

Ancient parishes at Talbot county. The Whitemarsh churchyard. Restoration of the Robert Morris tomb. A return from the grave, the experience of a rector's wife. "Plinhimmon." "Peach Blossom." "Orem's Delight." "Belleville." "Mt. Pleasant." "Hope." "Isthmus." "Pleasant Valley." "Grosses." "Delmore-end." An old Edmondson place. "Wye," for more than two and a half centuries, the home of one family. The burial ground and quaint inscriptions. St. Luke's, Wye Mills, and its traditions. St. Michael's and an early rector. "Rich Neck" and a fortunate couple described by the husband in an epitaph: "In love and Friendship all our years were spent, In Moderate wealth and free from want, content." "Spencer Hall." "Hampden." "Spring Hill cemetery, Easton. The Quakers of Tred Avon and Wenlock Christison. A day when there were no old maids and when widows were scarcely allowed time for mourning.

CHAPTER XI 225

Cecil, a part of Baltimore county until the year 1674. Site of first Baltimore town. Parishes of North and South Sassafras. Early rectors and vestrymen of St. Stephen's. St. Mary Anne's, North Elk. Augustine Herman and Bohemia Manor. Six generations buried in the Baldwin-Milligan-McLane graveyard. "Success" farm and Cromwellian traditions. What an "Old Mortality" of Cecil county has to say. The churchyards of Somerset county. Old Monie churchyard and the Stoughton tomb. The cradle of the Presbyterian church in America. Burial place of Rev. Francis Mackemie, the first pastor. Madam Mary Hampton. Her father the Irish baronet, her three husbands and her distinguished sons. "Tusculum." "Workington." "Westover." "Cedar Grove." "St. Bartholomew's or the Green Hill church. An interesting page in its history. Spring Hill or the Quantico church. All Hallows, Snow Hill. The Presbyterian churchyard. "Beverly." Old Dorchester county parishes. The ancient churchyard at Cambridge. Tribute of a disconsolate husband. The "Old Brick Church," Vienna. Restoration of the churchyard.

CHAPTER XII 244

The District of Columbia once a part of Maryland. Georgetown a social center long before the Federal city was thought of. Some of the notabilities living there early in the nineteenth century. The "Holland House of America" and its graveyard, now extinct. Oak Hill cemetery. A victim of the Baltimore riot of 1812. His stately funeral. How Arlington passed from the hands of the Lees. The grave of the first bishop consecrated in America. Something about the first of the Roman Catholic Hierarchy. The grave of Charles L'Enfant. The plan of the city of Washington, so beautifully realized, his only monument. The oldest places of burial in the city now no more. Partial list of bodies removed. The Congressional burying ground. Rock Creek cemetery—a churchyard covering fifty acres. Worthies who edited the first newspapers published in the Capitol. The Broad Creek churchyard. Some relatives of Joseph Addison. "Oxen Hill" and "Barnaby."

ILLUSTRATIONS

Slab from the Francis Sourton tomb . . . . *Frontispiece*	
	FACING PAGE
The Burning of the *Peggy Stewart*	20
A Tablet in Middleham Chapel, Calvert County	50
Top of the Tomb of John Rousby	60
Portrait of General William Smallwood	70
St. Paul's Church and Churchyard, Baltimore	112
St. Thomas's Church, Garrison Forest	120
The John Eager Howard Statue	122
The Vault Yard at "Hampton," Baltimore County	148
Christ Church, Queen Caroline Parish, Howard County	156
The Graveyard at Wye, Talbot County	212
The Old "Tred-Avon" Friends' Meetinghouse	222
St. Mary Anne's, or North Elk, Parish Church	232
Entrance to an Old Family Burying Ground	244

HISTORIC GRAVES OF MARYLAND AND THE DISTRICT OF COLUMBIA

CHAPTER I

THE early history of Maryland is so closely interwoven with that of the county which provided it with its final seat of government, that there is hardly an old graveyard in Anne Arundel but yields a record of important names.

A survey of the city of Annapolis in 1718, gives to the Church Circle an area of 94,025 feet. At that time all the citizens were nominally parishioners of St. Anne's, and the churchyard was their common burial ground. It was more than twice as large as it is now, extending as far as the present Court House, and into the grounds of the Executive Mansion. By the year 1786, every inch of the space was full, and much of it had been used over and over again. A piece of land, given to the parish by Elizabeth Bordley about the year 1790, supplied the pressing need for a larger graveyard, and this, until within recent years, was always known as St. Anne's cemetery.

Most of the bodies around the church were removed to the new place of burial; and in course of time the churchyard itself became confined within its present limits. Some of the broken gravestones have found their way into the street crossings near St. Anne's; others have been utilized in various ways. In one case fragments have been made to serve the purpose of steps to the wing of the Brice House. These, through the courtesy of Mr. Martin, owner of that historic mansion, were removed from their position and turned over for the purpose of investigation. On the under side of one of them were discovered the words: "died July 14th, 1765." The rest of the inscription had become obliterated, but by searching among the obituaries of the *Maryland Gazette*, a probable clew was found by which to reconstruct the whole. "Sunday last died here of smallpox at the house of her brother, Mr. Chief Justice Brice, Mrs. Anne Denton, widow, a gentlewoman of pious and exemplary life and conversation." The date of the *Gazette* where this extract appears is Thursday, July 18, 1765.

John Brice, the Chief Justice mentioned above, was the son of John Brice of Haversham, England. He outlived his sister about one year. Besides the position he holds in local family tradition, he is among those to whom complimentary allusions are made by Governor Sharpe in his correspondence with Lord Baltimore preserved in the Maryland archives. Designated by his Excellency as a man of "Good Abilities and Fortune," he is recommended to the Lord Proprietor as a gentleman fitted to fill the vacancy in the Council left by the death of one of its members. This position, however, he never held, as he died shortly afterward.

To return to St. Anne's and its funeral records, one reads in the Register of 1707—the oldest volume preserved—of the burial of such distinguished personages as "His Excellency John Seymour, Capt. Gen., also Governour of the Province and Vice Admiral," August 5, 1709; of "Marylandia, daughter of His Excellency John Hart, Governour," September, 1716; of "Madam Margaret Lasonby, aunt of His Excellency Charles Calvert, Governour," August 8, 1722.

Among the interments mentioned is also that of Capt. Ezekiel Gillis, which took place on January 9, 1749, at Mrs. Hill's, South River Neck. This entry points to the existence of an old burial ground which so far has escaped identification by members of the Memorial Committee.

In the cemetery of St. Anne's are to be found many names familiar to the older residents of the capital, as well as to the kindred families throughout the state; such, for instance, as Calvert, Mackubin, Randall, Steele, Murray, Maynadier, Steuart, Shaw, Nicholson, Mayo, Brewer, Harwood, Grammar and Munroe. The oldest date is 1763. It is preserved on a slab inscribed with the initials M. & E. In point of age that of Fr. de la Landelle, a French officer, comes next. He was born in Brittany, France, and died in 1800. A third without dates bears the names of John Kilty and William Kilty, "Brothers, and revolutionary officers" and on the title-page of *The Landholders Assistant*, printed early in the nineteenth century, and appearing in nearly every gentleman's library of that day, we find the same name perpetuated. Besides these are other ancient stones of later date:

Osborne Ridgely, born 1742, died 1818.
Thomas Duckett, died in 1806 in his 64th year;
Miss Elizabeth Fulks, died in 1830 in her 73rd. year.
Mrs. Mary Miller, died in 1830 in her 71st. year;
Sarah Ann Terry, died August 29th, 1841 aged 68 years;
John T. Barber, Esq., died April 6th, 1822, in the 51st. year of his age.
Honorable Peter Rich, late a delegate from Caroline County, departed this life on the 30th day of January A. D. 1805.

It appears that the monument to the above was erected by the "Honourable the General Assembly of Maryland" as a testimonial of respect to the memory of the deceased.

The Bordleys lie in a family vault. Thomas, the progenitor of the family in Maryland, was attorney-general of the Province from 1715 to 1726. He was born in Yorkshire, England, about the year 1682 and came to Annapolis about the year 1694, with an elder brother, the Rev. Stephen Bordley, who in 1697 was duly installed as second rector of St.

Paul's Parish, Kent county. Thomas studied law and was considered to be the first lawyer of his day. He married, first, Rachel Beard of Annapolis, who died in 1722. Four of their children lived to maturity—Stephen, William, Elizabeth and John. On September 1, 1723, he married, secondly, the Widow Frisby. Their sons were named respectively Thomas, Matthias and John Beale, the last of whom was born in February, 1726, old style, four months after his father's death, which occurred while on a visit to England for his health. A portrait painted by Gustavus Hesselius before he sailed, represents him as thin and pallid and dressed in gown and wig.

Although the gift of land made by Elizabeth Bordley was conveyed to the vestry of St. Anne's parish, its old name of St. Anne's cemetery has been lost through its incorporation of late years with graveyards of other denominations. It is now more popularly known as the "City Cemetery."

Clustered about the doorway and sides of St. Anne's church, Annapolis, are to be found several ancient tombs of the tabular kind, placed there in recent years to insure their preservation, also others erected in the year 1826, to replace the original ones that had occupied the same spot at a much earlier period. To the right is that of Maj. John Hammond, one of the commissioners appointed in 1694 "to survey and lay out the said town into lots, streets and lanes." It stood formerly in a field at the head of "Hammond's Creek," an estuary of the Severn river, about three miles from Annapolis. Amos Garrett's tomb occupies a corresponding position to the left, while those of Henry Ridgely and Nicholas Gassaway complete the number of the first group. The inscriptions read as follows:

Here lieth interred the body of Major General John Hammond who departed this life the twenty-fourth day of November 1707 in the sixty-fourth year of his age.

Anne Arundel County

Here lieth interred the body of Mr. Amos Garrett of the City of Annapolis in Anne Arundel County of the Province of Maryland, Merchant. Son of Mr. James and Mrs. Sarah Garrett late of St. Olives Street, Southwark then in the Kingdom of England now a part of Great Britain who departed this life March 8th 1707. Ætatis 56.

Here Lyeth the body of Mr. Henry Ridgely who was borne the 3rd of October 1669 and departed this life on ye 19th day of March 1699–1700.

Here Lyeth Interred The Body of Nicholas Gassaway Son of Coll Nicholas Gassaway who Departed This Life The 10 Day of March Anno Domini 1699, And In The 31 Year of His Age.

In the second group appear the following:

Here lies the remains of Rebecca late wife of Daniel Dulany of Annapolis and fourth daughter of Colonel Walter Smith. She faithfully and diligently discharged her duty in all relations of Daughter and Wife, Mother, Friend and Neighbor. She was virtuous and charitable. She lived an unblemished life and died universally lamented the 18th of March 1737 Aged 40 years. (Coat of Arms.)

Sacred to the Memory of Margaret Carroll Relict of Charles Carroll and daughter of Matthew Tilghman. She was born on the 13th day of Jan. 1742 and died on the 14th day of March A. D. 1817.

In Memory of Benjamin Tasker Jun. Esq late Secretary of Maryland Who died on the 17 Oct 1760 in the 39th year of his age.

In Memory of William Bladen Esq. Who died the 9th of August Anno Domini 1718 in the 48th year of his Age.

Here are deposited the remains of the Honourable Benjamin Tasker who departed this life the 19th of June A. D. 1768 in the 78th year of his Age, which though of a constitution naturally weak and tender, he attained through the efficiency of an exemplary temperance. At the time of his decease he was President of the Council a station he had occupied for thirty-two years. The offices of Agent and receiver general and judge of the prerogative Court he successively exercised. Such were his qualities, his probity, equanimity, candor, benevolence, that no one was more respected more beloved. So diffusive and pure his humanity, so singular the influence of his deportment that he was no one's enemy nor any one his.

These tombs are erected in the year 1826 in the place of the original ones, which have decayed, by the liberality and filial affection of Mrs. Ann Dulany of the City of London, still longer to perpetuate the memory of those of her respected ancestors whose remains are deposited beneath them.

Several years ago it was proposed to have the Greenberry tombs transferred from the Greenberry's Point farm to the same shelter, but here an unexpected difficulty arose, and one that had its humorous side.

The "Farm," having had its ups and downs (like most of the old estates), had finally passed into the hands of a worthy farmer, who provided the "Ancient City" with milk. Being approached about the removal of the stones, he offered no objection, but his wife opposed it vigorously. Upon being questioned as to the motive of her refusal, she answered that the stones were bought with the place, and she did not intend to part with them as they were her's and "company" for her! She then explained that people came from all parts of the United States to visit them and she evidently appreciated the social intercourse thus provided her in her seclusion. As no descendant of the former chancellor and "acting" Governor has appeared to dispute her right, the stones, which are not thought to mark the graves of the departed, have been allowed to remain, though a movement has been set on foot to inclose them where they are, in order to protect their crumbling surfaces from the greed of merciless relic hunters.

Col. Nicholas Greenberry was also one of the commissioners appointed for the laying out of Anne Arundel Town. This community, originally designated as the "Town at Procter's," received the name of Annapolis in 1695, when its life as a naval station began.

The inscriptions on the stones read:

Here lieth Interred The Body of Colln Nicholas Greenberry Esqr Who departed this Life The 17 Day of December 1697 Aetatis Suae 70.

Here Lieth Interred The Body of Mrs. Ann Greenberry Wh Departed This Life The 27th Day of April 1698. Aetatis Suae 50.

. . . Lyes interred the . . . Roger New[man] . . . born at London . . . in Talbot County in . . . 25 years and . . . The 14 of . . . 1704.

In Roger Newman's will, dated June 14, 1704, and probated June 28, he appointed his friend, Charles Greenberry, his executor. This trust, for reasons best known to himself, the latter declined, and yet we find Newman's tomb, or at least what remains of it, near those of Greenberry's parents.

Tradition says that the old meetinghouse of the Puritan settlers stood somewhere hereabouts—on Greenberry's Point, in fact—and was accessible by water to those who lived miles apart by land. It is possible that a graveyard surrounded this meetinghouse. However that may be, these tombs, which no longer cover the dust of those whose names they bear, form an interesting group to speculate about.

At the top of the Newman slab, otherwise much broken, is an elaborate escutcheon still distinct. Strange to say it combines the Bennett coat-of-arms with that of the Lloyds— the three demi-lions of the one and the lion rampant of the other. In *Heraldry in America*, Zieber gives these arms as "on the tomb of Newberry, 1704, near the Greenberry tombs." This, of course, is a mistake. It might not be unreasonable to suppose that a fine slab, such as the Newman stone undoubtedly was, had survived the Puritan graveyard of the earlier period, and that it had simply been recut with Roger Newman's name, when a stone was needed to mark his burial place. Knowing as we do how closely the names of Lloyd and Bennett were associated with the arrival of the Puritans in Maryland, it would not be irrational to infer that this escutcheon pointed to the union of the two families in previous times, and that this stone had covered the remains of some relative of an earlier generation, buried near the old meetinghouse on Greenberry's Point. In fact, unless it be known to the contrary, it might have been originally devoted to the memory of Richard Bennett, the first husband of Henrietta Maria Neale of revered memory, the commissioner's son who was drowned while quite a young man. The date of the third Richard's birth is given as September 16,

1667, which, if our inferences be correct, would approximate the age of the Newman stone.

Newman's friend, Charles Greenberry, appears to have been the owner of "Whitehall," afterwards the home of Governor Sharpe; for upon his death, in 1713, he left it to the church. Whether it was ever used as the glebe of St. Margaret's, Westminster, or was turned to money for the use of the parish, cannot be ascertained now; but the present graveyard at "Whitehall" dates from the time of Governor Sharpe's ownership. Nearly a century and a half ago the first interment took place there. It was that of an indentured servant, name unknown, whose only monument is the beautiful carving in the hall and adjoining rooms of the mansion. His pathetic history has been handed down as one of the legends of the place. Transported to this country as a convict, though innocent, he served his term in creating these forms of beauty, which were completed just before his death. The proof of his innocence came only in time to gladden his last hours. By his side lies a faithful old gardener—a redemptioner also.

Governor Sharpe returned to England just before the Revolution and the estate passed into the hands of his secretary, John Ridout. The first family grave is that of Meliora Ogle, youngest daughter of John and Mary Ridout, born August 14, 1780, and died July 11, 1781. A kindly letter of condolence written at the time by Governor Sharpe to his former secretary, is characteristic of the loyal friendship borne by him through life. On October 7, 1797, John Ridout himself was laid in the same ground, but having witnessed even at this early day the frequent mutilation of family graveyards, especially that on the neighboring estate of Greenberry's Point, he positively directed that no tombstones be erected on his or other graves at "Whitehall," an order religiously obeyed by four generations. This, of course, obscures the identity of individual graves. However, the interment of direct descendants only, besides a few family connections, has kept the names in memory by a simple arrangement of family groups. St. Margaret's, Westminster, Parish Register adds also to our knowledge of who is buried there, as the following extract shows:

"Be it remembered that John Ridout, Esquire, a native of Dorset, in England, departed this life on the seventh day of October, Anno Domini 1797 and was buried at Whitehall in this Parish, the funeral ceremony being solemnized by the Rev. Ralph Higgenbottom of St. Ann's Parish. And Mary Ridout (his relict), Daughter of Samuel Ogle Esquire and Ann his wife, departed this Life in the month of Aug. 1808 and was buried at 'Whitehall.'"

On the shore of South river, on his old plantation of "Brampton," lie presumedly the remains of John Macubin, or Mackubin, the original owner of the land in 1658, and the founder of the family in Maryland. John Mackubin died in 1685, and, dividing his property among his five sons (each one of whom apparently elected to spell his name differently, as their signatures appear William Macubin, Samuel Mackieubin, Zachariah Maccubbin and Moses McCubbin, in old parchment deeds in the possession of their various descendants), left this the homestead to his oldest son John Mackubin. The old graveyard lies in the middle of a ploughed field on the farm now belonging to Mr. Thomas Gaither, beyond "Three Oaks," and though intact and unmolested at the last visit of the chairman of the Memorial Committee, it was uninclosed and overgrown with trees and brambles and bore no sign of having once served as a graveyard, save the oblong holes or indentations which mark the graves of those buried there. The tenant on the place bore witness that there were old stones there within his memory, but they were carried away and used in the foundations of some neighboring houses.

On the other side of Annapolis, across the Severn river and on the road to "Whitehall," lies "Bellefield," once the home of James Mackubin, grandson of John Mackubin, and whose wife, the beautiful Martha Rolle, was distinguished by General Washington's selection to open the magnificent ball given in his honor at the State House on the night of December 23, 1783, after his resignation as Commander-in-Chief of the Revolutionary army. The graveyard at "Bellefield" is in fairly good preservation and bears the following inscriptions on stones still erect and in good condition:

To the memory of James Mackubin who departed this life on the 31st day of August 1834 in the 75 years of his age "He lived respected and died lamented."

In memory of Martha Mackubin who departed this life on the 11th day of November 1823 in the 63 year of her age.

Two smaller stones are to the memory of their sons who died in early manhood, and are inscribed:

James Mackubin died on the 19th of April 1816 aged 30 years.

Frederick Mackubin died on the 30th of January 1816 aged 28 years.

Frederick was killed by a fall from his horse.

In memory of Charlotte Sudler who departed this life on the 2nd. of May 1825 in the 41 year of her age.

Wm. M. Sudler died Feb. 18th 1813 aged 22 months and 7 days.

The oldest stone in the little inclosure is the only other on which the inscription is legible, and indeed this, like most of the oldest stones that have come down to us, is the best preserved. It is to the memory of Capt. Thomas Homewood, and there is a tradition that "Whitehall," which joins, together with "Bellefield" was once called "Homewood's Lot."

Here lyeth interred the Body of Captain Thomas Homewood late of this Parish who departed this life May 19th in the year of our Lord 1739 in the 35 years of his age.

"Bellefield" was also at one time the home of John Hesselius, the portrait painter, who has left in Maryland so many good examples of his work. He was born in 1728, died April 9, 1778, and was buried at "Bellefield" in an unmarked grave.

Another interesting cluster of graves is to be found on a farm belonging to the late General Steuart. It retains the name of Mt. Stewart, differently spelled, being after that of a former owner, Anthony Stewart, whom we shall have occasion to mention later. Here remain in a fairly good state of preservation the Burgess tombs. Col. William Burgess, who lived here in the seventeenth century, took an active part in the life of the period, holding among other offices, that of councillor, and having also served as deputy governor and as general of the military forces of the Province.

As he married three times, he left a number of descendants, some of whom are interested in having these tombs removed from the field where heretofore they have been carefully protected to the more certain shelter of St. Anne's at Annapolis. Colonel Burgess married, first, Miss Elizabeth Robins, daughter of Edward Robins of Accomac county, Va., secondly, Mrs. Sophia Ewen, widow of Maj. Richard Ewen of Anne Arundel county, who left children, and, thirdly, Ursula, who survived him and became the wife of Mordacai Moore. Madame Ursula Moore died December 12, 1700, and was buried by the side of her first husband.

Among the old Maryland wills, two testators mention the children of Col. William Burgess: George Puddington makes George, William, Susanna and Edward legatees, while Nicholas Painter leaves property to Charles, William, Benjamin, Joseph, Elizabeth and Anne.

Susanna is also mentioned by Susan Billingsly in her will made December 7, 1663. As this lady, the widow of James Billingsly, alludes also to her brothers Richard and John Ewen, the sequence of names would lead one to suppose that family loyalty had gone so far as to cause the widow Ewen to name her daughter by her Burgess marriage after her first husband's sister.

The inscription on Colonel Burgess' tomb is:

Here lyeth ye body of Wm. Burgess Esq who departed this life on ye 24 day of Janu Anno Domini 1686 Aged about 64 yrs. Leaving his dear beloved wife Ursuhla & Eleven children viz: seven sons and four daughters and 8 grandchildren. In his life time he was a member of His Lordships Counsell of Estate, One of his Lordships deputy Governours a Justice of ye High Provincial Court Collon of a Regiment of the trained Guards and sometime Generall of all the Military forces of this Province. His loving wife Ursulah his Execut. in testimony of her true respect and due regard to the worthy deserts of her dear departed husband, hath erected this Memorial.

On the tombs of his son, William, and his daughter, Anne, are the following inscriptions:

Here lyeth the Body of William Burgess the eldest son that coll. William Burgess had by his Dear and Loveing wife Ursella, he departed this life the 28th Day of June in the . . . year of his age, Anno Domini 1698.

Here lyeth Interred ye Body of Anne the wife of Thomas Sparrow daughter of William Burgess and Ursulla his wife, who was born on Thursday the 7th of Oct. 1680 Married on Tuesday ye 8th June 1697 Sickened the 25th day of ye same month and dyed on Sunday ye 25 of July 1697. This stone is erected as a Lasting Memorial of the person above Mentioned, by her surviving husband Mr. Thomas Sparrow.

In a field some distance from the imposing mansion at "Belvoir," which stands about seven miles from Annapolis, is a plain upright slab bearing simply these words:

Mrs. Ann Arnold Key Died Jan. 5th, 1811 Aged 84 years.

Until a few years ago tradition made this lady the mother of Francis Scott Key of "Star Spangled Banner" fame. To rectify the mistake a block of white marble placed there through the efforts of the Memorial Committee of the Maryland Society of the Colonial Dames of America, in co-operation with three of Mrs. Key's descendants, now establishes her identity as the poet's grandmother. She was the wife of Francis Key, clerk of Cecil county, and daughter of John Ross, who arrived in Maryland about the year 1721, and held a succession of important public offices until his death in 1766. Her mother was Alicia Arnold, the granddaughter of Rev. Thomas Knipe, Prebendary of Westminster, and headmaster of Westminster School, who is buried in the Abbey. Through the letters of her great-aunt, Helen Wolseley Sprat, directed to "Madame Alicia Ross at her house at Annapolis in Maryland, in the West Indies," her maternal ancestry is preserved. It includes names of interesting personages figuring in the stirring events of that day. Mrs. Sprat herself was the wife of the Bishop of Rochester, of whom Macaulay says: "He was indeed a great master of language and possessed at once the eloquence of the preacher, the controversialist and the historian." About him the pages of history are not silent, and so we shall pass on to persons more intimately associated with the subject in hand. To quote from my Lady Rochester's correspondence we have the following: "I hear send you your great-grandfather's [picture] In Littel; he was Colon'll Devereux Wolseley, he was third son of Sr Thomas Wolseley of Wolseley's Bridge in the County of Stafford, Knight. My mother, his wife and your great-grandmother always wore it by her side and gave me it when she died. She was Elizabeth Zouch, third daughter and Co-heiress of Sr John Zouch of Codnor Castle in the Co. of Darby, Knight."

This same Sir John Zouche was in 1631 one of the "commissioners" for the better plantations of Virginia. He was, moreover, brother-in-law of Vincent Lowe, a name not only well known in the archives of Maryland, but, also, as that of the father-in-law of Charles, third Lord Baltimore. In every turn the allusions in this correspondence bring one in touch with families descending from the same source, who have contributed not only to the making of our history, but to the social life of the Province and thence to that of the state.

Thus are we able to link with the name of Mrs. Key's

grandson, our immortal bard, those of Calvert, Sewall, Rozier, Chandler, Pye, Brooke, Wharton, Whettenhall and many others, whose family ramifications might form a volume by themselves.

Mrs. Ann Arnold Key was well known in her day, and by the community in which she lived. She was not simply the mother, or grandmother, or daughter, or granddaughter of "somebody." When her home at Carpenter's Point near Chestertown was destroyed by fire, she insisted upon returning into the burning house to rescue some servants, supposed to be left there, and lost her eyesight from the injuries then received. A letter from her daughter, Mrs. Elizabeth Maynadier, gives the particulars of her last days, showing that she was entirely sensible of her approaching dissolution, was entirely composed, said but little, but now and then began to repeat some of the hymns that had been her solace and delight, for many years past. In this she but carried out the tradition of the women of her race, for from Anne Wolseley Knipe, down, to use an expression of Madame Helen Wolseley Sprat, they were "such good women."

It is said that "Belvoir," where Mrs. Key and her Maynadier grandchildren are buried, was once the home of her father, John Ross. At all events her sister Elizabeth, who had married Upton Scott of Annapolis, lived there with her a part of the time, which will account for a tradition of the latter's ownership.

Near her grave is a small stone with this inscription:

In memory of the infant daughters of Henry and Elizabeth Maynadier, one who died on the 19th day of September 1780 the other on the 2nd. day of December 1783.

The lot was inclosed in the year 1900 by a pipe and post fence at the expense of the Maryland Society of the Colonial Dames of America.

"Belvoir" is beautifully situated, and from a slight ele-

Anne Arundel County 15

vation across the lawn a fine view of the Chesapeake may be had. It is easy to picture to ourselves the days of the past when the Ross, Key, Scott and Maynadier connections came here to enjoy the hospitality of the fine old mansion and to be fanned by refreshing breezes from the "Mother of Waters."

Nearer by several miles to Annapolis than "Belvoir," and reached by a slight deviation from the same road, lies the old Ridgely-Worthington estate that has been divided into several holdings owned or leased by small farmers.

The old family graveyard has been more than usually abused, and one may say in this case, profaned, in that a rough cellarless cottage was built on the site some twenty years ago over the actual graves, many of the footstones still remaining upright in the ground and visible under the floor of the house. The oldest and best preserved of the gravestones was a gray granite slab to the memory of Henry Ridgely, the second of his name. This full length stone served as a step to the cottage porch at the time of the visit of the ladies of the Memorial Committee and had been broken in two places by wagons driving over it. The inscription, however, was in good preservation and also the skull and cross bones carved inside a circle at the top.

In view of its being a seventeenth century stone and to the memory of a man distinguished alike for his own personal services and as the son and namesake of one of the earliest founders of the county, an honored Councillor of the Province, it was decided to make an effort to remove the tombstone for preservation in the churchyard of St. Anne's in Annapolis. This was ultimately accomplished in the year 1899 with the pecuniary assistance of several of his descendants.

The only other stones in this graveyard on which the inscriptions are not obliterated by time or abuse are two in white marble of much later date, erected in memory of Beale

M. Worthington and his wife Elizabeth, who was the granddaughter of Henry Ridgely II. The inscriptions read:

In Memory of Beale M. Worthington Died December 22nd 1824 in the 40th year of his age.

In memory of Elizabeth R. Relict of Beale M. Worthington who departed this life April 22nd 1837 in the 52nd year of her age.

In the third election district of Anne Arundel county, is a farm known as "Pendennis" belonging to the estate of the late Tilghman Brice. About 100 feet north of the house, which stands on a hill across the Severn Bridge, is the tomb of the founder of the Worthington family, inscribed as follows:

Here lyeth the body of Captain John Worthington who departed this life the 9 day of April 1701, aged 51 years.

The Quaker burying ground is an inclosure about a mile from the village of Galesville, and marks the site of the old meetinghouse mentioned by Thomas Story in his journal while visiting West river in 1698, as the guest of Mr. Richard Galloway of "Rokeby." In spite of the age of the graveyard there are no very old stones. This may be explained by the sumptuary laws of the early Quakers, which forbade that stones should be more than six inches in height. The earliest gravestones with inscriptions are as follows:

Mary Deale [Deak] Consort of James Deale Died March 25th 1812.

Capt. James Deale Died 1837.

Eliza Beloved wife of Thomas Franklin of Annapolis Daughter of John C. and Anne Mackubin Born April 29th, 1788 Married Nov 27th, 1808 Died Nov. 13th 1815.

Jacob son of Jacob and Mary Franklin 1743–1819.

In a large lot are to be found the following names and dates:

Captain James Dooley May 19th 1829 aged 38. (58?)

George Gale 1799–1856.

>Affliction sore for years I bore
>Physicians were in vain
>At length God pleased to give me ease
>And freed me from my pain.

Anne Arundel County

Lloyd Gale May 2nd 1823 aged 27.
Martha Gale December 20th, 1826 aged 40.
Ann wife of Samuel McDonnel 1765-1843.
William Cathell 1787-1822.
Samuel McDonnel 1768-1828.
Elizabeth Ann, wife of Thos. M. Crouch, Jan. 18th 1845.
Sarah, wife of William Cathell 1795-1845.
Elizabeth M. wife of John Thomas Born May 27, 1798 Died Oct. 15, 1847.
Elizabeth, 1826-1838, John, 1832-1837, Mary, 1818-1821, children of John and Mary Thomas.
Ann Thomas 1778-1848.
Leanna J. McDowell 1802-1841.
William Lingon [Lingan] Son of Daniel L. and Selina H. Lazenby 1848-1849.

The late Miss V. King, from whom the above data was received, continues: "There are three little graves standing in a row, so that the three little inscriptions read like a sentence. *All. Hel. Wel.* I have found that at least two generations are buried in known but unmarked graves, while in the present century the same families invariably use tombstones showing, I think, the date of the wane of Quaker influence in this county. It is said that the old unmarked graves in the Quaker burying ground can be identified, though the methods for so doing are not indicated. At all events the ancestors of the Murrays, the Masons, the Cooks, the Mercers, the Chestons, the Thomases, the Richardsons, the Mifflins, the Chews, the Amblers and a number of others are buried here with no stones to mark the spot."

An interesting story linked with this little cemetery is that of Captain Dooley. During the war of 1812 he was in command of one of the privateers fitted out with letters of marque to harass the English, but having remained at sea to prey upon the world's commerce after peace had been declared, he was branded by the name of pirate. After some years of successful venture but with failing health, Dooley invested his gains in a plantation on West river and, though the law was on his track, again and again he escaped arrest. His death warrant, however, was signed at last, but by a higher power, that carried him beyond the reach of human courts. In his last moments he wished to unburden his soul by confession, but his partners in crime guarded his deathbed so that no alien might hear his story. Could he have spoken, names well known to all of us might have been forever lost to good fame, for there had been city merchants with their capital behind the hardy seaman. The land bought with the ill-earned gold is said to bear a curse. Tradition thus steps in and adds its quota of local interest.

At Tulip Hill, a Galloway estate, the two oldest stones are to the memory of:

Virgil Maxey Born in Attleborough Mass. Killed by the bursting of a gun on board the Princeton 28th Feb. 1844 in his 60th year.

Mary Maxey Born 1787 At Chestertown Md. Died 16th July 1849 in her 62nd year.

Mrs. Maxey was Mary Galloway, granddaughter of Samuel Galloway who built "Tulip Hill." There is a family vault at Tulip Hill which was sealed after the burial of Mrs. James Cheston in 1838; Mrs. Cheston was the grandmother of Mrs. H. M. Murray.

At "Cedar Park," another Galloway estate, is an old family graveyard, inaccessible on account of tall weeds, briers, etc.

At "Tudor," owned by generations of Halls, is a graveyard, but no stones are visible.

At "Java," in an old field, is the grave of Major Francis who was drowned when returning from a visit to "Tulip Hill." The inscription on his tomb appears:

Here lyeth the body of Major Thomas Francies who deceased ye 19 March Anno 1685 Aged 42 years.
   Tho' now in Silence I am lowly laid
   Ha! 'tis that place for mortals made.

> O ther'fore doe not thou thyself more greive
> Mourne ye noe more doe yeself Releive
> And then in time I hope you'l plainly see
> Such future Comforts as are blessing mee.
> For tho' grim death thought fitt to part us
> Rejoyce & think that wee shall once appear
> At that great day when all shall sumonds be
> None to be Exempt'd in this Eternitie.
> Cause then itt soe greive ye no more
> In fear that God should the Afflict most sore
> Even to death and all to Let you see
> Such greives to him offencive bee.

At "Browsley," lately purchased by Mrs. Bowie Duckett, there are two graves before 1850.

Elizabeth wife of John Clator 1779–1820. John Clator 1783–1840.

In the graveyard at "Dodon," now the home of the priests, is a monument bearing these inscriptions:

Mrs. Ann Steuart widow of Dr George H. Steuart died in 1814 in her 96th year She was the Mother of Several children who are buried near her.

Ann and Jane Steuart daughters of Dr. Geo. H. & Ann Steuart died before the Revolution of '76.

William Steuart son of Dr Geo. H. & Ann Steuart died in 1838 aged 84 years.

David Steuart Son of Dr Geo. H. & Ann Steuart died in 1814 aged 64 years.

Dr. G. H. Steuart was the ancestor of the late Dr. James Steuart, Health Commissioner of Baltimore. There are also graves of later date than 1850, marked by smaller stones.

In a grove, within three miles of Laurel, on the pike running from Baltimore to Washington, is to be seen a handsome white stone with the following inscription:

Sacred to the Memory of William Reely who departed this life March 30, 1849 Aged 64 years, 4 months, and 19 days.

Near Annapolis Junction, is the Dorsey graveyard, which stands about two hundred yards from the house, on land appearing among the original Dorsey grants. Graves bearing date prior to 1850, are:

Owen Dorsey Died Aug 20, 1797. Aged 12 mos and 6 days.

Catherine, Consort of Lloyd Dorsey Died Nov 9, 1809 Aged 47 years.
Lloyd Dorsey Died May 12 1812 Aged 50 years.
James Madison Dorsey Died Sept 9, 1827 In the 20th year of his age.
Catherine daughter of Noah E and Sarah H. Dorsey Died Sept 17 1836 Aged 1 year 11 mos 9 days.
Catherine Dorsey Died Oct 10 1845 In the 57th year of her age.
Ann Dorsey Died July 30 1846 in the 56th year of her age.
Emma Elizabeth, daughter of Noah E. and Sarah H. Dorsey died Aug 12, 1848. Aged 10 years 3 mos 25 days.
Achsah Ann daughter of Noah E. and Sarah H. Dorsey Died Sept 9 1849 Aged 4 years 5 mos, 6 days.

All Hallows, or the South River church lies about half a day's journey from Annapolis. The main interest of its graveyard centers in a cluster of old graves associated with the name of Anthony Stewart, a name yoked with that of the ill-fated brig *Peggy Stewart*, the incidents of whose burning furnish a companion picture to the performances of the Boston tea party of Revolutionary fame. The occasion has been fitly commemorated by Turner on the walls of the Baltimore Court House. There Stewart is seen in his shirt-sleeves holding the smoking brand by which he has just set fire to the brig, and from a safe distance is watching, with others, the burning of his property. The sacrifice has been necessary to propitiate public sentiment, for the *Peggy Stewart* had arrived shortly before laden with a cargo of tea. The dramatic incident is accompanied by a certain element of tragedy, and its significance has taken hold of the imaginations of a later generation. To destroy another man's property in the name of the public good is one thing, to destroy your own through the councils of other men and under the pressure of expediency is quite another. The first, as illustrated by the revenging masqueraders of Boston harbor, may be historically picturesque, but the second is a drama in which the struggles of a human soul are terminated by one heroic act.

Copyright, 1908, by C. Y. Turner

THE BURNING OF THE PEGGY STEWART
A reproduction of the first panel of the series painted by C. Y. Turner, of New York, in the Baltimore Court House

Anthony Stewart lived at "Mt. Stewart," an estate which a century earlier had belonged to the Burgess family. It is owned at present by the Steuarts. In the spelling of their name we find a departure from the original, showing French influence. Afterwards a still further change occurred, when the descendants of the royal house of Scotland mounted the English throne as Stuarts.

Anthony Stewart married a daughter of James Dick, elsewhere styled "Merchant of London Town." His wife is buried at All Hallows in her father's lot. Here lies also Margaret Dick, the wife of James, who died October 23, 1766, aged 65 years. Her virtues are recorded in Latin and her tomb, with that of her daughter Margaret, who died November 12, 1762, are both in a good state of preservation.

In the parish records of All Hallows, South River, we find the following account of James Dick given by himself: "Be it known to all whom it may concern, That I the subscriber James Dick, heretofore of Edinburg in Scotland, Merchant, Burgess and Gild Brother, and son of Thomas Dick formerly of said city, Merchant, Bailey and Dean of Gild, Did come into the Province of Maryland on or about the first day of June, in the year one thousand seven hundred and thirty-four (1734) and settle in London Town on South River in the Province aforesaid. That in the year one thousand seven hundred and forty (1740) I made a trip home .... bringing back wife Margaret" &c. &c.

The name of James Dick also appears on the list of the South River Club members in 1742. He was a member of the firm of Wm. Lux and Co., in 1767, along with William Lyon of Baltimore county and Charles Graham of Calvert county.

One of the handsomest tombs in this churchyard is a large one of the tabular order, bearing the simple inscription " My

Louisa." This lady was the sister of Rear Admiral Brenton, K. C. B., of the British Navy, who had married the youngest daughter of Anthony Stewart. While traveling in this country for her health, she was making the Stewarts a visit, and died at their house. Her bereaved father feeling that as a stranger in a strange land she could be enshrined in no heart but his own, sought to bridge the gulf of separation by his solitary claim, and hence the enigmatic inscription that meets the eye of the wanderer among the old tombs of All Hallows churchyard.

One ancient slab broken in several pieces, but held in place by being imbedded in the ground, gives the following record:

In Memory of Capt. Thomas Gassaway Son of Colln Nicholas Gassaway who Departed this Life the 12th Day of September Anno Domini 1739 Aged 55 [56 ?] years 6 months & 22 days. Born ye 20th Day of February 1683.

Also in Memory of His wife Mrs. Susanna Gassaway Daughter of Captain Henry Hauslap who departed this Life the 24th Day of February Anno Domini 1740 Aged 58 years and 16 Days. She was born the 8th Day of February 1682.

Another of the same kind, but better preserved, is the stone to the memory of Samuel Peel of London Town, who died in 1733. On the same stone is also inscribed the name of Robert Peel, 1773, and above the names is a coat of arms showing a bar dexter between two stars.

This represents an imperfect record of the many parishioners who undoubtedly found near All Hallows their final resting place. The church itself, a quaint structure with interesting traditions, was built after the year 1727 in place of an earlier place of worship that had stood in hereditary succession from a time antedating the establishment of parishes by the Act of 1692.

The Herring Creek church, christened St. James, and built in 1760 as a successor of an earlier church, possesses records dating back to 1695. It is here that the oldest gravestone in Maryland is to be found. The inscription reads thus:

> This Register is for her bones
> Her fame is more perpetual than ye stones
> and Stil her Vertues through her life be gone
> Shall live when earthly monuments are none.
> Who reading this can chuse but drop a teare
> For such a wife & such a Mother deare.
> She ran her race & now is laid to rest
> & Allalugia singes among the blest.
> 1665

Nearby lies a memorial to Christopher Birkhead, who died in 1676. For more than 200 years these stones lay at "Birkhead's Meadows." This was doubtless a portion of the tract of 1,300 acres confirmed to Christopher Birkhead in 1666, and possibly lay near the house of Abraham Birkhead, the scene of one of the many triumphs of George Fox, the Quaker, by whom the "Speaker of the Assembly was convinced." In 1888 the Birkhead tombstones were moved to St. James parish churchyard and their scanty history shows a custom in Maryland—namely, that of burying the dead in private grounds—which has been the cause why so few graves from remote times have been preserved. Where nearly every freeman, whether a gentleman adventurer or otherwise, was a "planter," and his home, cut off from those of his kind often by miles of territory, became the nucleus of a small community like the castle of some feudal lord, what more natural than that he should provide a place of burial for members of his family and his dependents, which sacred spot, by the lapse of time and change of ownership, was first neglected, then forgotten and finally lost.

There are only a few ancient tombs in this churchyard. Among them is one to the memory of Rev. Henry Hall, an early rector who died in 1723, and another to the Hon. Seth Biggs, a dignitary who departed this life July 31, 1708, in his fifty-fifth year.

In the old parish churchyard of St. Margaret's, Westminster, on Severn Heights, a few tombstones are still to be seen clustering about the foundations of the church, long since destroyed by fire. Governor Eden is supposed to be buried here. He was the last of the Provincial governors and was obliged to return to England at the breaking out of the Revolutionary war. That he should have died here and have found in so inhospitable a soil a final resting place, seems strange, but tradition hath it so.

In St. Stephen's churchyard, Millersville, Severn parish, memorials of a later date as follows, are found:

John A. Reigle born 1786, died Feb. 28th, 1829.

Eliza, wife of John A. Reigle born 1799, died Nov. 20th 1854.

William H. Turton born April 1st. 1778 died Nov. 19th 1864.

Eleanor, wife of William H. Turton born Dec. 21st. 1783, died June 28th 1856.

In Memory of Dr. Asa Anderson died Sept 13th 1847 aged 55 years, 9 months, 23 days.

Genl Osborne Williams died Dec 28th 1819 in the 62nd year of his age.

Elizabeth wife of Genl Osborne Williams died Mar. 18th 1819, in the 61st year of her age.

In the Baldwin Memorial Methodist churchyard are found:

Rachel A. Woodward Born Nov. 19, 1807 Died Oct 6, 1865.

Eleanor R. Woodward Born May 6th 1810 died July 12, 1840.

Martha R. Woodward Born May 28 1812 died May 17 1832.

Henry Woodward, Son of Wm Woodward Jr. Born April 22, 1770 Died Oct 26th 1822. Eleanor wife of Henry, Born Sept 29, 1772. Died Aug 15th, 1850.

In memory of Henry Wm Woodward, son of Henry, Born July 30th, 1803 died in Stewart, Georgia, Oct 14th, 1841.

Abraham Woodward son of Wm. Born in London 1690 Died in this Country 1744.

Wm Woodward Sr. Born 1717 Died 1790. Wm Woodward Jr. son of W. W. Sr. Born 1742 Died 1807.

In memory of Mary Pitts Sewall wife of Francis Baldwin Born June 10, 1791 Died Dec 29 1848.

In memory of Francis Baldwin Born Nov 27, 1777 Died May 27, 1836.

In memory of Mrs Sarah Woodward Who Departed this Life Dec 18, 1833 Aged 31 years.

Maria Gambrill Relict of Augustine Gambrill who died 30th of Nov 1834 in the 67 year of her age.

Augustine Gambrill who Died 29th of Dec 1830 In the 58 year of his age.

Sacred to the memory of Elizabeth Woodward who departed this life Feb 14, 1847, aged 56 years

>Dear be this grave and blest this sod
>That shields a Christian Mother's clay
>Her spirit's gone to enjoy its Lord
>Where life shall last without decay.

Near Millersville is an old Hammond graveyard, where several distinguished members of the family are buried. Philip, son of Charles, Speaker of the Assembly, and also Treasurer of the Western Shore, died 1760; his wife Rachel, daughter of John Brice, born 1710, died 1786; Col. Rezin Hammond, their son, a noted patriot, born 1745, died 1809; Maj. Charles Hammond, another son, died 1777 and lies buried in an unmarked grave; possibly Matthias, a third son, conspicuous in civic affairs, also Mordecai and Isaac, Captains of the 7th and 8th companies in the Maryland troop at Long Island.

At "Summer Hill," the home of the late Col. Nicholas Worthington, about three miles south of Crownsville, are buried the following members of the Worthington family:

Brice John Worthington, son of Nicholas and Catherine Worthington, died Nov. 14, 1837, aged 73 years, 9 months and 14 days.

Anne Lee, consort of Brice John Worthington, died Sept. 27, 1824, aged 34 years and 8 days.

Elizabeth, daughter of Nicholas and Catherine Worthington, died April 29, 1820, aged 53 years, 10 months and 2 days.

John G., son of Nicholas and Catherine Worthington, died Feb. 14, 1797, aged 33 years and 4 days.

Nicholas, son of Nicholas and Catherine Worthington, died Dec. 6, 1782 [1792 ?] aged 25 years, 1 month and 11 days.

Col. Nicholas Worthington, died Nov. 1, 1793, aged 59 years, 7 months.

Mrs. Catherine Worthington relict of Col. Nicholas Worthington, died Dec. 8, 1793, aged 61 years, 6 months and 18 days.

Mrs. Hester Ann Mackubin, wife of Dr. Richard Mackubin and daughter of Brice John Worthington, Esq., died Feb. 22, 1848, in her 30th year.

Mary Dulany Worthington, daughter of Brice, John and Anne Lee Worthington, died May 2, 1835, aged 19 years, 5 months and 23 days.

CHAPTER II

IT is natural to think of St. Mary's county, the first place of settlement under the rule of a Roman Catholic Lord Proprietary, as a spot well provided with venerable memorials to the Catholic dead. Such, however, is not the case; for a diligent search throughout the county has brought to light very few ancient tombs belonging to members of that faith. Even in St. Inigoes churchyard near Priests Point, where the first Jesuit mission was established shortly after the arrival of Governor Calvert and his colony, only the later Jesuit Fathers laboring in the same field, are represented. One of them, the Rev. James Walton, who died in 1803, served the mission in Maryland for more than thirty-six years. Another, the Rev. Joseph Carbery, died in 1849.

The earliest death recorded in St. Inigoes churchyard is that of Joseph Jenkins, who died January 16, 1796, the next that of Richard Fenwick, April 10, 1799. The latter surname keeps in memory an early dignitary of the Province, whose Christian name, Cuthbert, descended to his son, with the title of "Lord of the Manor." In the will of the first Cuthbert, dated March 6, 1654, two priests, Mr. Starkey and Mr. Fitzherbert, are mentioned as legatees. His second wife, Jane, who died between November 24 and December 12, 1660, also showed her love for her church by leaving to it a contingent legacy of a half of her personalty.

The following inscriptions may be found in St. Inigoes churchyard:

Here lies the body of James Fenwick, who died on the third day of Feb. 1806 in the 56th. year of his age. He was a nobleman, candid, honest and generous, and truly attached to the liberties of his country. His fore-fathers were among the first settlers of this ancient County and he left a numerous connection; for all of whom he felt like a father. May his virtues be long revered and perpetuated among them.

Sacred to the memory of, Richard Fenwick who departed this life April 10, 1799, aged 52 years.

In memory of Joseph Jenkins, died Jan. 16th, 1796 aged 22 years 4 months and 12 days.

I.H.S. In memory of Walter Leigh, who departed this life Feb. 26th 1806 aged 46 years. Kind, benevolent, humane, charitable, Fatherly to some, and enemy to none.

Joseph Daffin, consort of Mary Daffin, who departed this life July 26th, 1820, aged 57 years. R.I.P.

I.H.S. Here lies the immortal remains of Captain Benjamin Williams, who departed this life on the 15th, of July 1821, aged 73 years.

> Now God has called him to his rest,
> From out this vale of mortal tears
> Hope whispers that his soul is blessed,
> Beyond the realms of mortal fears.

R.I.P. Hoc Morens conjunx posuit.

Jesus Hominun Salvator. Sacred to the memory of, Mary Williams, consort of Benjamin Williams, St. Mary's County, who departed this life the 3rd, day of August 1814, aged 56 years.

> Alas 'tis done, the busy scenes of life are oer,
> Wealth, children, fortune, smile on me no more,
> Virtue fair virtue lives beyond the grave,
> And she alone the immortal soul can save.
> Ye friends and kindred cease your sorrowing tears,
> If aught indeed 'tis not your gone out prayers.
> Where I am gone, prepare you all to go,
> Death veiled in darkness stabs his fatal blow.
> R.I.P.

Here lieth the body of Ann Dunkenson, consort of Robert Dunkenson, who departed this life the 25th, of May 1823, aged 42 years.

Here lieth the body of Eleanor Goul, who was born the 10th day of our Lord 1763, and departed this life the second day of Jan. in the year of our Lord 1800.

Here lies the body of The Rev. James Walton, of the Society of Jesus, who died on the 19th, of February 1803, aged 88 years. He was born in England and served the Mission in Maryland during 36 years 8 months and seventeen days, with indefatigable zeal, Perseverance and fortitude. His brethren the Roman Catholic clergyman of Maryland, erected this monument as a tribute due to his singular merits, and to perpetuate the remembrance of his zeal in the vinyard of the Lord. R.I.P.

In Memory of Joseph Carbery S.J. born May 2nd 1776, died May 26th 1849.

The following Jesuit Fathers are also interred here:

Jacob Spenks, S.J. 1815. James Alexander Dobbins, S.J. 1840. P. Livres, S.J. 1789. Father O'Hare, S.J. 1840. Father Botine, S.J. 1848. Father Lane, S.J. 1850. Father Spankes, S.J. 1845. Father Nicol Flant, S.J. 1854. Father Robertson S.J. 1842.

Fenwick's Manor no longer exists as a whole, nor is there any trace of a family graveyard to show where the first Fenwicks were buried. But the interesting home of the Briscoe family, Briscoe's or St. Cuthbert's Wharf, and the old Roman Catholic church of St. John are ancient local institutions that have preserved the traditions of early settlement. And then on the north side of the road leading from Oakville to Forest wharf is a part of Fenwick's Manor, which was presumably the estate of Henry Lowe, as his wife is buried there. Her gravestone, a heavy flat slab, bears a record worth preserving, but unless something is done to protect it from the ravages of time and neglect, it, too, before long, will be a thing of the past. The date, 1714, places it amongst the oldest memorials of the eighteenth century. The inscription runs:

Here Lyeth interred the Body of Susannah Maria Lowe, Late wife of Henry Lowe of the Family of the Bennetts, who departed this life the 28th Day of July 1714 in the 48th year of her age.

"Sotterly," within easy driving distance of Briscoe's wharf, was also originally a part of Fenwick's Manor. It passed by purchase into the hands of the Hon. James Bowles and was known as "Bowles Separation." Thence, through the marriage of his widow, Rebecca Addison Bowles, to the Hon. George Plater, it came into the possession of the Plater family and received its present name after the Plater homestead in England. The house was built about the year 1730. It is beautifully situated on the Patuxent river, opposite St.

Leonard's creek, and is a fine example of antique architecture. Having been for more than 100 years the home of a family prominent in public affairs, it is truly historic; and an atmosphere of romance is added by the existence of a secret passage that runs from the cellar to the river at the foot of the hill. The Hon. George Plater, moreover, was one of those uncompromising individuals who leave an impress upon their times. Endowed with a primitive force of character that often thrives under simple social conditions, he bitterly opposed innovations of any sort. Consequently, when the division of All Faith parish was decreed by act of assembly in 1744, and the formation of a new parish projected under the title of St. Andrews, he urged that the chapel-of-ease, that had been built many years before for the convenience of his family, should become the parish church. With this in view, he provided for his burial in the chapel yard, and until within recent years a brick wall was indicated as the inclosure within which he and his wife Rebecca lay side by side. The chapel stood near "Sandy Bottom," and was known for many years as the "Four Mile Run" church, but its importance dwindled very soon after 1755, the year in which the Honourable George was gathered to his fathers. The parish records show that a vestry meeting was held under its roof on September 6, 1764, to arrange for the erection of St. Andrew's church. The saying "Le roi est mort! vive le roi!" is illustrated by another extract from the vestry proceedings, when in 1769 a meeting was held at St. Andrew's church and we find his son and heir, the future governor, eagerly bidding for pew No. one. This he held with Abraham Barnes, who, like himself, had married into the Rousby family.

Governor Plater is buried in the garden at "Sotterly," which, with its sundial, roses and traditions, conveys to the mind of the modern visitor an idea of continuity, or at least wafts to his senses a delicate fragrance from the life of a day that is gone.

Another Plater place is "Bloomsbury," where Judge Plater lived and where his descendants are buried. It is to be found on the road leading from Valley Lee to Leonardtown.

The following inscriptions are found at Bloomsbury:

In memory of Sophia Plater dau. of Wm. S. & Sophia Ridgely, born in Georgetown, June 16 1820, died at Bloomsbury, the residence of her grandfather Judge Plater, on the morning of Sept. 2 1829.

In memory of Evelina, consort of Edward Plater & daughter of Josias Young of Prince George's Co., died August 12 1848, aged 34 years.

In memory of Elizabeth, wife of Stephen Gough & dau. of John R. Plater, born 31 of May 1792, died 10 Feb. 1845.

Sophia daughter of Stephen & Elizabeth Gough, born 25 Oct. 1827, died 16 August 1848.

John Rousbie, son of Stephen & Elizabeth Gough.

In the forks of the Trent river stands All Faith church, built about the year 1765 in place of an earlier one, which had antedated the period of church building ushered in by the act of 1692. Its most venerable graves, like those surrounding nearly all the old churches, have gone through the usual leveling processes of time, aided by neglect.

All Faith church possessed formerly a chapel of ease, known as the "Red Church." It stood on the west side of the public road leading from St. Joseph's Catholic church to Oakville, and about 200 yards below where it forks with the Patuxent road. A graveyard, sadly neglected, is now the only thing left to show where the chapel once stood.

St. Joseph's Catholic church is a large brick edifice of modern construction on the top of a high hill several miles from Leonardtown. Its predecessor, which is said to have been built in the year 1740, stood about 300 yards to the south of the present site, and in the center of the old graveyard, which is still used as a place of interment.

Near Leonardtown is the old graveyard of St. Aloysius,

but the chapel has disappeared. About ten miles distant is that of the Sacred Heart, which with St. John's, St. Francis, St. Nicholas and those already mentioned, completes the list of the oldest Catholic graveyards possible of identification in St. Mary's county.

The Sacred Heart chapel is a modest wooden structure that has stood upon the land of "Bushwood"—a fragment of St. Clement's Manor—for more than 125 years. The graveyard may have been there before the chapel, and it probably was. In 1669, Capt. Gerard Slye, then proprietor of this beautiful plantation inherited from his father, Robert Slye, was a very active leader in the proceedings which debarred Catholics from holding office in the Province. This gentleman did not foresee that he was to marry a Catholic dame of intrepid character, that his will, probated in 1733, would direct that his children should be reared in the faith, that his wife should "think most proper and convenient for their souls' health," and that through her, his home, once the stronghold of Protestant intolerance, should pass into the exclusive possession of his Catholic posterity.

It is supposed that Capt. Gerard Slye was buried in the Bushwood family graveyard adjoining the Sacred Heart chapel, and that this chapel, so long the only place of worship allowed to the neighboring Catholic gentry, was built by his wife, probably after his death. At all events, their son, George Slye, who in turn inherited the plantation, bequeathed it to his nephew, "Mr. Edmund Plowden," and mentions "the two acres whereon the small chapel now stands," adding, "I further desire that the Church stuff, etc., now used in the chapel, may be kept for the use of said chapel and not appraised in my estate." This will was probated in 1773, and by its provision in favor of Edmund Plowden, the "Bushwood" property, 2,000 acres surrounding a fine Manorial dwelling, now passed to a representative of the colonial period in Southern Maryland, and, for more than a century the dead have rested here "upon the lap of earth."

Edmund Plowden was appointed Captain of the Militia in the battalion of Upper St. Mary's in 1777; he was a member of the Council of Safety, and a member of the earliest State Legislature in 1783, 1792 and 1798.

Directly opposite to Drum Point, where the Patuxent empties into the Chesapeake, lies the small promentory known as "Cedar Point." At Susquehanna on this point, is the tomb of Christopher Rousby, the story of whose death reveals the jealousy existing between the King's collectors of revenue and those of the Lord Proprietary. Rousby, the King's officer, suffered at the hands of George Talbot, " Lord of the Northern Marshes," and his tomb, which records also the death of his brother John, bears the following inscription:

Here lyeth the Body of Xphr. Rousbie Esquire who was taken out of this World by A voilent Death received on Board his Majesty's Ship the Quaker Ketch, Capt. Thos. Allen Commandr. the last day of Octr. 1684 and alsoe of Mr. John Rousbie his brother who departed this naturall Life on Board the Ship Baltemore Being arrived in Patuxon River the first day of February 1685.

Back of Cedar Point is the "Pyne Hill," a creek which was the boundary of Calvert county as laid out in 1654, when it embraced both sides of the Patuxent. A quaint old house owned by Miss Mollie Carroll, on what is now known as the "Bay Farm," is a part of Mattapani, the home of the Sewall family. No old graves are to be found here, but it is said that the Sewalls of past generations repose in a large lot railed in just behind St. Nicholas' Catholic church about four or five miles back of the Patuxent river. In the chancel of this church is a marble slab placed there by Mrs. Maria L. Key—a Sewall and the last of her line—to the memory of Rev. G. Derosé, who died in 1812. Among the gravestones in St. Nicholas' churchyard are several after 1850, on which the name of Delahay appears; a name that can be traced back to the year 1659, when members of that family are mentioned as legatees in the will of Thomas Dinian, a Roman Catholic of St. Mary's county.

The earlier graves are marked as follows:

I.H.S. † Sacred to the memory of Catherine Jarboe who departed this life 24 November 1826 Aged 31 years, 9 months, 27 days. This tribute of respect to her virtues is erected by her husband, who loved her while living, and lamented her when dead.

Elizabeth wife of Robert Jarboe Jr. who died Sept. 6, 1810. Aged 60 years, 11 months & 2 days.

Sacred to the memory of Robert Jarboe, who died Mar. 21, 1803, Aged 51 years, 2 months & 18 days.

George Cissell, born Sept. 12, 1780, departed this life March 27, 1832. R. I. P.

Elizabeth Heatherland, aged 70.

In memory of Elizabeth Sauner, who departed this life Nov. 22, 1829, aged 31 years & 19 days. I am the Resurrection and the Life. For as in Adam all die.

In memory Sarah R. Broome, Born Sept. 10, 1820, Died Aug. 25, 1853, Aged 32 years.

Sacred to the memory of Thomas N. Bean, who departed this life March 23, 1813, in the 47th [49 ?] year of his age, also his sons Edward and Aloizius in the eleventh year of their age. And his daughter Virginia, Aged 14 months.

I.H.S. † Pray for the soul of Col Jarboe, died 1846.

In memory of William Holton Esq., who departed this life April 11th, 1812. In the 62 year of his age & was buried 16th same month. Dearly beloved in his life, Sincerely lamented at his death.

In memory of Philip Abell, Departed this life August 30th 1811, aged 37 years 4 months & 3 days.

Underwood 1826 & 27.

In an old Catholic churchyard, which can be reached from Briscoe's wharf, there is but one tombstone of an early date that can be deciphered. It is to the memory of Mark T. Wilkinson, who was born July 4, 1765, and died April 12, 1819. On the later stones are to be seen the names of Fenwick, Tucker and Stone. The church, no longer used as a place of worship, serves as a dwelling.

Saint Mary's County

One Catholic place of worship that has stood the wear and tear of time is the church of St. Francis Xavier at "Beggar's Neck," a peninsula to the west of Leonardtown. It is known as the "Newtown" church. Through this name it keeps in memory the munificent gift of one Wm. Bretton, Esq., who in 1661 presented to the Roman Catholic inhabitants of "Newtown" and St. Clements Bay Hundred and their posterity an acre and a half of ground for a chapel and a cemetery. The church is of quaint design, having been built in 1767 during the ministrations of Father Ashbey, who died shortly after its erection. The wooden crosses near the front of the church mark the place where rest in peace twenty holy, zealous men of God, also six of their humbler brethern. Fortunately a list of their names can be given:

P. James Matthews, December 8, aged 36, 1694; P. Francis Pennington, February 22, age [?], 1699; P. Henry Poulton, September 27, age 33, 1712; P. Robert Brooke, July 18, age 51, 1714; P. Francis Lloyd [or Floyd], November 13, age 37, 1729; P. Peter Atwood, December 25, age 52, 1734; P. James Carroll, Nov. 12, age 39, 1756; P. Michael Murphy, July 8, age 34, 1759; P. James Ashby (Middlehurst), September 23, age 53, 1767; P. James Beadnall, April 9, age 54, 1772; P. Peter Morris, April 19, age 49, 1784; P. Bennett Neale, March 21, age 44, 1787; P. Ignatius Matthews, May 11, age 60, 1790; P. Augustine Jenkins, February 3, age 53, 1800; P. John Bolton, September 9, age 67, 1809; P. John Henry, March 12, age 58, 1823; P. Leonard Edelen, December 21, age 40, 1823; P. Ignatious Combs, June 27, age 56, 1850; F. Richard Jordan, died October 20, age 32, 1827; F. Mark Faherty, died September 28, age 32, 1841; P. Walter Baron, died July 27, aged 80, 1855; F. Edward Nolan, died January 15, aged 63, 1852; P. John Franklin, died September 18, 1819; P. Cornelius Mahoney, 1805.

The last two were secular priests.

As is often the case with parish churches in Maryland, that of "King and Queen" has an official as well as a popular name. Owing to this fact and to the imperfect memory of man, it has been consecrated twice. With no bishops in Maryland before the Revolution, and with the general disorganization of the church, leading to conditions not improved by the war of 1812, the first consecration did not take place until the year 1817, when Bishop Kemp performed the sacred rite. On this occasion the records speak of "Chaptico Church." In the *Diocesan Journal* of 1841, Bishop Whittingham reports having consecrated "Christ Church, Chaptico," under the representation of the rector and vestry that "in spite of its age," this had never been done.

"Chaptico" is a survival in name of one of the baronial manors of the Lord Proprietary, and in the massive structure with its vaulted nave, its columns and aisles, we detect influences, not brought to bear upon the construction of most of the Maryland churches at the end of the seventeenth or at the beginning of the eighteenth century. The church has an apsidal chancel, which is the case with several of our old churches, but the rest of its design favors the tradition that it was the work of Sir Christopher Wren, the celebrated architect of St. Paul's, London, to whom are accredited many less ambitious creations.

The churchyard at Chaptico has its traditions also. As late as the year 1860, a slab of slate, eighteen inches or two feet square, was pointed out as the stone covering the last resting place of a pirate buried here at his particular request in an upright position. As a matter of fact, the person thus interred was Capt. Gilbert Ireland, high sheriff of St. Mary's county in 1745, who, making his will in 1755 as Gilbert Ireland, Gent., directed that he should be buried in Chaptico churchyard at the distance of three feet from the feet of his "good" friend, Mr. James Dickon, and that a slab of black "marblestone" be sent for to Philadelphia "with a proper inscription to be put upon it." The writer learned the above facts from a descendant of Captain Ireland more than ten years ago. Behind the church is the vault of the Key family. The coat of arms there displayed in a reversed position is the same that appears on a pair of candlesticks and a pair of salvers in possession of a member of the family. These heirlooms were handed down by Philip Key, who came to Maryland about the year 1720. In his will he mentions having bought them from the estate of "the Reverend Humphrey's," and it is presumable that the coat of arms engraved on the silver, on the feminine side of the shield, was the Keys by adoption and not *olim et de jure*.

In the church is a stained glass window placed there in 1882 by Thomas, Samuel and Thomas J. C. Maddox, to the memory of their ancestors: Samuel Maddox, 1666; Samuel Maddox, 1728, and Lydia Turner, his wife; Samuel Maddox, 1842, and Sarah Fowler, his wife.

In the churchyard the name of Turner appears again, and the initials C. T. on an irregular bit of stone, with the dates April 21, 1745, and January 4, 1796, may have belonged to a member of that family. It is to be found near the Carpenter graves, which favors the supposition, as a Turner married a Carpenter.

The gravestones and monuments remaining in the churchyard after the usual vicissitudes attending so many of our burial places, bear inscriptions as follows:

In memory of John Carpenter who departed this life 25th Feby 1803 aged 68.

In memory of Susannah wife of John Carpenter daughter of Edward Turner, who departed this life 26th Sept 1805 aged 56 years.

In memory of Susan E. Consort of Aquila Burroughs died March 20th 1849, aged 25 years 3 mos. 25 days. May she rest in peace.

In memory of Joseph Dunbar who departed this life February 27th 1801, aged 83 years.

In memory of James Cook Sen. died March 13, 1820, aged 60 years. Also Mary, his wife. Died April 11th, 1818 aged 55 years. For nearly 30 years they sojourned together on earth bearing each the others burdens and sharing each the others joys. Respected in life, in death lamented. They rest in peace.

Ann McPherson 1800, aged 44.

In memory of Zoba Columbia Zalute Eldest daughter of Jas. & Rebecca

W. B. Cooke, who was born Sept. 8 1833 & died March 9 1846 in the 13th year of her age.

> Thus our hopes & our prospects are shaded
> For the Plant which inspired them hath shed
> Its foliage all green and unfaded
> Ere the beauty of springtime hath fled.

I will ransom them from the power of the grave. I will redeem them from death. Hosea 13:14.

Sacred to the memory of John Briscoe, who died May 29th 1822 aged 81 years, emphatically it may be said that his life was a life of scrupulous integrity, rigid Justice and temperance with great moderation and self-denial.

To the memory of Cecelia Brown Lyles, who departed this life May 30 [10?] 1828 aged 40 years & 2 months
This tomb is erected by her devoted husband Wm. H. Lyles.

> O! here my friend the fair Cecelia's laid
> Too soon alas! the debt of nature's paid
> Such virtue would adorn each sphere of life
> And grace the friend, the parent, child and wife
> Sweet are the slumbers of thy virtuous breast
> Sweet is thy sleep & all thy cares at rest.
> Th' unfettered soul has bust the bars of night
> And winged its passage to the realms of light.

Sacred to the memory of Peregrine Hayden who departed this life February 29th, 1848, in the 84th year of his age. May he rest in peace.

Sacred to the memory of Henry Dade Burch, born July 17th 1817, Died Sept 19th 1850. He has left a wife and four children to mourn the irreparable loss. He was a kind and devoted husband, affectionate Father & indulgent Master. He lived beloved and died lamented.

> We shared our mutual woes,
> Our mutual burdens bore;
> And often for each other flowed
> The sympathizing tear.
> When we at death did part
> How keen, how deep the pain
> But we still are joined in heart
> And hope to meet again.

+ IHS Elizabeth W. R. Born May 26, 1843 Died Aged 3 months. Henry Dade Born July 28, 1850 Died June 6th 1854. Children of Catherine & Henry Dade Burch. And in their mouth was found no guile for they are without fault before the throne of God. Revelation XIV: 5.

To the memory of Philip Briscoe, who devoted his life to the education of youth, this marble is gratefully erected by those who received the benefit of his labors, that it may perpetuate his memory as a public benefactor, when they shall have ceased to be living witnesses to his unsullied honor, profound learning and extensive usefulness. He was born Nov. 9th 1786 & died Sep. 26th, 1842.

The "Three Notched Road," which passes the site of "Four Mile Run" church, is the main road of the peninsula. It served in the old days as a direct route from Point Lookout to Annapolis. Branching from it at intervals are the shorter roads to steamboat landings or to venerable estates overlooking the Patuxent. "Cremona," about eighteen miles from "Sotterly," is one of the latter, and although no old graveyard is to be found there, the house itself is a pleasant *pied-à-terre* on the dusty road of investigation. It has the large hall and high ceilings of the stately homes of the best building period, and its hanging staircase is among the most beautiful specimens of the kind in Maryland. Adjoining Cremona is De la Brooke Manor, an historic spot bringing to mind the fortunes of one of his Lordship's Counselors, Robert Brooke, who was seated here on a much larger tract in 1650. He held a commission as Commander of Charles county, whose metes and bounds differed entirely from the later creation of the same name, but he was degraded and his charter was annulled owing to a suspicion that his sympathies were with the Cromwell party, under whom he acted in an official capacity during its short ascendency in Maryland. To his son Baker, however, was granted the De la Brooke tract; but neither tombs nor traditions of tombs are to be found here. These are to be sought after on the other side of the Patuxent, where Robert Brooke retired in 1652 and where many of his descendants settled.

At Trent Hall, a few miles further up the river, are some very solid and handsome tombs, or rather what is left of them, for they are in such a state of neglect that their disappearance altogether is only a matter of time. Two are upright and four are in a fence corner, badly broken. The tobacco grows up about these stones, and the tenant who farms the place, while congratulating himself upon his fine crops, quietly ignores the claims of the dead. Little cares he for the memory of Maj. Thomas Truman, his wife Mary, or his brothers, Nathaniel and James; and yet this group of stones is among the oldest yet discovered in Maryland. They are inscribed as follows:

Here lyeth the body of James Truman, Gent, who died the 7th of August 1672 being aged 50 years.

Here lyeth the body of Thomas Truman Esqr. Who died the 6th day of December Anno. 1685. Aged 60 years. "The Memory of the Just is Blessed." Prov. ye 10ch. & ye 7th verse.

Here lyeth the Body of Nathaniel Truman, Gent. Who died the 4th of March 1678 being Aged . . .

Here lyeth the Body of Mary, wife and Relict of Thomas Truman Esq: who died the 6th of July, Anno 1686 Aged 52 years.

Other inscriptions at Trent Hall are:

Here lyeth the Body of Thomas Truman Greenfield who departed this life the 10th of December, 1733 in the 51st. year of his age.

Here lies ye Body of Walter Truman Greenfield son of Col. Thomas Truman Greenfield & Ann his wife. He Departed this life ye 28th of May 1739 in ye 14th year of his Age. A Dutiful Son, the Glory of his Mother.

"Trent Hall" was granted to Maj. Thomas Truman; it now belongs to Miss Eliza Thomas of Baltimore. It is situated immediately on the Patuxent river, and is the terminus of the road leading from Charlotte Hall to Trent Hall wharf.

At Charlotte Hall is the Dent Memorial, a pretty little modern church. Back of it lie several flat tombstones that were transferred here from the glebe of Trinity parish. They are to the memory of the Rev. Hatch Dent, his wife Judith, and members of his family. On the wall of the sacristy is a tablet bearing the following inscription:

In Memory of Rev. Hatch Dent one of the founders of Charlotte Hall School and its First Principal 1796-1799.

Among the other memorials are a font placed there in 1883 to Henry Hatch Dent, who died in 1848 at the age of four; a rose window in the chancel end to Katherine and Anne Maria Dent, tablets to Henry Brawner, an officer of the school from 1799 to 1802, and to his son Henry, "an honoured and valued trustee of said school from 1826 to 1835."

The Dent inscriptions are:

Rev. Hatch Dent, Son of Hatch and grandson of John Dent of Yorkshire, England, One of the early settlers of the Province of Maryland, was born May 1757 and died Dec. 30 1799. An honored officer in the Army of the revolution of 1776, and an Eminent Teacher and Minister of the Church. Ordained by Bishop Seabury in 1785. Removed from the Glebe of Trinity Parish July 30th, 1883.

Judith Poston, wife of Rev. Hatch Dent, born Jan, 10, 1758, died Mar, 3, 1814.

Henry Hatch Dent, born Feb 11, 1815 died Nov 19, 1872.

Ann Maria Adlum, wife of Henry Hatch Dent, born Mar 27, 1813. died June 10, 1849.

Dr William Hatch Dent, born Jan, 22, 1787 died Feb, 1, 1818.

Katherine Brawner, wife of Dr William Hatch Dent, born Oct, 10, 1789, died April 24, 1860. Her last words were "I may not live to see the spring flowers, but I shall soon see more glorious things. It is nothing to die, Jesus can make the dying bed feel soft as downy pillows are. While on his breast I lay my head and breathe my life out sweetly there."

"Chesley's Hill" is above "Trent Hall" a few miles and overlooks the Patuxent river. It is on the east side of the road leading from Charlotte Hall to the "Plains." A monument marks the grave of John Chesley, and bears the following inscription:

This monument is erected to the memory of John Chesley, of Saint Mary's County, who died December the 5th, 1767, in the 64th year of his age. He was Magistrate of this County upwards of 30 years, during several of which he presided as judge of the Court and always distinguished himself for Ability and uprightness.

> Beneath this stone the cold remains are laid,
> Of one who has the debt of nature paid,
> Truth as she passes drops the silent tear,
> Laments the husband, Parent, Friend

Duty and love have thus inscribed his name,
But virtue ranks it in the Book of Fame.

At Colonel Sothoron's place, "The Plains," are found the following:

Here lies interred the body of Col. Henry Peregrine Jowles, who departed this life the 31st. day of March 1720, in the 39th year of his age.

Here lies interred the Body of Mr. John Forbes, who departed this life on the 26 day of January 1737, in the 37th year of his age.

Here is interred the body of Mary Sotheron, wife of Henry Greenfield Sotheron, only child of Major Zachariah Bond. Born the 14th of January 1736 and died the 11th of October 1763 aged 26 years.

Under this tomb is deposited the body of John Forbes, who was born on the 19th of March 1757. He departed this life on the 31st. of December 1804 in the 46th year of his age. He was a good man.

Returning down the peninsula towards Point Lookout, a goodly number of private burying grounds have been explored. On St. Michael's Manor, granted to Gov. Leonard Calvert in 1639, and traversed by the historic "Three Notched Road," are no less than three estates where well known county names are perpetuated in stone. These are "Corn-Field Harbor," a Jones place, now owned by Mr. Ackerly of Long Island, N. Y.; "Fresh Pond Neck," the old home of a branch of the Bennett family; and "William's Fortune," or "Long Neck," patented in 1745 to John Biscoe and remaining in the possession of the Biscoe family until the year 1898, when it was bought by Austin Ridgel.

"Corn-Field Harbor," is situated on the Potomac river near Scotland P. O., St. Inigoes district, St. Mary's county, about five miles from Miller's wharf and on the right hand side of the "Three Notched Road," leading from the Pine to Point Lookout. In its graveyard the following inscriptions are found:

In memory of Mordecai Jones, born April 19th, 1747, died June 6th 1829.

In memory of Mrs. Mary Jones, Born Au 13th 1747 Died Oct. 19th 1818.

William Henry Jones, Born Dec 24th 1817 Died July 29th 1836.
Alex Claxton Jones Born Aug 20th 1840 Died May 8th 1863.

There are stones marking the graves of three children and eleven unmarked mounds.

"Fresh Pond Neck" is near Scotland P. O., St. Inigoes district, St. Mary's county, Md., and about four miles from Miller's wharf. It is on the left hand side of the road leading from the Pine to Point Lookout. Here the following are found:

In memory of Joseph Bennett who departed this life Aug 19th 1815, Aged 62 years.

In memory of Susanna Bennett, who departed this life Feb 28 1806 aged 49 years.

To the memory of William Bennett, died May 10th 1816 aged 38 years.

To the memory of Ann Smith, who departed this life Jan 22nd 1814 in the 36 year of her age.

In memory of Susanna Crane, wife of George Crane, who died Jan 18th 1839 aged 30 years.

In memory of Susan J. Crane, wife of George Crane, who departed this life Aug 22nd 1811, aged 36 years.

In memory of Jane R. Artis, who died February 9th 1856 aged 19 years.

In memory of Samuel Bean, who departed this life Jan 24th 1831 aged 42 years.

In memory of Mary Bean, born November 25 1788, died Nov 19th 1855.

In memory of William Greenwell died Octo 30th 1801.

"William's Fortune," or "Long Neck," is near Scotland P. O., St. Inigoes district, about five miles from Miller's wharf on the left hand side of the "Three Notched Road," leading from the Pine to Point Lookout. The inscriptions are:

In memory of Thomas Biscoe Died Apr 29th 1816, Aged 60 years, 11 month and 21 days.

In memory of Margaret Biscoe Born Apr. 14th 1764 Died July 20th 1833.

Mary Biscoe Died Aug 15th 1800, Aged 31 years.

In memory of Bennett Biscoe, who departed this life Dec 22nd 1822, aged 54 years 6 months and 23 days.

In memory of Bennett Biscoe Died Aug 28th 1821, Aged 15 years, 6 month and 23 days.

In memory of Elizabeth Biscoe, Died March 9th 1804, Aged 71 years.

Thomas Biscoe, her husband, is buried near her, his grave not marked. These are the parents of Gen. George Biscoe, the father of Mrs. Henry Edward Calvert of Mount Airy, Prince George's county, Md.

In memory of Richard W. Bennett died May 4th 1821 aged 50 years and 6 months.

In memory of Ann Bennett, Died Jan 14th 1824 in the 37th year of her age.

Thomas Bennett, who was born March 8th 1785, Died Aug 27th 1828.

Mary Artis, Died Aug 10th 1826 Aged 32 years 8 months and 19 days.

Jeremiah Artis, Died Feb 13th 1838 aged 55 years, 10 months and 16 days.

Elizabeth Artis, Died July 10th 1824 Aged 40 years 6 months & 15 days.

Joseph Artis, Died May 3d 1829 in the 32 year of his age.

Margaret Smith Died Dec. 30th 1816, Aged 31 years.

Thomas Smith, the husband, is buried by her side, but his grave is not marked. Five children have their graves marked with headstones and there are seven mounds unmarked.

We can show no monument to indicate the spot where our first settlers were buried, but we have our traditions about the Indian building converted by them into a Christian chapel; and Mr. James W. Thomas, an antiquarian who has given much time to the subject, has drawn a map of St. Mary's City showing where its successor stood. Around this chapel was "Ye ordinary burying place in St. Maries Chapell Yard," alluded to in John Lloyd's will, dated 1658. This was the earliest of which we have any record. As late as 1683, about fifty years after the landing of the Maryland Pilgrims, we find the following provisions, made apparently for a new graveyard:

Ordered and granted by his lordship in council that what quantity of land shall be thought necessary to be laid out for the Chapell, Statehouse and Burying place at the City of St. Maries shall (to save any man's particular Right and Property there whole and entire) be supplied by some other of his lordship's land thereunto contiguous, least prejudicial to his Lordship.

This land at least has been identified, for the State House was converted into an Episcopal church at the time of its establishment in the province, and was standing till the year 1829. Near its site, which within recent years has been marked by low granite pillars, a subterranean vault was discovered where tradition says a Colonial Governor is buried. The question has been settled beyond a doubt, that this was Sir Lionel Copley, the first Royal Governor. He was sent over in 1691, and died in less than two years after his arrival, and it is a matter of record that he and his wife were buried in a vault at St. Mary's.

On the left hand side of the road leading from Trinity church to St. Inigoes, is what is known as the "Graveyard Lot." Here lie in unmarked graves inclosed by a brick wall the ashes of Margaret Mackall Brome, wife of James M. Brome, who died April 13, 1814; John Mackall, who died August 18, 1813, aged 75 years, and Margaret Gough Mackall, the wife of John Mackall.

The marked graves in the "Graveyard Lot" are as follows:

In memory of James M. Brome who departed this life Feb. 9th 1823, aged 31 years 9 months and 11 days.

Sacred to the memory of John Ashcom, who departed this life in the full hope of a happy immortality, on the 3rd. day of April 1839, aged 44 years 10 months and 20 days.

Sacred to the memory of George Ashcom. Born Aug. 8th 1792. Died April 24th 1846. aged 53 years 8 months and 16 days.

Porto Bello was the Hebb homestead. It is on the St. Mary's river, nearly opposite St. Mary's City, and the terminus of the road known as the road leading from Leonardtown to Porto Bello. The property is now owned by the Hyatts. Three inscriptions are noted here.

In memory of Mr. William Hebb who dyd May 25th 1758 in the 46th year of his Age.

Vernon Hebb, Son of William and Ann Hebb, Departed this Life Oct. 26 in the sixth year of his age.

Elizabeth Thompson who departed this life July 18th 1802, Aged 49 years ten months & 21 Days.

"Ellenborough," now owned by William D. Henry, is about a mile distant from Leonardtown, and on the left-hand side of the road leading south. P. O. address and steamboat landing "Leonardtown." Formerly it was the Reeder home and for more than a century the Harris home, Col. Joseph Harris marrying Susanna Reeder, the latter part of the eighteenth century. In the graveyard may be found the following:

In memory of Judith Townley Reeder and her three little children, Jane, Thomas and Susannah, by her Affectionate Husband & their tender Father, Henry Reeder, to whom she was married ye 7th of July 1767, from whom he departed this Life the 24th of October 1771, Aged 27 years, being born the 26th of January 1744.

> How loved, how honored once availes thee not
> To whom related or by whom begot
> A heap of dust alone remains of thee
> Tis all thou art and all the proud shall be.

The verse to the children begins:

> Happy the babe who privileged by fate—

The rest of the inscription is illegible.

Henry Reeder, the husband of Judith Townley Reeder, is buried near, but grave unmarked. There were Reeders also at "Westfield," St. Mary's county; Dr. Gustavus Brown is buried there.

Susannah Harris, wife of Joseph Harris, born June 20th 1782 died April 17th 1827. She loved and was beloved by her family, was benevolent to all and charitable to the poor, devoutly hoping for the mercy of God, through the merits of the Redeemer.

Joseph Harris, born August 7th, 1773. Died March 27 1855. He enjoyed the respect and esteem due to an intelligent, upright and benevolent gentleman.

Jane Harris daughter of Joseph & Susanna Harris. Born Jany 21 1813. Died Oct 22 1831. Our loss is her eternal gain.

Martha M. Harris, daughter of Joseph and Susanna Harris, born Oct 4th 1811. Died May 30th 1837. All who knew her loved her.

In memory of Elizabeth Sanders, wife of John Sanders, who departed this Life December 13th 1802, Aged 23 years 8 months and 3 Days.

> Weep not for me my Husband dear,
> I am not dead but sleepeth here.
> Remember well as you pass by,
> As you are now, so once was I
> As I am now so must you be,
> Prepare for death and follow me.

There are three other gravestones and several unmarked graves, those of Col. Benjamin Gwynn Harris and his wife being among the number.

"Rosecroft," as it is now spelled, is reached by a road running through "St. Mary's Manor," formerly known as Mattapony street. It is about two miles from Brome's wharf and St. Mary's City P. O., is owned by the Kennedys, having been formerly the home of the collector of the Potomac district, Daniel Wolstenholme. In the old graveyard we find the following:

In memory of George Campbell who departed this life May 11th 1806 aged 32 years.

In memory of Ann Campbell consort of George Campbell who departed this life March 21st. 1807 aged 30 years.

There are two gravestones of children of George and Ann Campbell—two unmarked graves, and evidences of two.

In the "Deep Falls" graveyard are buried the following:

Major William Thomas Sr. died March 25th. 1795. A soldier of the Revolution.

James Thomas, son of Major William Thomas Sr, wounded at "Long Island" and died at home April 21st., 1781.

Elizabeth, wife of Major William Thomas Sr. died Aug 15th, 1808 aged 94 years.

Major William Thomas Jr, died Aug 1st, 1813.

A tablet, marking the resting place of Maj-Gen. James Thomas, reads:

In memory of Major Gen James Thomas, Ex-Governor of Maryland born March 11th, 1785, died Dec 25th, 1845, aged 60 years, 9 months and 14 days. This Monument is erected as a tribute of affection by his children.

> Green be the turf above thee
> Friend of my better days,
> None knew thee but to love thee
> None named thee, but to praise.

Jane Armstrong, his wife, is buried near, but her grave is unmarked.

These tablets also are found:

In memory of Geo. Thomas born Feb 23 1794, died November 22nd 1857 This monument is erected by a bereaved and sorrowing wife.

Mary Tubman, wife of Geo Thomas, died Aug 8th 1870, aged 80 years. Grave unmarked.

Eliza Courtes, wife of Gov, James Thomas, born Aug 16th 1789 died Nov, 3rd. 1851. This monument is erected to her memory as a tribute of affection by her children.

Richard Thomas, born June 20, 1797, died Octo. 30th. 1849. He was long a member of the Legislature of Maryland, and for many years President of the Senate with unanimous applause. Standing always honorably high in public confidence and private affection.

There are twelve other graves marked, and fifteen unmarked.

A unique memorial was exhumed in 1886 by the sexton of Old Poplar Hill, or St. George's church, while digging a grave. The Rector, Rev. Maurice Vaughan, reported the discovery to the Maryland Historical Society shortly afterward, but nothing was done until about the year 1896, when, through the instrumentality of the late Mr. Buck, Rector of Rock Creek parish, Washington, D. C., it was removed to the east wall of the vestry room. It is in a fairly good state of preservation, but the meaning of the heraldic devices that adorn its lower half has so far defied the skill of those supposed to be proficient in the ancient art of heraldry. The inscription, which is entirely in Latin, records the name of Francis Sourton, who died in 1679, and a portion of it forms a border around the edge of the stone. It reads:

Francis Sourton, Anglo-Devon Francisi Filius Veritas Evangelical Atque Ecclesiastes, Heic Sedulus Vita Rrevi & Saepius Aflicta Functus est Sep. 1679.

The legend following the above is much defaced by time. A version of it, translated, reads as follows:

And thou reader, living in the Lord Jesus Christ, keep the faith, and thou also though dead shalt live.

CHAPTER III

CALVERT county lies between the Chesapeake bay and the Patuxent river, consequently its shores are indented by innumerable coves and creeks, that, through their names, challenge investigation and bridge over the distances of time and space. Battle Creek is one of these names, and, linked with that of Brooke, it carries us far into the field of conjecture.

Robert Brooke, who with his second wife, ten children, and a retinue of servants, came from England in 1650, to take command of a newly projected county, had first married Mary, daughter of "Thomas Baker of Battle, Esq." in England.

At Battle Creek farm, owned by Thomas Watt Williams, we find traditions of Brooke occupancy and of an old family burying ground, where there was once quite a number of tombs. Now one alone remains, bearing this inscription:

Elizabeth Dare, Born 31st. Dec. 1780 [1782 ?], Died 6th Oct. 1805. She was the wife of Doctor John Dare and the daughter of Basil and Anne Brooke.

Fond affection weep no more
I am not lost but gone before
Prepare to follow.

Not far from Battle Creek is a farm known variously as "Duke's Adventure," "Old Orchard," and "Old Place." This is owned by Col. Thomas Brooke.

At "Brooke Place," a knowledge of the exact spot, where the unfortunate progenitor of the Brookes was buried, has been transmitted as a sacred heritage from father to son up to the present day. Robert Brooke died here at the age of

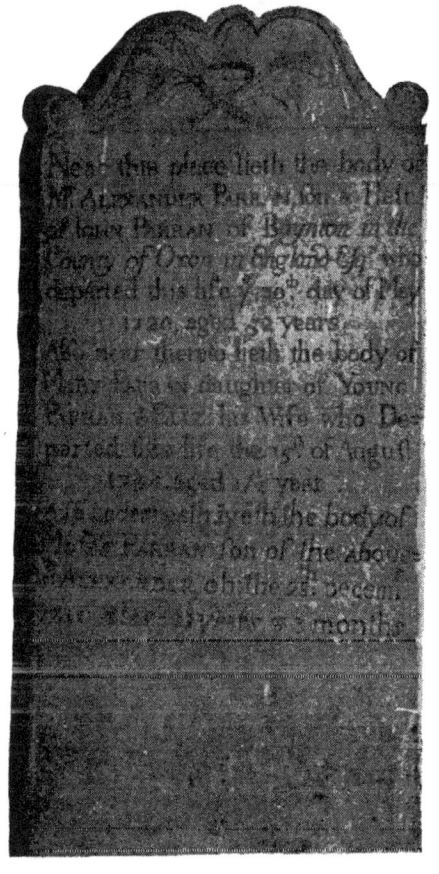

A Tablet in Middleham Chapel
Calvert County

fifty-three, on July 30, 1655, not surviving long the loss of the Lord Proprietary's favor. A spring near by serves to keep his memory green, but there is no monument. To Old England, we must look for "storied urn or animated bust" to ascertain the prominence of the family there.

At Whitechurch, Hants, we find as the "pietatis opus" of another Robert Brooke the following epitaph:

This grave (oh griefe) hath swallowed up with wide and open mouth
The body of good Richard Brooke of Whitechurch, Hampton South,
And Elizabeth his wedded wife, twise Twentie years and one.
Sweet Jesus hath their souls in heaven, ye ground flesh, skin and bone.
In Januarie, worne with age, daie sixteneth died hee.
From Christ full fifteene hundred years and more by ninety-three;
But death her twist of life in Maie, daie twentieth did untwine,
From Christ full fifteen hundred years and more by ninety-nine.
They left behind them, well to live and grown to good degree,
First Richard, Thomas, Robert Brooke the youngest of the three;
Elizabeth and Barbara and Dorothee the last
All six the knot of nature, love and kindness, keeping Fast.
This toomstone with the plate thereon, thus graven fair and large
Did Robert Brooke, the youngest sonne, make of his proper charge.
A citizen of London State by faithful service Free,
Of Marchant greate Adventurers a brother sworne was hee;
And of the Indian Companie, come gain or loss or lim
And of the Goldsmith liverie, All these God gifte to him
This monument of memorie in love performed hee
December thirtie-one from Christ, Sixteen hundred and Three.
              Anno Domini, 1603–
              Laus Deo.

The parish register of Whitechurch tells us that Thomas Brooke, Esq., was buried September 17, 1612, and that Susan, his wife, was buried the following day. There is a tradition that their monument once stood in the church near the altar. They are the parents of Robert Brooke of Brooke Place, and among their numerous descendants in Maryland are many who have added credit and distinction to the name.

A full account of the Brooke family is given in the *Mary-*

land Historical Magazine, beginning with March, 1906, but an unusual incident connected with one of the names may be of interest here. Thomas Brooke, a relative of Charles Carroll's wife, and a "Popish Priest" was tried *after death* for having during life exercised the functions of his mission. This trial took place somewhere between the years 1702 and 1714, the period covered by the reign of "Good Queen Anne." The provincial government had become absorbed by the crown upon the accession of William and Mary and the laws in force against "Jesuits and trafficking Papists," in England, were attempted here. In fact the celebrated "Act of Toleration," passed by the General Assembly of Maryland in 1649, became for a time more honored in the breach than in the observance.

Another name, well known in the annals of our state, is recorded on gravestones in Calvert county. On a farm, owned by Mr. John B. Mackall, St. Leonard's Creek, are to be found three massive brown stones, two of which are to the memory of the parents of Thomas Johnson, our first governor. The graves are on a knoll, a few hundred yards from the residence of Mr. Mackall, and the inscriptions are:

In memory of Thomas Johnson Born February 19th 1702. Died April 12th 1777.

In memory of Dorcas Johnson Born November 2nd 1705. Died November 11th 1770.

In memory of Rebecca McKenzie Born November 8th 1730 Died March 11th 1767.

The first Thomas Johnson arrived in Maryland in 1690. He married Mary, daughter of Roger Baker of Liverpool, and died in 1716. His wife died also, leaving an only son, born February 19, 1702. The latter, also named Thomas, married Dorcas Sedgwick of Connecticut. They had five children, of whom Thomas, the youngest, became Governor of Maryland at the outbreak of the Revolution. He was born in 1732, married, in 1776, Ann, daughter of Thomas Jennings of Annapolis, and died in 1809. He is buried in All Saints cemetery at Frederick.

The Mackalls of Calvert county have a distinguished record also. Benjamin Mackall, Judge of the Court of Appeals and member of the Maryland Convention in 1776, is buried at "God's Graces," his father's place on the Patuxent. At "Hallowing Point," opposite "God's Graces," another Benjamin Mackall is buried, besides members of the Covington family. His wife's mother was a Miss Hollyday.

The name of the Point may have been originally "Hallooing Point," or the spot whence a shout for the ferryman could be heard across the water. There are places in Maryland to this day where the same custom prevails. During a three days' driving trip taken a few years ago by the writer with a friend, the ferry near Bennett's Point was reached. We wanted to cross to Wye Island, but there was no visible means of doing so. Had it not been for the services of an obliging countryman, whose vocal chords had evidently been trained by long practice, a very interesting trip might have been cut short. Ferries were of so much importance to the settlers in early times, that they were provided for by Acts of Assembly.

Christ Church in the lower end of the county, and still the parish church of that section, stands for much in its religious life. On the south wall of the present edifice, erected about the year 1772, is a tablet to the memory of Col. Alexander Somervell, the builder of the church. The name of Somervell, spelled in different ways, is found in many of the private burial grounds of the county, and it represents a family known for its attachment to the traditions of the Episcopal Church. The inscription is:

In memory of Col. Alexander Somerville and Rebecca his wife Decessus 1783 Ætatis 49 Decessa 1812 Ætatis 72.

In this church which he built and of which she was the ornament this taken of affection is reared by their grand-daughter Mrs. Sarah H. Bond. May we always remember them and asPire to imitate their virtues.

An inscription commemorating a former rector is:

Here lieth Interred the Body of ye Reverend Mr. Jonathan Cay, son of Mr Robrt Cay of New Castle uPon Tine, Rector of this Church 22 years. He died the 9th of May 1737, Aged 57 years.

The active religious life of the community dates from the preaching of George Fox, the Quaker, who was in Maryland in 1672. The first known church register of births, deaths and marriages, alluded to on the records, was begun at this time. Very possibly the Rev. Ambrose Sanderson, who by a chain of circumstances has been indicated as the minister of the earlier church, reaped the harvest of another's seeding. It is thought that his ashes repose beneath Christ Church. After his death, in 1682, his daughter Mary, wife of Michael Taney, the County Sheriff, a post of honor in those primitive times, made an appeal for aid to the Archbishop of Canterbury, which led to a serious consideration of the colonist's religious needs among those in high circles. The Rev. Paul Bertram was sent over to take charge of the church, in answer to this demand. Thus we find the name of Taney, so well known at a later period in the person of our distinguished chief justice, one of significance in the early history of the province.

Many of the descendants of Richard Smith, who arrived in the Province with his wife, Eleanor, in 1651, are buried in Calvert county, and having intermarried with the Brookes, the Mackalls, the Holdsworths, the Parrans, the Somervells and other prominent families, the blood of the attorney-general is pretty well distributed in every part of the state. One son, Capt. Richard Smith, was vestryman and warden of Christ Church. He was also surveyor-general of the Province. Born in England, before 1651, he died in Maryland in 1714. Another son, Col. Walter Smith, was among the vestrymen of All Saints parish church in the northern part of the county. He was also born in England and died in 1710.

At Middleham Chapel, Christ Church parish, built in 1748 on the site of an earlier church, are two marble slabs of quaint design. The inscriptions on these suggest the tombstone lore of Old England, and well they may, for one is from the pen of Pope and the other from that of Joseph Addison. The first is copied from a mural tablet in a church at Northampton, England, where a certain Anne Shorthouse reposes; the second, in Old-English lettering, indicates the place of burial of John, the young son of Dr. George Cook, a former rector. The old bell, given in 1699, by John Holdsworth, is still used to call the congregation to worship. These interesting slabs are inscribed:

Here lies the Body of John Cook son of the Rev'd Dr George Cook, Rector of this Parish. He dyed 5th Jan'y 1759 Aged 15 years 6 months. "The Soul Secur'd in her Existence smiles at the drawn dagger and defies the point. The stars shall fade away the sun shall grow dim with age, and nature sink in years. But thou shalt flourish in immortal youth, unhurt amidst the Wars of Elements and the wrecks of Matter and the Crush of Worlds." (ADDISON)

In memory of Robert Addison who died suddenly Dec 30 1785 Aged 59 years and 8 mos.
"How lov'd how valu'd once avails thee not
To whom related or by whom begot
A heaP of dust alone remains of thee
Tis all thou art and all ye Proud shall be." (POPE)
LIFE HOW SHORT, ETERNITY HOW LONG.

In the south wall is a tablet, with this inscription:

Near this place lieth the body of Mr. Alexander Parran, Son and Heir of John Parran of Baynton, in the County of Oxon, in England who departed this life ye 30th day of May 1729, aged 52 years.

Also near thereto lieth the body of Mary Parran daughter of Young Parran and Eliz: his wife who DeParted this life the 15th of Aug. 1744 aged 1½ years.

Also underneath lyeth the body of Moses Parran son of the above Alexander, ob; the 28th Decem 1740 Ætas-33 years and 3 mos.

An old tomb, near the north wall, bears two inscriptions:

Here lies the Body of Ann Parran who DeParted this Life August 3rd 1775 Aged 31 years.

Near this Place lies the Body of Moses Parran who DeParted this Life September the 5th 1773 Aged 22 years.

Inscriptions of a later date are to the memory of:

Thomas Hart Benton Bourne Son of Sarah J. and James J. Bourne died 1860 aged 26.

Sarah J. Bourne died 1884 aged 71.

William Coster died 1870 aged 72.

James Bourne son of James J. and Sarah Bourne born 1825 died 1868.
Walter Hellen born 1833 died 1887.

Soloman's Island was once Bourne's, and the oldest house on it, now occupied by the Obertons, was the home of Dr. Bourne.

The graves in this burial ground are mostly of a late date, as above, but they transmit the following names: Somersville, Sedwick, Wilson, McDaniel, Darel Parran and Coster. Those earlier than 1850 are as follows:

Ellen D. Tongue died 1805 aged 41.

James Tongue died 1843 aged 64.

Anna Tongue wife of Dr James Tongue died 1843 aged 61.

Jonathan Needham died 1811 aged 47.

Elizabeth Dare died 1815 aged 69.

Alexander Dawkins died 1845, aged 27.

Francis Parran died 1842 aged 49.

Ann B. Parran wife of Francis K. Parran died 1857 aged 60.

Marietta Hodgkin Dare wife of Nathaniel Dare died 1852 aged 41.

James M. Sollers died 1842 aged 26.

Sarah Sollers.

Jane Sollers died 1849 aged 59 [39?].

Mary Parran died 1818 aged 57.

Alex. Parran died 1805 aged 45.

Charles S. Parran died 1785 aged 26.

On the McDaniel, or Parran, place, the following were found:

Sacred to the Memory of John Ireland who departed this life March the 24th In the year of our Lord 18— aged 66 years and 3 weeks.

In memory of Dr Joseph Ireland who departed this life in the City of Baltimore on the 2 December 1823 Aged 57 years.

Mary J. Peyton born Nov. 24th 1843 died January 30th 1844.

James John son of Dr Joseph and Mary Ireland Born Sept 12th 1821 Died April 15th 1828.

These six stones were found in an almost inaccessible spot back of Drum Point, on what was once a part of the "Mill Mount" property.

Sacred to the memory of John B. Tolley Who departed this life on the 25th March 1840 in the 40th year of his age.

> He lived in peace with all mankind
> And died regretted by all who had
> his friendship.
> Ye living men come view the ground
> Where you must shortly lie.

Sacred to the memory of Elizabeth wife of John B. Tolley and daughter of John Willoughby who departed this life Jan 10th 1830 in the 26th year of her age.

> Here where this silent marble weeps
> A friend, a wife, a mother sleeps
> My Saviour shall my life restore
> And raise me from my dead [dread] abode
> My flesh and Soul shall part no more
> But dwell forever with my God.

Sacred to the memory of John Willoughby who departed this life on the 3rd April 1826 Aged 59.

> A man sedate of sober mind
> To wife and children ever kind
> [Rest lost by break in stone.]

In memory of Rebecca Willoughby who departed this life March 15 1827 Aged 52 years.

> Kind angels watch her sleeping dust
> Till Jesus comes to raise the just
> When may she wake, with sweet surprise
> And in her Saviour's image rise.

Sacred to the memory of Captain Alex Beard who departed this life the 31st of August 1821.

In memory of Mary Cryer who was born May 29th 1792 and departed this life June 29th 1831 Aged 39 years and one month.

The Dare Place, now inhabited by Wallace Dalrymple, has a very old graveyard, all grown up with trees, briars and swamp. Only two tombs could be found. Nothing legible but the names of John Dare and Elizabeth Dare.

At Mr. Hellen's farm on Mill Creek, under some old gnarled trees in the orchard, are two stones:

In memory of Mrs Elizabeth Pattison who departed this life February 20th 1808 Aged 60 years.

Affliction sore long time I bore
Physicians were in vain
Till God alone he heard my moan
And eased me of my pain.

In memory of John Pattison, who died in 1805, Aged 62.

In solemn silence let him lie
Nor dare disturb his dust
Till the archangel rends the sky
And wakes the sleeping just.

At the Preston place, below Mrs. Wilson's, may be seen these two inscriptions:

To my husband Richard J. Wells, born Feb. 24th 1823; died Sept 8th 1857. Aged 34 years 6 months and 25 days.

Elizabeth Gantt, daughter of Richard and Susannah Wells, born January 10th 1851 departed this life August 12th 1852 19 months and 2 days.

On the old Duke place, between Mutual and Hellen's church and Battle Creek, known as "Dukes," now in possession of Col. John Brooke, are a number of old stones, among which are:

James Duke, son of James and Rebecca Duke Born August 27th 1797, Died April 16 1843.

Ann Maria Duke, wife of James Duke, daughter of John Thomas and Ann Laveille. Born Sept 4th 1801 died August 28 1839.

Eliza Howard, daughter of James J. and Carrie Owen Duke, born Feb. 25th; Died Oct 28th 1862.

Dr. James J. Duke son of Ann Maria and James Duke Born Oct 22nd 183– died Sept 3rd 1876.

Alexander Duke son of James and Rebecca Somervell Duke born Sept 13th 1788 died Feb. 7th 1885.

Mary Broome Duke his wife.

John J. Brooke born August 11th 1789 married Oct. 25th 1810 departed this life April 16th 1856.

Mrs Juliet Brooke wife of John J. Brooke Born 25th Sept 1791 died Oct 11th 1810.

Ann Rebecca Duke daughter of James and Ann Maria Duke, born Dec. 1822 died Dec. 1823.

Ann Maria Duke daughter of James and Ann Maria Laveille born 1832 died 1838.

Mrs Mary Bausman wife of the Rev John Bausman departed this life Jan. 29th 1826 in the 31st year of her age.

Basil Duke Bond Born April 4th 1817 died December 28th 1890.

Mary Wheeler wife of Basil Duke Bond born Oct 22nd 1820 married Nov. 15 1838 died March 13th 1853.

The old Laveille place, on Battle Creek, was bought of Moses Parran Duke. Here are buried:

Col. Uriah Laveille born 1800; died 1855.

Mary Laveille, daughter of Joseph and Mary Harris, born 1806; died 1877.

At the Pardoe place, near the Wilson place, on the bay side, are buried:

Samuel Parran, born 1780; died 1845.

Elizabeth, his wife, born 1799; died 1850.

Another inscription here reads:

Here lies Interred the Body of Mr. John Rousby (only son of the Hon'ble JOHN ROUSBY Esq.) who departed this life the 28th day of January Anno Domini 1750 Aged 23 years and 10 mos.

Three miles from Prince Frederick, on the Huntingtown road, is the old Holdsworth house, owned of late by the Gaunt family. Three of the Gaunts are buried here:

Dr. Thomas C. Gaunt [Gantt] Died January 29th 1829 In the 43rd year of his age.

Dr. Thomas C. Gaunt Son of Dr. Thos. and Susan Gaunt Born Sept 18 1818 Died Jan. 4th 1844 Aged 25 years 3 months and 16 days.

James Edward son of Dr. Thos. C. and Susan Gaunt Born Nov. 26th 1826; Died Sept 3rd 1831, Aged 4 years and 9 months.

James Truman in his will, dated 1672, mentions his daughters Martha, Mary and Elizabeth, whom he left to the care of his two brothers in case of his widow's marriage. This lady was named Anne, and her tomb, found after much diligent search, on a farm owned by Mr. Basil Duke, near Prince Frederick, Calvert county, shows that she consoled herself for her loss by becoming the wife of Robert Skinner, "Gent." The inscription is:

Here lyeth the Body of Mrs Ann Skinner, first the relict of James Truman, Gent., afterwards that of Robt. Skinner, Gent., who died the 3rd day of August 1717, about 75 years, having lived near half that time a widow.

This most elusive stone, incorrectly reported to members of the Memorial Committee as that of Robert Skinner, was found, after three years' search, in a thicket on top of a plateau, buried several inches below the surface of the ground.

On the Morton farm, at Hunting Creek, Stokely, near the stable, is a family burial place, all grown up with weeds. Some stones are down, others are standing. Some of the inscriptions we give:

Mrs Ann Somervell departed this life 28 . . . 1789 aged 22 years 10 months and 15 days.

Mr. John Somervell departed this life Dec. 24 1826 Aged 70 years 7 months and 9 days.

Mrs Sarah Ireland departed this life Sept 1st 1809 Aged 48 years 1 month and 29 days.

Mr. James Somervell departed this life Oct. 10th 1773 Aged 43 years 8 months and 6 days.

Susan Somervell departed this life May 15th 1840 Aged 66 years 10 months and 2 days.

Mr. Hone Somervell departed this life October 6th 1821 Aged 58 years 10 months and 27 days.

Ann Truman Somervell departed this life Sept 1st 1814.

Sacred To the memory of Mrs Susan Harris Consort of Alexander Harris and daughter of Hone and Susan Somervell Born March 20 1816 Died April 28 1857 Aged 31 years.

TOP OF THE TOMB OF JOHN ROUSBY
In the graveyard at "Rousby Hall," Patuxent River, Calvert County

Calvert County

Nathaniel Aged 10 months Nathaniel D. Aged 15 days Children of Hone and Susan. Of such is the Kingdom of Heaven.

Leonard Hollyday Somervell Departed this life April 15th 1814 Aged 12 months and 10 days.

Sacred To the memory of Sarah Jane, wife of James Somervell of Prince George's County and daughter of the Hon. Thos H. Williamson, of Calvert County, Died May 27th 1844 Aged 26 years.

She lived and died a Christian Her bright example inspired many hearts with love and her name is still uttered with praise by many lips.

In fond remembrance of Thomas Truman Son of James and Ann Magruder Somervell who died July 26 1845 Aged 39 years one month and 7 days.

Mrs. Susannah Somervell departed this life August 5th 1787 Aged 55 years 3 months and 13 days.

Mrs. Elizabeth H. Somervell departed this life April 27th 1815 Aged 54 years 5 months and 21 days.

On a place formerly owned by the Dares and Allnutts, but now in the possession of Mr. Schemell, we find the following:

Here lyeth the Body of Sarah Dare, who departed this life December the 7th 1787 Aged 58 years.

John Dare Ireland [dates illegible].

D. [dates illegible].

Sarah E. daughter of Rich'd and Priscilla Dare departed this life 9th mo 5 1842. Aged 2 years and 9 days.

Thomas C. Dare Jr. departed this life 8th mo 7 1843 Aged 35 years 1 month and 29 days.

Gideon Allnutt son of Francis and Sarah Allnutt born Dec. 10th 1815 died Mar. 30 1879.

Priscilla D. wife of Richard S. Dare departed this life . . . 12 mo 25 1858 Aged 49 years 3 months and 25 days.

Dr. George Dare Born August 19th 1795 died March 15th 1813.

Sally S. Dare Born April 2nd 1818 died March 5th 1851.

John Thomas Ireland, Mary Dare Ireland, M. S. D. 1821.

Thomas C. Dare Sr departed this life 9th month 29 183–8 Aged 59 years 9 months and 19 days.

Elizabeth Snowden The wife of Thomas C. Dare Sr. departed this life 3rd month 26 1851 Aged 75 years 7 months and 9 days.

Richard S. Dare Son of Thomas C. and Eliza Dare Born Nov 16 1805 Died Jan. 6th 1868.

Also about six other stones with only the letter "D," no dates.

The last of the Calvert county inscriptions noted, are in an old cemetery on the farm of Mr. John G. Roberts, near the bay. They are:

Sarah Waters Born Oct. 27th 1779 Died December 30th 1848.

Mrs. Betty H. Beckett born August 31st 1764 died Oct 15 1831.

Mr. John Beckett husband of Mrs. Betty H. Beckett born March 16 1764 died Sept 2 1803.

Captain John Beckett died May 20th 1850 in the 59th year of his age.

Richard Beckett born Sept 23 1802 died April 2 1855.

Mary Heighe Blake died March 24th 1840 in the 70th year of her age.

Miss Mary H. Beckett born February 22 1788 died Feb. 19th 1852.

John Beckett son of Richard and Maria Beckett born Sept 30th 1835 died December 21st 1852.

In that portion of Charles county, which is indented by a bend of the Potomac river, lies Port Tobacco Creek, anglicized from "Pertafacca," an Indian name, descriptive of its position in the hollow of the hills. Port Tobacco was one of the original centers of the Church of England, established in 1692, as well as one of the oldest stations of the Jesuits in Maryland. On a bluff overlooking the creek, stands the venerable mansion of St. Thomas' Manor, which for years has been the home of the Jesuit Fathers, the cornerstone of the church attached to it having been laid about one hundred years ago. In the little graveyard repose some well-known sons of St. Ignatius, including Neales, Barbers and others who have labored in the missionary field. Unfortunately, there are no stones here of a very early date, that of Rev. John H. Pile, who died in 1813, seeming to be the oldest.

Col. William Chandler directed in his will, executed about the year 1731, that he should be buried in old St. Thomas' graveyard on Chapel Point. Here also we must look for the graves of his sister Mary, the wife of Boswell Neale, who died before him, and of his sister Jane, the wife of Henry Brent, who was living at the time his will was made. In "Chandler's Hope," a homestead on a steep hill overlooking Port Tobacco, the ancient county seat, and in Brentland post office, across the creek from Chapel Point, we have a survival of these names. One ancient tomb recorded as having been at St. Thomas' chapel, is that of Elizabeth, wife of Edward Diggs, Gent., who died on May 9, 1705. She was the daughter of Col. Henry Darnell, of "The Woodyard," and Ellinor (Hatton) Brooke, his wife.

We naturally ask, "Where are the ashes of those, who like the Jesuit Fathers, William Winter and Robert Brooke, and the Franciscan, Rev. Basil Hobart, labored as missionaries here, and suffered persecution during the period of transition from the government of a Catholic Lord Proprietary to that of a Protestant king?" All trace of these seems to be lost forever, and even Father William Hunter, Superior of the order in Maryland, who died in 1723, and to whom is accredited the founding of the Newport mission, in 1697, has no stone to mark his grave.

Newport is situated about six miles from Lothair, the nearest railroad station. In the shadow of its church, built in 1840, is a venerable burying ground, where a tombstone bearing the date 1790 is reported to be the oldest.

"Rose Hill," near Port Tobacco, is an old homestead associated with the name of Dr. Gustavus Richard Brown, one of the many physicians accredited to the "Father of his Country." He was born in 1748, graduated in Edinburgh in 1768, married Miss Graham of Prince William county, Va., was elected in 1774 to serve as representative of Charles county in the Legislature, was one of the judges of Charles county court in 1777, and died in 1804. He was enterprising and public-spirited, and is said to have founded a hospital for the inoculation of smallpox, which was opened about June 15, 1776.

Dr. Brown is buried in the family burying ground:

> Sacred to the memory of Dr. Gustavus Richard Brown. This Tomb Stone is erected by his relict Margaret Brown in testimony of her respect and affection and as a Monument of his Skill as a Physician and his Learning as a Scholar; of his Wisdom as a Philosopher and his Generosity as a Friend; of his Elegance as a Gentleman and his hospitality as a Neighbour; of his kindness as a Master and tenderness as a Husband; . . .

His father, Dr. Gustavus Brown, the fourth of that name, was born in Scotland in 1689. He settled at Port Tobacco, was Justice of Charles county from 1726 to 1762, also chief justice from 1748 to the same period. He married Frances Fowke, who was buried at "Dipple," an estate of her son-in-law Rev. James Scott, on the Virginia side of the Potomac. Her tomb bore this record:

> Here lyeth the body of Frances, wife of Dr Gustavus Brown, of Charles County, Md. By her he had twelve children, of whom one son and seven daughters survive her. She was a daughter of Mr Gerard Fowke, late of Md., and descended from the Fowkes of Gunston Hall in Staffordshire, England. She was born Feb. 2nd 1691 and died much lamented on the 8th of November 1744, in the 54th year of her age.

A third Dr. Gustavus Brown is buried in the Reeder family graveyard at Westfield, St. Mary's county. He died on July 3, 1801, at the age of 50.

To the west of Port Tobacco creek, is Nanjemoy, which has its associations also. The land granted by Lord Baltimore to William Stone, the first Protestant governor, 1649–54, is described as "lying west of Nanjemi Creek on the Potomac." Tradition says that he is buried on the manor (his portion of the tract going by the name of "Poynton Manor"), and a spot on the farm called "Cherry Field," is still pointed out as his grave. He had many children whose descendants lived on "Poynton Manor." Upon a portion of the estate known as "Equality" the founder of another family, well-known and honored in the annals of the state, is buried. This is Samuel Hanson, both father-in-law and grandfather-in-law of David Stone, a great-grandson of Gov. William Stone and the "inheritor of Poynton Manor, with Court Leet and Court Baron." Samuel Hanson's will, made in 1740, helps us to approximate the date of his death. He was a grandson of the Swedish colonel of the name who fought for and died with Gustavus Adolphus at Lützen, November 16, 1632. Samuel Hanson was prominent in county affairs, and his numerous descendants were more or less conspicuous in the public life of their times.

All that section of the county lying between the Nanjemoy creek and the Potomac river was included in "Durham," one of the four Church of England parishes, which after many mutations now remain. The others are, William and Mary, embracing its eastern portion and the peninsula between the Wicomico and the Potomac; Piscataway, or St. John's, extending along the Potomac to the north, and now included in Prince George's county, and Port Tobacco parish. Charles county, during one of these changes, obtained a portion of St. Paul's parish, originally laid out in Calvert. Oldfields' chapel near Hughesville is a part of this later-acquired territory. No eighteenth-century gravestones have been discovered in this churchyard, although the chapel has stood for more than a hundred years, and only one bearing an ancient date appears in the Catholic cemetery of St. Mary's church at Bryantown. It reads:

In memory of Raphael Boarman who died 19th May 1829 Aged 80 years Also Near this lies the remains of Mary, Consort of R. Boarman who died 15 Aug 1786 Aged 21.

The husband outlived the wife 43 years.

The rest of the names antedating the year 1850 are listed as follows:

Raphael Edelen died Sept 13, 1845 aged 33.

Austin Miles died Sept. 19, 1840 aged 28.
>And Thou, oh Heaven! keep what Thou has taken.
>And with my treasure, keep my heart on High
>The Spirit meek, and yet by pain unshaken
>The Faith, the Love, the lofty Constancy
>Guide me where these are, and with my loved one flown
>They were of Thee, and Thou
>Hast taken Thine own.

Alex. Johnson died June 13, 1816 aged 49.
>Vain, vain the transient views of man!
>Deaths stroke subverts each earthly plan
>Oh dreadful . . . Yet all must come.
>You, Reader, too, must meet this doom.
>Reflect your own frail life must tend
>Revere your God, his laws attend
>Your sins wash out with timely tears.
>To God for me direct your prayers.

Mary Carrico died Dec. 11 1849 aged 53. May the Lord be merciful to her.

Augustine Burch	died	Aug.	6, 1834	aged	56.
Susanna D. Burch	"	Feb.	25, 1846	"	63.
John H. Hardy	"	Mar.	25, 1827	"	27.
Igns F. Gardiner	"	Apr.	26, 1841	"	52.
Cath.	"	".	Oct.	24, 1864	"	65.
Mary Rose	"	"	June,	24, 1838	"	17.
John F. Gardiner	"	Sept.	12, 1831	"	78.
Cath.	"	"	"	17, 1823	"	52.
Benj D.	"	"	"	27, 1832	"	23.
Benj Franklin	"	May	10, 1831	"	11.
Marsham Bowling	"	Aug.	2, 1847	"	75.
Margt.	"	"	June	15, 1819	"	56.
Aloysius	"	"	Jan.	1, 1850	"	40.
John H.	"	"	July	17, 1837	"	5 days [?].
Thomas	"	"	Sept.	17, 1829	"	27.
Mary A.	"	"		1829	"	24.
Elizabeth Boswell	"	Sept.	24, 1852	"	26.

>My fraim only lies here in the deep
>My soul is with my God above
>My dearest William, why do you weep?
>May you meet me there to love.

Charles County 67

Mrs. Susan Spaulding died Mar. 1, 1850 aged 54.
Thomas Semmes " Sept. 2, 1829 " 56.
Elizabeth Semmes " July 18, 1853 " 78.
Dr. Geo W. Jameson " Oct. 5, 1827 " 23.
Georgianna " " " 4, 1827 " 5 y 6m.
Sophia Dyer died Sunday " 2, 1831 " 31.

Rev. Edwin M. Southgate, who furnished this list, remarks that the custom of raising stones to the dead was less common before the war than now. With some few exceptions it is still difficult to get the parishioners to look after their burial lots. This curious neglect prevails in spite of the fact that most of them are of the old colonial stock, and very much attached to the memories of their ancestors. An old register of Upper and Lower Zachaiah and Mattawoman congregations is preserved at this church and from it Rev. Ed. Southgate has made the following extracts:

1794.
Ann Johnson, wife to John Johnson died June 28, born 1729.
Martha Morice, wife to Joseph Morice died Aug. 6 " 1707.
Susanna Neale wife to Jeremias Neale died Aug. 10 " 1711.
Martha Hagon.................... " Oct. 29 " 1730.
Jas. O'Brien..................... " Oct. 25 " 1730
The widow Ann Sanders........... " Dec. 23 " 1725.

1795.
The widow Sarah Jameson, died April 9 born 1710.
The widow Elizabeth Simpson, " " 18 " 1719.
John Harbin.............. " May 1 " 1702.
Henry Osbourn............ " May 15 " 1716.
Catherine Harbin .... " June 8 " 1709.

The record is missing up to the year when it continues.

1816-1820.
Patsy Beavin; Joseph Carricoe; Sally Dyer; Ann Gardener; Nancy Middleton; Walter Edelen; Green Dyer; Franc Edelen; Sam Berry; Teresa Berry; Margt. Mudd; Benj. N. Mudd; Mrs. Geo. Edelen; John Boswell; Mrs. Worthing; Ed. Stewart; Julia Boone; Philip Edelen; Julia Mudd; Pres. Langley; Mrs. Hill; Mrs. Jos. Montgomery; Mrs. Leond. Mudd; Willm. Cooke; Eliz. Queen; Eliz. Simms; Tom Jameson; Mrs. Hill; Polly Middleton; Eliz. Smith; Tom Langley; Jas. Montgomery; Mrs. J. Smith;

Jas. Smith; Ally Montgomery; L. Boarman; Margt. Bowling; Walter Mudd; Nic. Langley; Th. Stansberry; Mary A. Gardiner.

1821.
Nancy Jameson; Polly Bowling; Robt. Young; Polly Richard; Teresa Gardiner; Charlotte Gardiner; Sally Boarman; Eliza Dyer; Harriet Jameson; Wm. Stewart; George Jameson; Sally Gardiner; Mrs. Hardy; Monica Reeves; Henry Parker.

1822.
Philip Gardiner; Mrs. Stonestreet; Mary Fenwick; Mrs. F. Diggs; Leonard Mudd; Mrs. Schell; Ann Langley; Hilary Burch; Adeline Harbin; Mary Harbin; Josiah Hamilton; Abel Carricoe; Raphael Jameson; Oswald Dyer,

1823.
Theodore Dyer; Ned Jenkins; Josh Montgomery; Ann Wright; Mrs. Miles; Jeremiah Dyer; Jas. Fenwick; Cath. Gardiner; Rev. Mr. Heath; George Dyer; Rosella Middleton; Sally Jameson; R. L. Edelen.

1824.
Mrs. W. Beaven; Francis Boarman; Wm. Holton; Mrs. L. Smith; Eliz. Jenkins; Theod. Hardy; Rev. Mr. Vergnes; Alex. Langley; Nancy Thompson; Jerry Dyer; R. T. Wilson; R. Willet; Cecilia Gardiner; R. Harbin.

1825.
Thos. C. Reaves Nov. 29th; Louisa Carricoe Dec. 21st; Dr. Donatus Middleton, Dec. 15th.

1826.
Clemintina Queen Jan. 9; Mary Grey, Jan. 20th; Ann Middleton, Mar. 11; Sally Mudd, March 12; Matilda Boarman died May 13, buried 15; Alex. Smith, July 23rd; James Gates; Harriet Gardiner; Susan Murray, Sept. 13. Cath Baker, Sept. 14; Mary A. Bowling Oct. 12, buried 14.

1827.
John H. Hardy, May 21.

1833.
Benj. Dominic Gardiner, Sept. 10; Jas. Boarman, Aug. 5.

1836.
Mary Rose Dyer, wife of Horatio Dyer, Aug. 30th, 1836.

1837.
Ann Boarman, widow of James Boarman, May 23rd; Mary Emily Montgomery, June 24th; Maria Jameson, Sept. 13.

1838.
Mary Rose Gardiner, June 23rd; Rose Langley, July 10th.

1839.
George Boarman, May 25th.

1840.
Ann Middleton, Feb. 18, buried 20th; Cath. Simpson, Apr. 4, buried 6th;

Sarah Jenkins, April 18-19; Elizabeth Reeves, Aged 85, April 22-23; Maria Green, daughter of Cath. Simpson, April 22-23; Ann Queen, Mother of Dr. Queen, Aug. 11; Augustine Miles, Sept. 18-20; Anne Boarman, widow of Raphael, about 90 years of age, Nov. 17-18; Alexius Boarman, died suddenly Dec. 15.

1841.

Henry Montgomery, Jan. 23-25; Mary Bowling, wife of Richard Bowling, April 1-2; Francis Gardiner, April 27-28.

The record from 1841 to 1850 is missing.

We thus occasionally come across in out of the way places, surnames well known in the early history of the Province, and many a name, which in these old graveyards fails to arouse an interest among the present generation, takes a new significance when it appears in the quaintly worded proceedings of Council or Assembly, sometimes directing a captain of a troop to range with his men in one direction, sometimes sending a second in another, in order to be on the lookout for hostile Indians, and when found, to treat with them in a way to win their friendship; or to investigate cruelty and injustice, on the part of either race. It is thus that the personages in a drama long since enacted on Maryland soil are brought before us once more, with suggestions of the picturesque, the pathetic and the tragic. Charles county and Prince George's are both rich in names connected with our early struggles with the Indians, and the discovery of old tombstones within this territory, would furnish materials for a hitherto unwritten chapter of romance.

William Smallwood was the last male representative of a Maryland family that was always prominent in colonial history. His grandfather, Maj. James Smallwood, settled in Charles county at an early date, being a delegate to the General Assembly in 1696. His father, Bayne Smallwood, Esq., was both a merchant and a planter on a large scale, and filled various public offices, among them that of justice of the peace besides being a member of the House of Delegates for a number of years. His mother was Miss Priscilla Heaherd of Virginia, a lady of birth and fortune. She outlived her husband, who died before the Revolution. Like so many of the sons of the affluent in colonial times, William Smallwood was sent to England to be educated. He never married, but, excepting when in the field, fighting for his country, lived with his mother until her death in 1783.

In a letter written by William Smallwood to Governor Paca in 1784, he speaks of his home "Mattawoman." This may be the place known as "Smallwood's Retreat," for this old mansion, about which cluster the traditions of his occupancy, is in the Chickamuxon district, which is near Mattawoman creek. The Smallwoods had a road cut from their place down to the Durham church, which to this day is known as "Smallwood's Church Road."

The Sons of the American Revolution have won glory by erecting a monument in the private burying ground at "Smallwood's Retreat," where General Smallwood lived the greater part of his life, and where it is supposed he is buried. The benighted later generation of this locality will no longer have to consult the *Century Dictionary* or the *Encyclopædia Brittanica* for a record of him and his deeds, as one of our correspondents confesses having done. The inscription on his monument, tells the story thus:

> In memory of General William Smallwood, a hero of the American Revolution, and a native of Maryland. Commissioned Colonel in 1776, Brigadier General in 1777; Major General in 1780. Elected Governor of Maryland in 1785. Died February 14, 1792. Erected by the Maryland Society Sons of American Revolution, July 4, 1898.

The Durham church was built of brick about the year 1732. It was repaired in 1792, and a list has been preserved of those who contributed money or tobacco towards the furtherance of the work. William Smallwood's pledge was for three thousand pounds of crop tobacco, or three times as much

GENERAL WILLIAM SMALLWOOD
From the original in the picture gallery of the Maryland Historical Society

Charles County 71

as any of the subscribers gave in legal tender, and exceeding the most liberal donations in money. This list is interesting, in as much as it furnishes family names, many of which had descended from the early settlers. It acts also as a substitute for those that ought to appear in the churchyard on monuments or slabs of quaint design. The records are full of interest as showing customs that no longer prevail. They extend from 1772 to 1824, all those before 1772 being lost. A history of the parish has been written by the Rev. William P. Painter, and to him we will refer all those who care to pursue the subject further.

In the churchyard is one monument which must not be passed by, modern though it be. It stands on the left side of the walk leading from the gate to the front door of the church, and marks the grave of the Rev. Robert Prout. He died in 1880, but his ministrations began here in 1826, and continued with an intermission of seven years, until within a short time before his death.

The Charles county names, alluded to above, are as follows:
Adams, Addison, Allen, Anderson, Armstrong, Baillie, Barker, Barnes, Bastin, Beale, Bell, Benson, Bloxton, Bowie, Brawner, Brooke, Bullman, Burchell, Burris, Bush, Bradshaw, Channing, Chilton, Clarke, Clinkscales, Cobey, Coffer, Craik, Crawford, Davis, Dent, Doyal, Dunnington, Evans, Franklin, Flowry, Fairfax, Ferguson, Fowke, Fowler, Filbert, Flanagan, Ferril, Fleming, Gardner, Garner, Gaskin, Gilbert, Golden, Gray, Green, Griffin, Groves, Haislip, Hall, Hamilton, Hanson, Hatcher, Harrison, Hayward, Hudson, Jackson, Jenifer, Jenkins, Jones, Keibeard, Kennedy, Lanakin, Leftwitch, Lomax, Luckett, Maddox, Martin, Mason, May, McConkie, Meek, Milstead, Middleton, Mitchell, Muncaster, Murdock, Muschett, McBayne, McLemon, Nally, Nelson, Perry, Picken, Posey, Poston, Price, Ratliff, Retler, Rice, Risen, Rye, Robertson, Russell, Scott, Sennet,

Simmons, Shepherd, Shields, Skinner, Smith, Smoot, Speake, Smallwood, Stoddart, Stone, Stormatt, Stewart, Southerland, Strange, Tallmarsh, Taylor, Thomas, Thompson, Vein, Williams, Waple, Ward, Woodward, Worden, Wright, Young.

At Old Christ Church in the Piccawaxen district, we find no such list of names to bridge over the gap between the old days and the new. The nearest post office is "Wayside," and by the wayside, in a sparsely settled part of the county, stands one of the oldest of our brick churches, amidst its weather stained graves. The locust trees and young cedars overshadowing them, form a belated but voluntary guard of honor.

The writer visited this spot some years ago, when an aged incumbent was in charge. This was before our patriotic societies had begun to arouse a general interest in the antiquities of the state, and before the division of the Diocese of Maryland infused new life into out of the way localities. It is a matter of regret that the inscriptions in the old churchyard did not then appear to her sufficiently venerable to be copied; for there were very few, if any, before the thirties of the last century. She could not foresee, at that time, how important even these more recent names might be to the old mortality of future generations, nor the difficulties in the way of obtaining information afterwards.

William and Mary parish, to which Christ Church belongs, was one of those originally laid out in St. Mary's county. By the change of boundaries and the creation of new parishes, the Charles county section now occupies a solitary position on its peninsula. Here, indeed, have we met the silence of the grave.

The church of St. Ignatius, attended by the Jesuits, stood at Waldorf. The oldest tombstone in the cemetery of St. Peter's is that of Thomas C. Reeves, died 1825, aged 70.

He or his heirs donated his old house to the priests. It still exists, but is no longer the priest's house. Other tombs are:

His wife Elizabeth, died 1840, aged 85. Geo. Dyer, 1822; Dorothy Dyer, 1843. John H. Gibbons, 1843. Robert Merrick, 1834. Thos. M. Dyer, 1835. Eliza: Ellen Wildman, 1854.

She had an aunt in the Carmelite order.

At Marshall Hall, is a stone with this inscription:

Here lyes the body of Sabrina Truman Greenfield Wife of Thomas Marshall deceased and daughter of Thomas Truman Greenfield and Susanna his wife, who departed this life in the 53 year of her age, 1 March, 1768.

From the family burying ground at "Pamonky," on the Potomac, we have the following inscriptions:

In Memory of Henrietta Maria, wife of James Fenwick and daughter of John Lancaster, Who died Feb. 14th 1792.

Sacred to the memory of James Fenwick, who departed this life September the 3rd 1823, in the 60th year of his age. He was the eldest son of Ignatius Fenwick and Sarah Taney his wife.

May he rest in peace.

CHAPTER IV

TO vary the monotony that must inevitably ensue from following names and dates too closely, and from contemplating the skull and cross bones at every turn, it is proposed in this chapter to make a slight digression. As a means to this end the notebook of one of the members of the Colonial Dames, who accompanied the writer on a trip through Lower Maryland, will be largely drawn upon.

The season chosen was the month of June, but the day opened with clouds in the sky. Our first objective point was Old St. Barnabas church, Queen Anne parish, Prince George's county, standing about a mile distant from Leeland, on the Southern Maryland Railroad. Arrangements had been made with a liveryman of Upper Marlborough, the county seat, to have a team awaiting the party at the station, but it failed to materialize. Nothing daunted by this hitch in our plans, we climbed into a lumber wagon, the only thing available going in our direction. Our sable driver proved to be an encyclopedic compilation of facts as to the surrounding neighborhood, and promised valuable assistance in the shape of a conveyance to Upper Marlborough, our next stopping point, if nothing better could be found.

St. Barnabas church stands in a beautiful old grove. It is one of those barn-like brick structures remaining from the past, that derive much of their picturesqueness from the shape of their roofs. This happens to be something between a gambrel and a mansard without windows, dominated by a ridged peak. According to the vestry books, St. Barnabas was erected between the years 1772 and 1773. Cut on a brick near one of the windows at the chancel end, is the date July 3, 1774, the meaning of which is left to conjecture.

In the churchyard no ancient tombs are visible, but it was ascertained from Mrs. Turner, the rector's wife, that the earliest graves lay in front of the church and on the side nearest the public road; also that the dead were so thickly buried there, that no other interments could be made. A lych gate, built in recent years, marks the front boundary of this ancient God's acre, and the land back of the church, where an earlier parsonage stood, has been turned into a graveyard to answer the needs of modern times. The stones here are of comparatively recent date, and among them we find one to the memory of the Rev. Thomas F. Billop, a former rector. He is also honored by a memorial window, one of twelve in the church.

Perhaps the ecclesiastic worthy of the most importance, whose memory is thus perpetuated, is the Rev. Jacob Henderson, commissary of the churches in the Province, sent here by the Bishop of London in 1717, and appointed to the rectorship of Queen Anne parish. His ministrations covered a long period of thirty-four years, and only ended with his death. The marble font, that stands in a recess between the two front doors, and also the communion service, which is still in use, date from the second year of his incumbency.

Our investigations around St. Barnabas church were about over when the Reverend Mr. Turner arrived on the scene. He very kindly put himself and his buggy at our disposal, and, by obtaining the escort of a lady parishioner, we were able to reach Upper Marlborough, five miles away, in time for dinner at the Marlboro' House.

Here our surroundings were nothing, if not historic. The house itself, tradition saith, was built for a bank, and is quaint and rambling; while our landlady—to preserve the historic harmony—was the descendant of Governor Ogle.

The grave of Doctor Beanes is in sight from the porch, surrounded by a brick wall. This inscription is:

William Beanes son of William and Mary Beanes was born January 24 1749 and was married to Sarah Hawkins Hanson November 25, 1773 Died 12th October 1828 in the 80 year of his Age.

Here lies the Body of Sarah Hawkins Beanes Daughter of Samuel and Ann Hanson Born August 12, 1750 Married to William Beanes November 25th 1773 And died 15th July 1822 In the 72nd year of her Age.

The remains of Gov. Thos. Sim Lee (1792–94), buried originally in the Catholic burying ground, now lie in the new churchyard at Upper Marlborough.

An old Clagett place is to be found a little off from the road going from Marlborough towards Rosaryville. The graveyard is indicated by a wooded knoll surrounded by a post and rail fence. Besides some children's graves, of recent date, there are only two stones of any prominence. A prostrate obelisk, inclosed by an iron railing, marks the burial place of its late owner:

Thos. Clagett born Jan. 10, 1791 died Aug. 27th 1873 In the 83rd year of his age. An upright man that feareth God.

On the other monument is inscribed:

Sacred to the Memory of Susan Clagett wife of Thos. W. Clagett born the 25th of October 1814 died the 18th of Nov. 1843. She lived the life of the Righteous and died with Confidence in Jesus.

On a farm between Leeland and Upper Marlborough are some Hillary and Belt graves. The widow Hillary married Benjamin Bowie.

At "Acquasco," formerly "Covington's Fields," now owned by Mr. Watson, and not far from Patuxent, is a stone to the memory of

Mr. Leonard Covington who departed this life the 19th of March 1742 in the 30th year of his age.

"Ranelagh," about six miles from Upper Marlborough and twelve from Washington, is the original home of the Contee family. Amidst the cypress trees in the graveyard is a large flat tombstone supported by four columns which bears the following inscription:

Underneath is interred the remains of Margaret Contee, wife of John Contee who died December 30th 1793 in the 68th year of her age.

A little farther off is buried Mrs. Mary Contee, consort of Richard Alex. Contee and daughter of David and Sarah Craufurd, who died in Upper Marlborough on March 11, in the year of our Lord 1787 in the nineteenth year of her age.

In the graveyard at "Belair," near Collington, once the residence of Governor Ogle, are the graves of Benjamin Ogle, who died April 4, 1845, aged 57, and Anna Maria Ogle, his wife, who died December 28, 1856, in the 80th year of her age.

In a graveyard on the road leading from Berwin to Springfield are buried the following:

W. W. Duvall, died July 27, 1827; Rebecca Duvall born July 28, 1787, died May 8, 1858; Rachel E. daughter of R. Bond & Mary D. Walker, born July 29, 1824, died Nov. 14, 1826.

After a brief refreshment, we renewed our journey, this time for Croome, where the rector, Rev. Frank Willes, was waiting for us. We examined the parish church, St. Thomas', and the churchyard, but found again not much to reward our labor. Bishop Claggett's home place lies between St. Thomas' Croom and Croom station. An effort was made some years ago to endow the church as a memorial to him, but so far it has not been accomplished. Since our visit his body has been removed from the family burial ground to the National Capital, and re-interred in the Cathedral Close.

On the old Claggett place, are the following graves and inscriptions:

Samuel Claggett Esq. Eldest son of Right Rev. J. T. C. Claggett born November 29th 1783 died November 5th, 1824.

Mrs. Mary Ann Eversfield Eldest daughter of Rev. Thomas John Claggett born September 8th, 1776 died August 28th, 1810.

Mrs. Elizabeth Laura Young daughter of Rt. Rev. Thomas John Claggett born March 3rd., 1787 died November 1864.

On a farm owned by Mrs. Fendall Marbury near Croom:

Robert William Bowie born March 3, 1787 died Jan. 3, 1848.
Catherine Lansdale Born Jan. 13th, 1800 Died Oct. 22nd. 1867.
Mary E. L. Bowie Born Sept. 10th, 1823 Died . . . 1838.
Robert Bowie Born Oct. 6th 1821 Died Jan 17th 1860.

From Croom, we pressed on to Nottingham, where we found only desolation. The port of entry once so famous, like its neighbor Benedict, now lies silent and forlorn, with only memories to keep it company. We found here that our cherished plan of an extension into Calvert could not be fulfilled at this time, the boat schedule preventing, so we retraced our road to the rectory, where under the old trees we had a restful little supper, and later drove home through the woody roads, the evening birds singing their sweetest in the cool shades.

Not far from Nottingham, on the old Waring farm, now belonging to Mrs. Wilkinson, daughter of the late E. S. Hollyday, is a genealogical table all on one stone:

Here lies the body of Leonard Waring, who departed this life in the year 1806, in the 60th year of his age; he was the son of Major Frank Waring, who was the son of Basil Waring, Gent; commissioned Capt. of Dragoons by His Majesty George the 3rd on 14th of July 1715, he was the son of Basil Waring the 1st, who was son of Capt. Sampson Waring of His Majesties Provincial Commissioners of Md. who died in the year 1663.

In the same district at Brookefield, the old Hollyday home, is a tombstone with a fine coat of arms and the motto:

Nulle virtute secundus. Here lyeth interred the Body of Coll. Leonard Hollyday who departed this life May 6th 1747 Aged 49 years and 2 days.

The graveyard at Brookefield Manor lies in the part of the estate owned by Mrs. Elizabeth Worthington Bowie, now living in Washington. Among those said to be buried there are Alexander Contee who died in 1741, and his son, Col. Thomas Contee, in 1811, whose stones have been covered by the sod; also Maj. Thos. Brooke, who died in 1676, and his son, Col. Thos. Brooke, in 1744, neither of whom is honored with a stone.

The next day we drove to the old Tyler place, now owned by Mr. Wilson of Calvert county, where there were gravestones in a private burial ground reached through plowed ground. Many of the stones have fallen, but the inscriptions can still be read, among which are:

In Memory of Truman Tyler Died Augt 13, 1849 Aged 53 years.

In Memory of Grace wife of Truman Tyler died Dec. 22–1851 Aged 74 years.

In Memory of Jane H. daughter of Truman and Grace C. Tyler Died July 10th 1844 Aged 34 years.

In Memory of Edwin M. Dorsey Died Oct. 16th 1833 Aged 30 years.

The Tylers were prominent people, and a part of the family, who moved further north, into what was formerly Prince George's county, composed that branch of the family to which Dr. Grafton Tyler and Dr. Samuel Tyler of Georgetown, D. C., and Frederick, Md., belonged. Some thirty years ago, a funeral took place from Dr. Grafton Tyler's home in Georgetown, leaving very early in the morning in order to reach the old graveyard in good season.

Our next quest was for the Craufurd place. To reach this we had to pass through the stable yard as the shortest way across a cornfield to a plateau, where in a clump of woods, now a perfect wilderness, lie the dead. Although the plantation, and indeed great possessions in land, belonged to David Craufurd, no trace could be found of his grave, but after we had cut away the vines and brambles, and cleared away the undergrowth, we found a tomb, much broken as to support, but a fair specimen of columnar slab. We were at first unable to decipher more than the name, but after vigorously scrubbing off the top of the tomb, a Latin inscription became visible, and was deciphered with much difficulty. Translated by Rev. G. A. Leakin, it reads as follows:

In this foundation is laid and ascends through travail into welcome regions, as much virtue as could permanently exist.

This was followed by the obituary and epitaph of Mrs. Martha Walker, daughter of David Craufurd, Esq.:

In Memory of Mrs. Martha Walker 3rd Daughter of David Craufurd Esquire who was born on the 11th day of February 1777, was married to George Walker of the city of Washington on the 16th day of December 1794, and died in childbirth on the 31st day of January 1796. This monument is erected by her affectionate Husband.

    Condemned to lose the partner of my breast
    Whose beauty charmed me and whose virtues blest,
    Formed every tie that binds the soul to prove
    Her duty, friendship, and that friendship love,
    Gone to our lovely offspring just before;
    Not parted long but now to part no more.
    Closed are those eyes that felt another's woe
    And cold those hands so ready to bestow.
    Unpitying Death has summoned her away
    And closed at morn our bright unclouded Day.
        Sed Mors Janua Vitae.

On the same hillock, and apparently the only other stone, was one to the memory of Sarah Forrest who died January 8, 1864, aged 70. She was the daughter of Sarah, second daughter of David and Sarah Craufurd, who was born in 1777, and died in 1832, and was the wife of Richard Forrest.

There may be other graves, but as has happened so often in our experience, there was absolutely no trace of them—and we left no bit of stone unturned or rather no thicket unexplored, to find one.

We sent our acknowledgments to Mrs. Sasscer, the present owner of the property, and drove along. Before we leave this Walker tomb we must record the fact that George Walker's signature is among those who disposed of their property to the Federal government for the site of the city of Washington, and that he was the original owner of that portion now known as Lafayette Square.

Our next drive was a long one, to the settlement of Baden.

We learned, all too late, that the old estates of Woodyard and Poplar Hill, were close at hand. We drove past the Brick Church, for so the parish church of St. Paul has been called for generations, and halted at the store of Mr. Baden, where we fed our horses and enjoyed the luncheon put up by our wholesome hostess of the night before.

We found the key of the church at Mrs. Hyde's, for which family this seems a rallying point, three of the name being within half a mile.

St. Paul's church is in very good repair, not half so ancient looking as its daughter, St. Barnabas, and evidently restored not so long ago. As there were no very distinctive features, and absolutely no very old tombs, we adjourned to the grateful shades outside, where we found re-enforcements in a party who had been engaged in the preparation of a site for a grave stone. We discerned our opportunity, and seized it, for a man who serves as a burial director for three counties, cheery by nature, Joy by name, is not to be met with on every expedition. So we held a session, seated on the spreading roots of a superb old oak tree, while Joy imparted great store of knowledge, topographical, genealogical, biographical and monumental. Among other points we asked for centers whence teams could be procured, and board arranged for. Here Joy was in his element and furnished us with several addresses, where we might get teams for a week if necessary, and where we could be accommodated with lodgings. He lamented the fact, that while he would be happy to have us stop over at Hughesville, he could not provide a team for more than a day at a time, as he never knew just when his horses "Brightly" and "Sprightly" might be needed for a funeral. Although we represented a memorial committee, this did not appeal to us as a safe or desirable alternative, and so we crossed out Hughesville for a sojourn, although in so doing we left Joy behind us.

Mr. Joy having given us most specific directions for our visit to Mrs. Skinner, to whom we had letters from Reverend Mr. Willes, we pursued our way along the old plantation road, lined with cedars, a mile and a half from Baden, to the old Key place where the Greenfield tombs were.

A short ride brought us into the plantation of Magounskin, delightful survival of Indian possession. This portion of the farm belongs to Mr. Edmund Key who now lives in Texas, Mrs. Wilkinson owning the other tract. The tenant, Mrs. Goddard, was a protégée of Miss Margaretta Key, a sister of Edmund. Mrs. Goddard was indisposed, but the children conducted us to the spot, where, under a little group of walnut trees, lay the graves of four of the Greenfields, very well preserved, with one exception, and in this case we had to avail ourselves of our driver's skill with broom and hoe. The slabs were of brown stone, clearly lettered save where the moisture from the overhanging trees has worn the stone away, and bear the following inscriptions:

To the memory of James Truman Greenfield who died 6th April 1760 Aged 32 years.

Here lies the body of Col. Thomas Greenfield late one of his Majesties Honorourable Councell of Maryland, who died the 8th of September anno 1715 in the 67th year of his Age.

Here Lyeth Interred the Body of Elizabeth Parker the Daughter of Coln. Thomas Greenfield and Martha his wife. She departed this life the 2 Day of August 1715 Aged 19 years. A Dutiful child is the Glory of the Mother.

Here lyeth interred the Body of Martha wife of . . . as Greenfield . . . This L . . . ber 171-.

Martha, wife of Col. Thos. Greenfield, was the daughter of James Truman, testator of 1672.

We were assured that in the adjoining field, we should find the grave of a colonial governor. When, however, we heard that his name was Swann, we had misgivings, and as no traces of the usual grove or indeed of even a stump appeared, we made note of the only person who could help us to explain the tradition, and, after getting our inscriptions down, we turned back to the main road.

From the many interesting bits of neighborhood history, given us by Mrs. Skinner, it seemed quite time for the chronicler to pass that way. At White's Landing, where Bishop Claggett was born, the gravestones had been taken up, hewn with a broad axe and thrown into the river, the perpetrators of this outrage averring that when they plowed the ground the crop of tobacco had grown seven feet high over the graves! We mentioned that a law existed which would punish such vandalism if reported, which greatly cheered and comforted Mrs. Skinner, who promised herself the pleasure of imparting it to the iconoclasts.

Another instance of wanton destruction occurred at "Bald Eagles," one of the Waring places, and which has its name from the eagles' nests built for generations in the old trees on the plantation. The owner had never allowed them to be disturbed, but when the last proprietor died, some of the more turbulent sort essayed to break the injunction. One of them, in coming down from the tree, after the total destruction of the nest, fell and broke his enterprising neck. Another of the band was murdered by one of his boon companions not long afterward.

We left Mrs. Skinner at her home, then turned back to the Three Notch road, waving our appreciation and adieux to Mr. Baden. We drove into Woodville, and found our way to Mr. Macpherson's, where we passed by far the most comfortable night of our pilgrimage. There were, at one time, two burial grounds on this plantation, which embraces parts of the old colonial grants of Brooke Court Manor and Joseph and Mary. All traces of these graves have passed away, and the impression on the minds of the present owners was that the bodies of the early proprietors were removed to

Bryantown. On the bluff, overlooking the Patuxent, they find even at this late day, traces of the aboriginal lords of the soil in flint arrow heads and sharks' teeth. There are many interesting traditions connected with the old manor house now torn down, dating back to the Digges, the Craycrofts and the Hoxtons.

Our next search was for reference and credentials as to our "Colonial" governor, and Mrs. John Compton, a daughter of the late Judge Key, had been named to us as having all the information we needed on this point. We found Mrs. Compton and her sister-in-law, Miss Compton, most hospitable and kind, but alas! no tiding of our official. We consoled ourselves, through the opportunity afforded by Miss Compton, of examining a very full and complete family record, contained in a quaint old Bible.

This fortunate find took up the parable of the Greenfields where the gravestones left off, containing entries of Wilkinsons, Trumans, Greenfields, Addisons, Smiths and others. Unfortunately, it was most illegible in some places, but Miss Compton's knowledge of family history helped us greatly.

The Burnt House farm was our next objective point. We followed our instructions minutely, with the result that after we had inquired for Robert Lyon's stable, traveled up one hill and down another, we found a cabin which stood on what looked like a primitive clearing, but where the owner was very civil, and showed us two outhouses, near the smallest of which was our goal. We had to toil for it though, but when we had driven up the cross-road, taken down some bars, traversed a plowed field and moved a harrow out of our path, and had climbed to the top of a steep slope, there was one of the most beautiful specimens of all that we had found.

Strange to relate, the very name is unknown and no one

seems ever to have heard of Mr. Randolph Morris, or Elizabeth, his wife! We looked in vain for the other tombs, which Mr. Joy told us we should surely find in the same place. A huge compost pile occupied the whole remaining space, and effectually checked any investigation in this direction. The farm belonged to Mr. Nicholson, and is now owned by Mr. Frank Hill. The inscription reads:

> Here lyeth interred the Body of Randolph Morris, born March the xv, . . . Married Elizabeth his wife September the XIV A.D. M. D. C. C. XXI, who departed ys life Sept the XXII M.D.C.C. XXXVII Aged XLI years.

As we drove away we met a colored man from Hughesville, who was very positive as to the existence of two other graves, one of these being that of Anthony Crabbe. He promised to investigate when the compost pile should have been removed.

Oldfields chapel was our next halt. We accomplished little or nothing here, except a rest under the trees, the only antique features to be found on the premises. The oldest inscription was that of James Kane.

> Here lieth the Remains of James Kane Native of the Waterside of Londonderry, Ireland, who departed this life March 26 1805 Aged 22 years.
>
> In Memory of Mable Hunter aged 1 year 1837.

There are Contees, Hunters, Goldsmiths and Swanns buried here, but all after the year 1850.

We reached Hughesville in the early afternoon, and revived at a glimpse of Joy, who with Mr. Harrison and a venerable gentleman, whose luxuriant beard was plaited and tied in a queue, directed us to Bryantown.

We needed all the aid we could get, as we were growing weary and our terminus seemed to recede before us. When St. Mary's Catholic Church was reached it seemed to rise right up out of the trees. It is a modern building, and the older graves are not now to be distinguished. The parish priest was, fortunately for us, at the church, and was much interested in our researches. We had so universally found the fathers foreign ecclesiastics, and this one had so much the air of an Italian, that it was a delightful surprise to find that he was a son of Bishop Southgate, and had been once an assistant at St. Luke's, Baltimore. He not only helped us to find the oldest inscription extant, but he sent us afterward a list of the departed from his parish register.

From Hughesville we drove to Charlotte Hall. It was getting to be twilight, very chilly, and, with as little delay as possible, we made terms with one of the landladies of the place.

Late as it was, we determined to go over to the rectory in order to get our plans for the morrow all laid to the best advantage. After driving through fields where we had no business at all, we found that we were on the wrong trail, and had entered the grounds of one, Mr. Smoot. We made as dignified a retreat as was possible, and, taking another turn, came suddenly round a corner into one of the loveliest of leafy lanes, so leafy, that only one carriage at a time could pass, and at the end of this verdant tunnel we came upon the venerable old parsonage, upon its surrounding glebe land. It is positively hoary and by far the most typical of all the colonial houses that we saw. The Reverend Mr. London met us and took us to the glebe graveyard.

On the glebe of Trinity parish is a stone with this inscription:

> Erected by the members of Trinity Parish to their Late Rector the Rev. James D. Nicholson Died Aug. 30th 1838 in the 30th year of his age. The deceased was remarkable for great simplicity of character, deep humility and unerring zeal in the service of his Master. Endowed by nature with a lovely imagination and rich poetic fancy, his preaching abounded with appropriate and original illustration. Whilst it delighted the mind it improved the heart. His ashes mingle here with their kindred dust. He will long survive in the affection of his grateful people.

Also, we find the following :

Anna Eliza Nicholson wife of Addison Daugherty of the City of New York Died in Woodville Prince George County April 19th 1849 Aged 56. Blessed are the dead who die in the Lord.

Here lies interred The body of John Reynolds Son of the Rev. John Reynolds and Ann his wife who departed this life Nov. 9, 1824, aged 2 years and 6 months. Also interred at the Plains of Plenty.

Inclosed by an iron railing placed there of late years by the Kirk family, are stones with the following inscriptions:

In memory of Ann Matthews who departed this life July 9, 1825 Aged 64 years 2 months and 5 days.

In Memory of Elias Matthews Who died on the 30th day of Dec. 1812 in the 45 year of his age.

In Memory of Alex Matthews, who died at the White Sulphur Springs on the 5th day of Sept 1847 in the 55th year of his age. Although far from home at the time of his decease His last request was that his remains might be laid by his relatives and friends at the family burying place in his native parish and in Pursuance of his wish they have been removed and are here deposited.

Elizabeth B. Matthews who departed this life 28th day of Sept 1851 Aged 61 years. Professing an humble belief In the Religion of her Savior.

The next morning we examined the Dent Memorial Chapel, and, returning to the glebe, wound up with the registers of Trinity parish, going back to 1750. We had a most interesting search therein, and endeavored to get them started to the Maryland Historical Rooms to be copied. It seems difficult to realize that Charlotte Hall was once so famous a place of resort, that the Colonial Government passed an act to "purchase lands adjoining to the Fountain of Healing Waters, called the Cool-Springs, Viz: in St. Mary's County, for building Houses, &c. for the Entertainment of such poor impotent Persons as should repair thither for Cure."

The "Fountains of Healing Waters" still flow on, undisturbed by the changes and chances of the two hundred odd years that have intervened, but little else is left save the humane law, which records the paternal care of those in authority, for the needy and indigent.

The school at Charlotte Hall was founded in 1796, and perhaps the brightest spot in the landscape is made by the cadets at their sports through the grounds, around the venerable old building, the first erected on the campus, over a century ago.

The Dent Memorial Chapel, of brown stone, has gathered the bodies of all the members of the family, from Oak Hill, Georgetown and other burial places, and mural tablets are erected, few of which have yet been filled. The inscriptions at Dent Memorial Chapel have been given in another chapter.

Returning to Charlotte Hall, we turned our team homeward, feeling that our interesting trip had enabled us to add much to the archives of the society.

Among other graveyards in Prince George's county is the Methodist churchyard on the northern outskirts of Laurel. The tombstones prior to 1850 are as follows:

In Memory of Horace Son of A. Alter Born March 18 1832 Died Sept. 10 1845.

> He has gone to the land of the blest
> From his prison of sorrow and night;
> He has snatched immortality's rest
> And mantled his spirit in light.

Here lies the body of Harriet Ann Vincent, who was born Jan. 29, 1825, and Departed this life Nov. 21, 1847.

> Dry up your tears and weep no more,
> I am not dead but gone before.

In memory of Albert S. Haslup Died April 21 1849.

> Short was my time,
> Strong my pain;
> To rest in Christ
> Is now my gain.
> Dry up your years and weep no more,
> I am not dead but gone before.

The earliest date to be found in the Episcopal churchyard, is 1851, when Chas. Edward, infant son of Peter and Mary Bogart, was buried, and the earliest in the Roman Catholic cemetery is as follows:

Prince George's County 89

Here lies Patrick Mulgare a native of Limeric Ireland. died in Anne Arundel Co., Md. Sept 7th 1845.

The graveyard at Birmingham, about two miles from Laurel, is on a part of the original tract granted to Richard Snowden, and has never gone out of the family.

Here lies the Body of Richard Snowden Jr. Eldest son of Mr. Richard Snowden Sr. by his second wife Elizabeth, who departed this life the 18th of March 1753 in the 34th year of his Age. He was a Dutiful son, a Tender Husband, a Good Christian and a sincere Friend. This erected by Elizabeth his Widow as a mark of her Affection for him.

Here Lies the Body of Major Thomas Snowden, who departed this Transitory Life on Thursday, the 27th day of October in the year of our Lord 1803. And in the 55th year of his age.

Here lies the Body of Mr. John Crowley, who Departed this life the 2nd of November 1748, Aged 52 years.

Sacred To the Memory of Dr. Gerard Hopkins Snowden who departed this life on the 27th of May 1828. Aged 40 years and 1 month. He was a practical Christian, Kind and affectionate son, Husband and father. As a Magistrate he was just and humane, as a friend and physician he was Charitable and Kind to the poor. When the ear heard him, then it blessed him, and when the eye saw him; it gave witness to him.

Because he delivered the poor that cried, and the fatherless and him that had none to help him.

The blessing of him that was ready to perish came upon him: and he caused the Widow's heart to sing for joy.

He was a father to the poor; and the cause which he knew not he searched out. Job, 29 Chapter, 11, 12, 13, and 16 verses.

This tribute of respect is erected by his affectionate wife, who feels that she can only cease to mourn her irreparable loss with life.

On a tall white marble shaft is the inscription:

To Louisa V. Capron wife of Horace Capron and daughter of Nicholas and Elizabeth Snowden, born June 3rd 1841 died March 27th 1849.

Richard Snowden of Birmingham, England, the founder of the family in Maryland as early as 1690, is supposed to be buried in this graveyard. The inscription on his tombstone has been obliterated by time, but there is a record of his burial, May 20, 1711. He was captain of provincial forces from 1700 to 1703.

To his son Richard was patented, in 1719, the tract of

10,000 acres, which included the plantations known later as Birmingham, Snowden Hall, Fairland, Montpelier, Oakland, Snow Hill, Avondale, Woodland Hill, Alnwick, Elmwood, Brightwood and Maple Grove. An account of the family is given in the Thomas book. (Laurence B. Thomas, D.D., 1896.)

"Montpelier" was the home of Thomas, son of Richard, who was born in 1751, died in 1803 and was buried at Birmingham. His third son, Nicholas, was born here October 21, 1786, and died March 8, 1831, and was buried here.

"Oakland" was inhabited by Richard, eldest son of Maj. Thomas Snowden and his wife Ann Ridgely. He and his two wives were buried here, also his son Thomas, the father of Mrs. Charles Marshall. He died September 3, 1823. It is said that members of the Contee family are also buried in this graveyard. This is probable, as Ann Louise Snowden was married to John Contee and had eight daughters and two sons.

The estate of "Riversdale," District of Bladensburg, was bought by Sieur Henry J. Stier of Antwerp about the year 1794–1795, and given to his daughter Rosalie Eugenia, wife of George Calvert, Esq. After his death, his son, Charles B. Calvert, Esq., owned the estate. It was sold in 1886.

On the east side of the graveyard is the Balto. & Ohio R. R., on the west side, the Balto. & Washington Turnpike.

In the center of the lot are the tombs of George Calvert and his wife; along the west side, are the graves of their four children, who died in infancy, and on the east side are the tombstones of Charles B. Calvert of Riversdale and his infant son.

On the principal monument is a bas-relief by Persico, representing the mother with outstretched arms, ascending to heaven, where the four angel children are waiting to receive her. The inscription reads as follows:

Here rests the body of Rosalie Eugenia Calvert Wife of George Calvert and Daughter of Henry I Stier of Antwerp, Who died March 13, 1821. Aged 43. May she be numbered among the Children of God and her lot be among the Saints.

At the base of the stone and on the sides are inscribed these lines:

We see the hand we worship and adore And justify the all disposing power. Death ends our woe And puts a period to the Ills of life.
Let me die the death of the righteous And let my later end be like his.
Here lies the body of George Calvert, Esq. Of Riversdale, youngest son of Benedict Calvert Esq. of Mount Airy, Prince George County Maryland and grandson of Charles Calvert, Sixth* Lord Baltimore, who died January 28th, 1838 Aged 70.

I. van Havre son of C. B. & C. A. Calvert Born Oct. 30th, 1848 Died Aug. 4th, 1849.

In Memory of Charles B. Calvert Born August 28th, 1808 Died May 12th, 1864. Blessed are the merciful for they shall obtain mercy.

A footstone bears the inscription:

C. B. C.   Sans peur et sans reproche.

---

* Error. It should be "fifth."—EDITOR'S NOTE.

CHAPTER V

BALTIMORE, erected into a county in 1659, formed one of the five divisions of the province that at that time lay west of the Chesapeake Bay. It embraced also the area to the east of the Susquehanna river, belonging later to Cecil county, where a meeting of the Baltimore county court was held as early as 1661. Cecil entered upon its separate existence in 1674, and just one hundred years afterwards, Harford also was taken from the parent county. Consequently, the history of Harford covers that of a part of Baltimore county until the year 1774, and we find many more traces of early settlement here than among the regions watered by the Patapsco.

On the Bush there was once a Baltimore town, though nothing now remains to approximate its site, except a few graves. Fortunately one of the latter is marked by a fine slab mounted on columns, and the inscription introduces us to some of the worthies, who helped to make the local history of their times.

Beneath this stone is reposed the body of James Philips, and in compliance with his dying request, the body of his wife, Martha Philips, daughter of John and Elizabeth Paca, born Feb. 3rd, 1744, married Jan. 25th 1776, died March 6th 1829. Having survived her husband 26 years.

May brightest Seraphs from the world on high
Spread their light pinions o'er the sleeping tomb
And guard the dust within till from the sky
The Saviour Comes to bid the dead rebloom.
Then may they rise!
Together meet their change,
Together hear the plaudit Rest! well done!
Through Spheres of light and Spheres of glory range
And sit with Jesus on his dazzling throne.

Martha Philips was the sister of William Paca, one of the signers of the Declaration of Independence, and the third governor of the state. Her husband was fourth in descent from James Philips, who arrived in Maryland in 1660 and married the daughter of William Osborne, said to be the first settler in Baltimore county. William Osborne was certainly the first patentee of the land on the Bush where Old Baltimore stood, the latter having passed eventually to the descendants of his son-in-law, James Philips. The Osborne graveyard lies on a broad peninsula between the Bush river and Rumney creek, not very far from the site of Old Baltimore.

Between Rumney creek and the Narrows separating Spesutie island from the mainland, is a place called Gravelly. Here, we are told, was the site of the first Spesutia church. Tradition, combined with a date on record, fixes the year 1671 as the period from which to reckon its organization. The book of vestry proceedings has been lost, but on the church register is recorded the birth of John Cook, son of John Cook, born at Bush river on September 28, 1681. As late as 1851, sunken graves and partially obliterated remains of a building were still to be seen here and a bridge in the locality, known from time immemorial as "Church bridge," helped by its name to locate the spot.

Though the Spesutia church of the past is no more, the Spesutia church of the present marks a continuance of the parish history from the year 1718. Here again we encounter the name of James Philips. He was the munificent donor of the two acres on which the church has found a permanent home. It stands amidst the dead of nearly two centuries and though rebuilt as late as 1851, it is an interesting monument of the past, and a striking feature in the landscape. St. George's, or the Spesutia church, took its more familiar name from the Hundred where it first stood. This, in its turn, was derived from the island, perpetuating alike the name and aspirations of its first owner, Col. Nathaniel Utie, for Utie's Hope, latinized, became "Spes Utie," then Spesutie and finally Spesutia.

In 1744, a James Philips appears with Col. Thomas White and other members of the vestry, appointed to acquaint the governor of the Rev. Stephen Wilkinson's death. This clergyman came to Maryland highly recommended by Edmund, Lord Bishop of London, and entered upon his duties as rector of St. George's in 1726. Toward the end of his ministry he and his vestry did not agree, hence the request of the committee at his death, "that the governor should not induct another minister disagreeable to the parishioners." This shows the spirit of the colonists, even in those early days.

The Philips, the Pacas, the Halls, the Whites, the Dallams, the Websters, and the Smiths were all more or less united by marriage. At Cranberry, the home of the Halls, and at Blenheim, were once old family burying grounds.

Nearly every Marylander who has been so fortunate as to have an anecdotal uncle, aunt, or grandmother has heard the couplet:

> Pretty Betty Martin, tip-toe fine,
> Couldn't get a husband to suit her mind.

As a matter of fact the dainty damsel had two husbands in close succession: Richard Dallam and William Smith. The latter, a nephew of Sarah, Duchess of Marlborough, lived at "Blenheim." He had a son Winston, and this name we still find used by the Churchill family on both sides of the water. His daughter Elizabeth was the wife of John Paca and mother of the "Signer."

It would be interesting to know where "Pretty Betty" was buried, whether with her Dallam descendants, including her gallant son Maj. William Dallam, who died in 1761, or with the Smiths at "Blenheim," or whether she lay in solitary state in the Spesutia churchyard. No tombstone remains to satisfy our curiosity on this point.

There is an old graveyard at Level between Mosquito creek and the Narrows, where some of the Uties and Boothbys were buried. In fact, throughout the whole region below the Old Post road from Havre de Grace or the Lower Ferry, to the Patapsco River Necks, family graveyards were once known to abound.

The following inscriptions are from the Spesutia churchyard, at Perryman:

In memory of John Hall of Cranberry, who departed this life June 8, 1779, in the 61st year of his age.

In memory of Barthia Hall, wife of John Hall of Cranberry, who departed this life Jan. 16, 1784, in the 60th year of her age.

In memory of Edward Hall born on the 10th of December, 1747, and died on the 18th day of July, 1788.

In memory of Elizabeth Hall, who was born Dec. 8, 1762, and died Nov. 11, 1840.

In memory of Martha Griffith, who died Dec. 1, 1807, in the 62nd year of her age.

In memory of Alexander L. Griffith, who died Apr. 1, 1815, in the 24th year of his age.

In memory of Cordelia Griffith, who died Oct. 25th, 1805, in the 19th year of her age.

In memory of John H. Griffith, who died Apr. 3, 1815, in the 33rd year of his age.

Sacred to the memory of Martha A. Hall, wife of Josias Hall, who departed this life June 24, 1804, in the 35th year of her age.

Sacred to the memory of Emieline Cordelia Hall, daughter of Josias and Martha Hall, who departed this life Apr. 26, 1820, in the 16th year of her age.

In memory of Martha Hall born on the 30th of Apr. 1760, and died on the 20th of Feb. 1845.

In memory of George Josias Ontario Hall, son of Josias and Martha Hall, who departed this life Apr. 2, 1845, in the 43rd. year of his age.

Sacred to the memory of Mary Clarissa Hall, daughter of Josias and Martha Hall, who departed this life Oct. 14, 1851, in the 60th year of her age.

In memory of Hannah Emily Griffith, who departed this life 16th day of June 1817, in the 22nd year of her age.

In memory of Daniel Palmer, who departed this life Oct. 1, A. D. 1845, in the 73rd year of his age.

In memory of Sarah A. Reasin, wife of William D. Reasin, born Sept. 29th, 1794, died Mar. 5, 1835.

Sacred to the memory of Frances Beaty, who departed this life Sept. 5, 1826, aged 76 years.

In memory of Elizabeth Barnes, who departed this life on the 20th of March [date illegible, and she was sister of the above].

In memory of Mary Garrettson, who departed this life Mar. 3, 1835, aged 78 years.

Thomas Hall, Esq., departed this life Aug. 9, 1804, aged 52 years.

Sacred to the memory of Isabella L., wife of Thomas Hall, who departed this life Oct. 1, 1828, in the 53rd. year of her age.

In memory of Eleanor Rodgers Stokes, who departed this life on the 7th of Aug. 1791, in the 8th year of her age.

In memory of Col. Alexander Lawson Smith, who departed this life the 24th of Jan. 1801, in the 48th year of his age.

In memory of Mary Monks, wife of John Monks, who departed this life the 14th day of Oct. 1800, in the 35th year of her age.

In memory of our mother, Elizabeth Chauncey, who departed this life the 2nd. of Feb. 1845, in the 69th year of her age.

Sacred to the memory of Mary Brown, who departed this life May 21st. 1812, aged 55 years.

Sacred to the memory of Jacob Brown, who departed this life March 2, 1826, aged 55 years and one month.

In memory of Charles H. Webster, who departed this life June 28, 1849, aged 28 years and 4 months.

Sacred to the memory of Mary Veazey, who departed this life Mar. 28, 1849, aged 53 years and 4 months.

Sacred to the memory of George Webster, who departed this life Thursday the 6th of May, 1847, in the 29th year of his age.

In memory of our mother, Emily Griffith, wife of George Griffith and daughter of Isaac Perryman, who died Aug. 13, 1824, in the 28th year of her age.

In memory of Sarah Hall, who departed this life on the 21st of Dec. 1827, aged 65 years.

Sacred to the memory of Mrs. Delia Rodgers, wife of Alexander Rodgers, who departed this life the 7th of Sept. 1827, in the 45th year of her age.

Peregrine Nowland born July 1763, died Oct. 1810, in the 48th year of his age.

To the memory of Gabriel Christie, Esq., who departed this life in the city of Baltimore on the 1st. day of April 1808, in the 53rd year of his age. He was at his decease Collector of the Port of Baltimore and had for a number of years served in the Congress of the United States, as well as in the Senate of the State of Maryland.

In memory of John Hawkins, died May 15, 1831, aged 31 years.

In memory of Matthew Hawkins, died Feb. 17, 1831, aged 36 years.

Sacred to the memory of Winston Smith, who departed this life Oct. 2, in the year of our Lord 1822, in the 50th year of his age.

Sacred to the memory of Cassandra Smith, who departed this life Nov. 9, in the year of our Lord 1815, in the 38th year of her age.

In memory of Mrs. Susanna Risteau, who died Sept. 20, 1806, aged 88 years and 5 days.

> Now well earned peace is hers and bliss Secure,
> Ours be the lenient not unpleasing tear.

In memory of Sarah Hawkins, who departed this life Apr. 27, 1803, about the 36 year of her age.

In memory of Matthew Hawkins, who departed this life Nov. 20, 1813, aged 62 years.

Sacred to the memory of Chas. W. Perryman, who died July 1835, aged 30 years.

In memory of Jacob Ergood, who died Nov. 23, 1846, aged 21 years 1 month and 18 days.

In memory of Jacob Suter, who was born July 25, 1791, and departed this life July 12, 1840, in the 49th year of his age.

Departed this life on the 12th of Sept. 1818, Samuel Jay, Esq., in the 49th year of his age.

Ah ever dear and much loved Samuel, how few, how very few has heaven made like thee.

Sacred to the memory of Sarah, wife of Samuel Jay, who departed this life in the 36th year of her age, on the 8th day of Dec. in the year of our Lord 1810.

In memory of Dr. Samuel Griffith, who died Jan. 14th, 1803, aged 36 years and 58 days.

In memory of Garrett V. Nelson, who departed this life Dec. 24, 1850, in the 55th year of his age.

In memory of Acquilla Nelson, who departed this life 10th of Oct. 1826, aged 60 years.

In memory of Frances Nelson, wife of Acquilla Nelson, who departed this life the 17th of Sept. 1847, in her 73rd. year.

In memory of Mr. Henry Van Sickkle, who died the 13th of Sept. 1801, aged 59 years.

In memory of Elizabeth Van Sickle, wife of Henry Van Sickle, who departed this life May 29, 1821, aged 77 years.

In memory of Jane Roberts, consort of Owen Roberts, departed this life 5th day of April, 1824, aged 44 years.

In memory of Elizabeth Allen, wife of Eben N. Allen, who departed this life June 14, 1816, in the 24th year of her age.

In memory of Martha Sutton, consort of Samuel Sutton, who departed this life June 10, 1824, in the 30th year of her age.

In memory of Elecia M. Allen, wife of Eben N. Allen, who departed this life Jan. 13, 1823, in the 28th year of her age.

Martha, Relict of Alexander L. Smith and of Samuel Jay, died Aug. 4, 1847, aged 76 years.

> Jesus thy heavenly radiance shed
> To cheer and bless her silent bed
> And from Death's gloom her spirit raise
> To see thy face and sing thy praise.

Samuel Griffith Smith died Apr. 18, 1845, aged 30 years.

> When by a good man's grave I muse alone
> Me thinks an angel sits upon the stone.
> And with a voice inspiring joy, not fear,
> Says pointing upward that he is not here.
> That he is risen.

Rev. John Allen, who departed this life Mar. 16, 1830, aged 69 years, for 20 years the faithful and untiring minister of this church, a profound scholar, and able divine, a sincere and humble Christian. Also his wife Brasseya Allen who departed this life Dec. 29, 1831, in the 69th year of her age.

In memory of Rebecca Godsgrace, wife of William Godsgrace, who departed this life on the 6th day of Sept., 1778, in the 26th year of her age. Also William, the son of William and Rebecca Godsgrace, who departed this life on the 21st day of July 1777, in the 22nd month of his age.

D. Allen died Dec. 24, 1801.

Col. Thos. White who died Sept. 29, 1779, aged 74 years. His relict Esther, daughter Mary and son William, the latter the first bishop of the diocese of Pennsylvania, are interred in the yard of Christ Church, Philadelphia. This stone is erected by Thos. H. White, son of the bishop, in 1847.

William Hall born at the "Dairy" on the 31st of July, 1756, and died at Constant Friendship on the 9th of Nov. 1818.

I am the resurrection and the life.

Sophia Hall relict of William Hall, departed this life at Constant Friendship on the 18th day of April 1853, aged 86 years.

In memory of Catherine, daughter of William and Mary Fulford, who departed this life 24th of February 1815.

In memory of John Patterson, who departed this life on the 7th day of Jan. 1787, in the 42nd year of his age.

In memory of Avarilla Patterson, relict of John Patterson, who departed this life the 16th day of Jan. 1819, in the 63rd year of her age.

Sacred to the memory of Dr. William Beatty, who departed this life on the 14th of April 1801, aged 29 years and 2 months.

In memory of Patrick McLaughlin, died July 23rd. 1829, aged 53 years.

In memory of Anne McLaughlin, consort of Patrick McLaughlin, who departed this life Nov. 2, 1813, in the 42nd year of her age.

In memory of Mary, wife of Benjamin Chandlee, died Jan. 6, 1827, aged 73 years.

In memory of Barthia Patterson, wife of George Patterson, who departed this life Aug. 25, 1806, in the 36 year of her age.

In memory of George Patterson, who departed this life Mar. 11, 1808, in the 60th year of his age.

Sacred to the memory of John Kirk, who departed this life Jan. 5, 1851, in the 50th year of his age.

In memory of Jane, wife of Archibald Beatty, who departed this life the 16th of Dec. 1782.

In memory of William T. Herbert, M. D., who departed this life on the 16th day of Aug. A. D. 1821, aged 24 years 5 months and 18 days.

"Like leaves on the trees the race of men are found
Now green in growth now withering on the ground."

In memory of Capt. John Herbert, who departed this life the 12th of Mar. 1825, aged 52 years 8 months 12 days.

In memory of James B. Herbert, who departed this life on the 10th day of July A. D. 1830, aged 36 years 9 months and one day.

In memory of my husband Edward Giles of New York, who died Jan. 10, 1813 aged 29 years 3 months 12 days.

In memory of Mary Ann, wife of Burt Whitson, who died Aug. 19, 1843, aged 37 years 8 months 9 days.

George Henderson, who died Oct. 3, 1847, in the 74th year of his age.

Col. William W. Ramsey born Nov. 29th, 1792 died Dec. 26, 1831. He survives in the memory of those who best knew him.

Here lies the body of William Moylan Lansdale, who died Feb. 16, in the year of our Lord 1831, in the 47th year of his age.

In memory of our mother Mary, consort of J. Nicholas Sutor a native of Pennsylvania, died at Havre de Grace, Md. June 17, 1832, in the 71st year of her age.

In memory of our father J. Nicholas Sutor a native of Germany, born Dec. 4, 1756, died at Havre de Grace, Md. Mar. 23, 1831, in the 75 year of his age.

In memory of Phillip Moore Hall, who departed this life Oct. 13, 1843, in the 23rd. year of his age.

In memory of Anna Mary, daughter of John and Ann E. Martin, died June 22, 1839, in the 22nd year of her age.

Sacred to the memory of John Martin, departed this life Sept. 26, 1841, in the 66th year of his age.

Sacred to the memory of Ann Elizabeth, wife of John Martin, departed this life Sept. 28, 1828, in the 50th year of her age.

In memory of John Clarke Monk a native of Bristol, Gloscestershire, England, who departed this life Dec. 9, A. D. 1827, aged 67 years., 9 months 14 days.

"Heaven raise its everlasting portals high
And bid the pure in heart behold his God."

Sacred to the memory of George H. Perryman, who died 19th Aug. 1843, aged 35 years.

Sacred to the memory of Isaac Perryman, who died June 30, 1831, in the 72nd year of his age.

Sacred to the memory of Ann Perryman, who died Oct. 7, 1837, in the 75 year of her age.

In memory of Hannah, consort of John Kirk, who departed this life on the 30th day of October, A. D. 1820, aged 32 years, 4 months and 19 days.

Sacred to the memory of Archibald Beatty, who departed this life on the 18th day of February 1813, aged 78 years.

Jonathan Sutton, died Jan. 19, 1825, aged 65 years, 2 months and 2 days.

Semelia A. Murphy, wife of Thomas J. Murphy, daughter of Col. Jacob J. Michael. Born Oct. 12, 1809, died Nov. 1, 1847.

In memory of Miranda Chauncey, who departed this life Oct. 17th, 1834, in the 30th year of her age.

In memory of Ann Eliza Chauncey, who departed this life July 1st, 1837, in the 36th year of her age.

In memory of Margaret, wife of Capt. John Herbert and mother of

Baltimore County 101

James B. and William P. Herbert, who departed this life June 19th A. D. 1849, aged 98 years.

Mary Sophia Thomas Higbee, wife of Rev. Edward Young Higbee and daughter of Abraham Jarrett Thomas and Mary S. Thomas, was born Aug. 25th A. D. 1815, and died July 1, A. D. 1836.

Beneath the same stone lies Edward Higbee, infant son of Rev. Edward Young Higbee and Mary Sophia Thomas Higbee.

"A cherished hope just born, baptised and gone."

Mary S., wife of A. J. Thomas, died Sept. 20th, aged 29 years.

In memory of Abraham Jarrett, son of Abraham J. Thomas, who departed this life July 4, 1841, in the 20th year of his age.

Abraham J. Thomas, who departed this life Aug. 31, 1841, in the 64th year of his age.

Herman S. son of A. J. and Mary S. Thomas, died at Monteray, Mexico, Sept. 23, 1846. A soldier of the Mexican War, conspicuous for gallantry in the front ranks, among his heroic comrades in the memorable charge of the height commanding Monteray, he fell mortally wounded.

William T., son of A. J. and Mary S. Thomas, died 1850.

Mary Michael, wife of D. Michael, died June 26th, 1842, in the 51st year of her age.

Sacred to the memory of Martha, consort of Ethan Michael, who died Feb. 1st, 1846, in the 34th year of her age.

In memory of Elizabeth, wife of Nathaniel Tuchton, who departed this life July 13, 1840.

Sarah Sutton, died Dec. 3, 1824, aged 56 years 8 months and 17 days.

Sacred to the memory of Martha Giles, who departed this life Mar. 24, 1815, in her 33rd year. Resurgiam.

Here sleep the mortal remains of Jacob W. Giles, born the 26th of June, 1776, died the 7th of Nov. 1851.

From Perryman going northward, we must look for the oldest churchyards of the different religious sects. Though in many cases obliterated, their sites are held in memory by members of the Harford County Historical Society, who have given the subject close attention in the past. A letter to the writer some years ago from the late George W. Archer, an enthusiastic follower after historic research, gives a good picture of these sacred spots viewed under the processes of time, neglect and so-called "progress." The letter referred to is dated February 3, 1898.

"About two miles northeasterly from Churchville, some twenty years since, there was a graveyard of about 100 feet square, enclosed by an old fence and over-grown with bushes and briars, where interments were made one hundred and sixty years ago, and for many years thereafter. It was the burial ground of the first Presbyterian congregation in what is now Harford county. I visited it a little more than twenty years since, for a few moments, while passing along the public road very near its site, and finding many rude gravestones with legible inscriptions, I resolved to copy them at some future time. But when I visited it for this purpose, I found that the owner of the surrounding land had torn down the fence, cleared up the thicket, grubbed out the roots, dug up the gravestones, plowed the ground and sowed a crop of grain which was then growing over the ashes of the dead. It is some comfort to know that this man left the earth soon afterwards for unknown abodes. I think I could say where he went, but refrain for obvious reasons. I found a great pile of these gravestones dumped in the adjoining woods and from them I selected one and presented it to our local Historical Society.

"The church was a log structure directly on the roadside where a depression and some remains are still visible. About 1750 its successor was built at the present Churchville, then called the Lower Cross Roads. From about that date interments took place at the more recently built church.

"My grandfather, one of our most active local patriots, was buried there; also his wife, a daughter of Capt. Thos. Harris, a member of the family who founded Harrisburg, the capital of Pennsylvania. Also Mary McKinney, the wife of Capt. Harris, to whose memory a fine monument was erected a few years ago by her descendants now residents of various states. Capt. Harris, who lived at Churchville, returned, after his wife's death, to Pennsylvania, and died about the year 1802, in Tuscarora Valley, aged over one hundred years, having lived in three centuries."

The beginnings of the Presbyterian church in Baltimore and Harford counties are enveloped in obscurity, although 1683 has been given as the date of its organization on the eastern shore. The Deer Creek congregation is the first of which there is any record in Harford county, and may be said to date from the preaching of Whitefield in this country, taking the year 1738 as its starting point. The old Bethel church dates from 1745. It stands in the northwestern part of the county between Jarrettsville and the Baltimore county line, and in its churchyard are many graves with inscriptions.

Near Priest's Ford, where the road from Churchville to Darlington crosses Deer creek, is the old Catholic graveyard. Interments were made here as early as 1750 and many graves remain marked by rude stones without inscriptions, or by wooden crosses. All the bodies that could be identified were removed some time ago to the more recent cemetery of St. Ignatius at Hickory. Priest's Ford got its name from the chapel established there by the Jesuits about the year 1747. The latter is alluded to in a public document of the year 1756, as "Priest Neale's Mass House."

This singular structure is still standing on a high hill on the borders of Deer creek. It is one story high, with thick stone walls, having almost the appearance of an old blockhouse used for defense against the Indians. An ancient document, quite respectable for its authority, mentions the Rev. Bennett Neale as its builder. "The central part of the building, running like a long and wide hallway through the house, was alone used for church purposes. The other rooms were the private apartments of the priests. This was conformable to the laws of the Province, which prohibited Catholics from having public places of worship, but tolerated these domiciliary oratories or chapels." We are indebted for this description to Mr. Walter W. Preston, in his history of Harford county. As these domiciliary chapels are fast disappearing, the manner of their arrangement is worth mentioning here. This house was sold in 1814, and has since been used as a dwelling.

The graveyard is near the foot of the hill and for more than half a century received the Catholic dead for many miles around. The land for St. Ignatius was purchased for a nominal sum in 1779, and so this spot, also, is of venerable age.

About a mile further on the road from Churchville to Darlington is Trappe church, successor to a chapel-of-ease of Spesutia parish, built in 1755. In the churchyard are some ancient stones with inscriptions. One of these is to the memory of William Smithson, possibly the nephew of William Smithson, Sr. The latter, a venerable judge and citizen, who took a prominent part in local affairs at the time of the Revolution, built a home for himself in 1774, later known as the Farnandis Homestead, but recently destroyed by fire. On a part of this place, adjoining the Fulford farm, is the old Smithson and Farnandis graveyard. William Smithson Senior's grave is marked by a stone bearing his name and the fact of his having

Departed this life January 17, 1809, Aged 64 years.

One of the few detached graves of which there is any report is that of Parson Coleman, as he was familiarly known in his day and generation. He at one time officiated at the Garrison Forest church, but in his latter years removed to Harford county. Near the ancient and primitive stone house where he lived, three miles from Belair and an equal distance from Fallston, is his grave:

Respectfully dedicated to the memory of John Coleman, Minister of the Protestant Episcopal Church, who departed this life in the full assurance of a blissful immortality.

Though his earthly tabernacle were dissolved, he had a building of God, a house not made with hands, eternal in the heavens. 20th January 1816, aged 58 years.

At "Street," we find the following inscriptions:

Here lieth Hannah Stokes, Aged 79 years, 10 ms. 26 days. Departed this life the 26th of Feb 1826. The wife of Joseph Stokes.

Here lieth the body of Dan Scarbrouch, who Departed this life the 23rd of January 1834, aged 13 years.

"Remember youth as you pass by,
Suple as you, so once was I:
As I am now, so you must be,
Prepare for death and follow me."

Here lieth the body of Hannah Hall, aged 59 years, 2 mo and 26 days, the wife of Rice J. Hall. Departed this life the 11 of Oct, 1832.

Among the detached graves of interest in the Trappe churchyard, is that of Capt. Parker Hill Lee, a gallant officer of the old Maryland line. It is to be found in a small enclosure with two or three others belonging to members of his family. The lot is on the left of the main road leading from Churchville to Priest's Ford.

On the farm of the late Jeremiah Silver, about a mile east of Harmony Presbyterian church, is the unmarked grave of Aquila Deaver. According to a well-founded tradition, he bore the illustrious Lafayette on his back from the boat to the Harford shore at the Bald Friar ferry. This occurred in 1781, when the French officer, at the head of the army on his way to Virginia, came to a stand-still owing to the grounding of his boat. He was about to wade ashore, when Deaver presented his brawny shoulders and saved him a wetting.

There are many old graves in the Methodist cemetery at Abingdon, which encloses the site of the first Methodist college in the world, for higher education. The latter was destroyed by fire in 1795 and was never rebuilt. Abingdon was started by the Pacas. Richard Dallam, one of the leading men of the county and quartermaster of the American army, lived there and it was from him the property for the

Methodist college was bought. The bell from the latter was saved and now hangs over Goucher Hall, at the Woman's college, Baltimore.

The Quakers had their religious organizations in Maryland at an early period, the two great meetings being the one at Tred Avon on the Eastern Shore, the other at West river. When they first came to Harford county is not known, for the book that might have thrown light upon their Bush River meeting is lost. With the Deer Creek meeting of 1736, their actual history begins. This was transferred later to Darlington. The Little Falls meeting near Fallston dates from 1738, and there were many Friends in the northern part of the county who, in 1780, attended the meeting at Fawn Grove over the Pennsylvania border.

The early burial customs of the Quakers were of the greatest simplicity. Sometimes neat little stones not much taller than footstones are found in their cemeteries, but inscriptions very seldom. They were advocates of a broad and liberal education and the institutions they have founded, whether in the cause of education or in that of benevolence, are their best monuments. The name of Moses Sheppard, who was born in Harford county, is of more than local significance, also that of David C. McCoy; whereas Amos, Tyson, Jewett, More, Hull, and many others, are well known in both counties.

The Harford Baptist church, though not established as early as Sater's Meetinghouse, over the Baltimore county line, has enjoyed an uninterrupted existence since 1754. A copy of its first records has preserved a list of early members and among them are several names to be found at Chestnut Ridge in the Saters graveyard. For instance, there are Burnhams, Walkers, Towsons, Cockeys, Boswells and Jones. Then also we find Slade, Hitchcock, Parks, Stansbury and others—names appearing quite frequently on the tombstones in St. James or the Manor churchyard. This is easy to account for. "My Lady's Manor," a term still used by the farmers of the locality, was a tract of 10,000 acres given by Charles, Lord Baltimore, in the year 1713 to his wife Margaret. At her death in 1731, it passed under her will to a granddaughter, whose husband's debts were the ultimate cause of its disintegration. This was before the division of Baltimore county. The settlers of kindred blood came pouring in and when the separation occurred, a part of "My Lady's Manor" lay on one side of the border and the rest on the other.

Near "My Lady's Manor," was a tract owned in 1705 by Wm. Bladen, Esq. In 1737 a portion of it was laid off under the name of "Blenheim," by Col. Thos. Franklin, and here we find the graves of his daughter Elizabeth Paca and others, with these inscriptions:

Elizabeth Paca, wife of Aquila Paca, and daughter of Thomas & Ruth Franklin, departed this life April 23d, 1771, aged 26 years.

Eleanor L. Owens, daughter of Larkin H. and Rachel Smith, died Jan. 4th, 1840, aged 39 years.

Larkin H. Smith, departed this life July 11th, 1844, in the 71st. year of his age.

Rachel, wife of Larkin H. Smith, who departed this life July 21st 1849, in the 72d year of her age.

Edward Price, born Jan'y 2d. 1799, departed this life June 6th, 1829.

It is a noteworthy fact that St. James' Episcopal church, or the Manor church, was built in 1753, just one year before the Harford Baptist congregation over the border was organized, and many of the settlers who attended the latter, turned to the established church for its ceremonials of marriage and burial. The Manor church was built as a chapel-of-ease to St. John's or Gunpowder parish, entering upon its existence as a separate parish in 1777. In the churchyard, there are but few graves dating from the eighteenth century, the disorganization that followed the Revolution, having borne fruit here as elsewhere. The most interesting of these inscriptions are given:

In Memory of John Mather, Who departed this life October ye 2d 1775, Aged 38 years.

> My Pilgrimage I run apace,
> My resting place is here.
> This stone is got to keep the Spot,
> Lest man should dig too near.

Elizabeth Mather, June ye 3d 1776, Aged 33 years.

> A Resurrection with the Just
> I hope for, though I sleep in Dust.

Elizabeth Bosley 1784.

John McClurg, August 17th 1777.

> Affliction sore long time I bore;
> All human help was vain;
> Till God did please to give me Ease,
> And fre'd me from my pain.

A variation of the above verse is found on the tombstone of Lydia Brookheart, "Consort" of Peter Brookheart, date 1833:

> Sickness sore long time she bore,
> Physicians' skill it was in vain,
> Till God revealed his tender love & took her away from pain.

Among the first to be buried in the nineteenth century was Elizabeth Talbott, wife of Thos. Talbott, who died December 8, 1801, aged 31 years. The largest family group is that of the Gwynns:

Samuel Gwynn, 27th day of August 1810.

William Gwynn, October 1st 1819, In the 70th year of his age.

Eleanor Gwynn, 30th day of July 1829, In the 77th year of her age.

John Gwynn, March 25th 1823, Aged 75 years.

John Gwynn Jr., March 16th 1822, Aged 44 years.

Our beloved Father, William Gwynn of R. Born 4th Dec. 1797; died 4th Dec. 1846.

Our beloved Mother Mary, Wife of William Gwynn, Born 11th May 1793; died 2d August 1849. Blessed are the dead who die in the Lord.

Among those who reached the good old age of three-score-years-and-ten are: Col. Wm. Hitchcock, who died June 8,

1835, in the 71st year of his age, and Jemima his wife, on February 16, 1824. Some of those whose lives were cut short were:

Capt. Aquilla Miles Feb. 18th 1808, In the 32nd year of his age. A tender Husband and an indulgent parent. and Elizabeth, his wife, who died January 9th 1805, aged 22 years.

Between Maj. Dixon Stansbury, who died June 5, 1841, in his 58th year, and Sophia, his wife, October 12, 1831, aged 40 years, lies John Stewart Calhoun, infant son of Capt. D. D. Miles, U. S. N., date, December 27, 1840.

The oldest graves of the Hutchins family, who were seated within the bounds of St. James parish before the church was built, are Zarey Hutchins, wife of Richard, who departed this life December 23, 1819, aged 78 years; Col. William Hutchins, in the year 1824, aged 70, and Nicholas Hutchins, who died May 24, 1845. The latter was doubtless a descendant of the Nicholas Hutchins at whose house the services were held, while the church was being built.

The name of Pearce is also well represented in the churchyard. Seven brothers of this name settled in Baltimore county, five of whom took part in the Revolutionary war.

The ancient parish of St. John's Protestant Episcopal church overlooks the border of the two counties, but the church itself stands at Kingsville on the Baltimore county side. In fact, there are at present two churches with the old graves about them, the one to suit the requirements of a congregation "up to date," the other to be reserved as a venerable connecting link in the romantic history of a church, subject to the migratory habit in the past. More than one hundred and seventy years ago, St. John's parish church stood at Joppa, a flourishing town and port-of-entry and a rival of Baltimore in its early days. When St. Paul's church was about to be erected at the latter place in 1730, St. John's was recommended as the model worthy to be copied. Of Joppa, alas! nothing now remains but the Rumsey mansion, built in 1760, traditions of a family graveyard and a stone,

To the memory of David McCullogh, Merchant of Joppa, who died the 17th day of September 1766, aged forty-eight years.

In the churchyard of St. John's we find the following inscriptions:

In memory of Dr. John C. Howard, Died December 1844. Also Ellen, Daughter of Dr. John C. and Marian Howard, Aged 7 years.

In memory of Marian, Wife of Dr. John C. Howard, Died November 17th 1864.

In Memory of Abraham Whisler, who departed this life March the 16th 1841, in the 77th year of his Age.

To Eliza, daughter of Edward Day and wife of John B. Bayleys, Died Augt., 1825. "A tribute of affection by her daughter Caroline."

Sacred to the memory of Charles Grupy, Died Oct. 29th 1845, aged 18 years 10 months. also Adolphus, his brother, Born June 17th 1830; Died Nov. — 1832.

> Who here side by side repose
> Till the resurrection morn.

In memory of Elizabeth Grupy, who departed this life October 2d 1830, Aged 32 years.

Jacob Grupy, Aged 47 Died Aug 18th 1835.

In memory of our grandfather, Edward Day, Born August 17th 1759; Departed this life September 10th 1842. Donor to the Vestry of this church in 1834.

On a wide, low stone with two inscriptions abreast are recorded the deaths of Stephen Onion and his daughter Elizabeth.

Stephen Onion Iron Master, Born February 10 1694, at Brewood in Staffordshire in England; departed this life Aug 26th 1754. his Body here Interr'd.

Elizabeth Russell Onion Born July 12th 1734 Departed this life June 10th 1742 her Body lies Inter'd.

> "How great God's pow'r is none can tell
> Nor think how large his Grace
> Not men below nor Sai'ts that dwell
> on High before his Face."

Another stone is inscribed:

Baltimore County 111

In memory of Juliana West Gittings, wife of Dr. D. S. Gittings, Born Sept. 26th 1798; Died Jan. 16th 1847.
Blessed with a heartfelt Christianity, the purity and Strength of which were evident by its consoling influence, May it, oh! most merciful Father, have caused her to be numbered with thy Saints in Glory everlasting.

Dr. David Gittings married three times. He was born August 17, 1787, died March 12, 1887, and was buried near his first wife.

A later generation is represented in this churchyard by the names of Dilworth, Blair, Whisler, Ringgold, Grover, Gorsuch, Murray, Tyson, Scarff, Altvater, Thompson, League, Freeman, Dutton, Bell and Falls.

In the churchyard of St. John's Roman Catholic church at Long Green, enclosed by a substantial fence, is the Jenkins burial lot. Each of the following inscriptions ends with "May she rest in peace," or "may he rest in peace," as the case may be, "Amen."

In Memory of Ann, daughter of Michl C. and Charity Jenkins, and wife of Charles Hopkins. Born 1772; Died 1836.

In Memory of Charity, wife of Michl C. Jenkins, and daughter of Thomas Wheeler. Died in the year 1820.

In Memory of Michael C. Jenkins, son of Wm Jenkins and Mary Courtney, Born in St. Mary's Co., Md. 1736; Died at Long Green 1802.

In Memory of Ignatius, son of Michl C. and Charity Jenkins, Born 1776; Died 1819.

In Memory of Michl F. Jenkins, son of Josias and Elizabeth A. Jenkins, Born 18th Sept. 1812; Died 18 June 1835.

In Memory of Josias Jenkins, son of Michl C. and Charity Jenkins, Born 17th March 1781; Died 20th April 1823.

Ports-of-entry were established by law in 1683, at which time the conditions of plantation were withdrawn. Among the ports of Baltimore county was Humphrey's creek, an estuary of the Patapsco lying west of North Point and south of where the battle was fought in 1814. In Patapsco Hundred where the Rev. John Yeo began his ministrations in 1683, the first brick church of St. Paul's parish was erected in 1702.

It stood forty rods west of where the Sollers' road leaves the North Point road, and when the writer was engaged in exploring the neighborhood in the company of Rev. George Leakin some fourteen or fifteen years ago, the traditional site was pointed out. It consisted of a triangular bit of woodland, extending down a gentle slope divided at the bottom by the rippling waters of a tiny brook—the Colegate creek of yore.

No one would have supposed that so insignificant a stream could have ever been of sufficient volume to float the craft used by the settlers on their way to worship. And yet, when we hear how the Patuxent river has in course of time lost fifty miles of its navigable waters, and that Elk Ridge Landing, a flourishing port on a branch of the Patapsco, is now high and dry, preserving only its name, we cease to find incredible the traditions about our minor water ways.

Baltimore town, at the head waters of the north branch of the Patapsco, was incorporated in 1730, and migration to this much more salubrious locality ensued. This left the old church and churchyard to take care of itself. By 1756, it was completely in ruins, and the bones of the dead were removed to the shelter of the new St. Paul's, which stood very near its present site. The church lot extended, at that time, nearly to Lexington street, covering the ground now occupied by the Masonic Temple.

On Back River Neck, lying between the Gunpowder and the Patapsco rivers, is a remnant of an old plantation given up to Poles engaged in truck gardening: but there are also tombs here that serve as links between the dead that lie beneath the sod and the original Anglo-Saxon owners, who settled these necks more than two centuries ago. The following epitaph, upon a stone curiously hidden by a tree, which has grown up under it and hides one side, was made out with some difficulty:

St. Paul's Church and Churchyard, Baltimore, 100 Years Ago
From an oil painting now owned by the Maryland Historical Society

Sacred to the Memory of Gould Smith D. Raven, Son of I. Raven, 1826, in the 20th year of his Age.

> How soon alas! here in his Early bloom
> In prime of life he meets an Early tomb
> As by the number of his days appears
> Which reached but just twenty Years.
> Where is that Stubborn Soul that can forbear
> Hearing this loss and not let fall a tear.

The footstone initials are "G. D. R." The father did not long survive the son, for on the next tomb is carved:

Sacred to the Memory of Capt. Isaac D. Raven, 1826, in the 53rd year of his Age.

> "My dear relations do not weep;
> I am not dead, but here do sleep
> Within this Solid lump of clay
> Until the Resurrection day.
> And here my body must remain
> Till Christ shall call me forth again."

There are also two other stones. That of Capt. Wm. G. Shaw, who died in 1834 in the sixty-second year of his age, contains the same epitaph as was written for a nameless suicide in potter's field of a much earlier date, and which is far more appropriate for him than for the respectable old denizen of the later tomb:

> "Fare Well, Vain World, I've seen Enough of thee,
> And now am careless, What thou sayest of me.
> Thy Smiles I court not, nor thy frown I fear;
> My Soul's at rest, My head lies quiet here.
> The faults you saw in me, take care to shun.
> Look you at home, enough there to be done.
> Whene'er I lived or died, it matters not,
> To whom related or by whom begot.
> I was, now am not; ask no more of me
> 'Tis all I am and all that thou shalt be.

Sarah Shaw, wife of the above in the 34th year of her Age, 1827.

> "Go home dear friend and Cease from tears.
> I must lie here till Christ appears
> Repent in time while time you have.
> [Last line wanting.]

Gould Smith Raven was connected with the Goldsmiths of

Goldsmiths' Hall, higher up in the county, the boundaries of which were found on the shore of the bay after the tide went out.

On Patapsco Neck, about twelve miles from Baltimore and in the neighborhood of North Point, are many places with traditions of early occupancy. Among them is the old Eager place, long since passed into the hands of strangers, where a broken tombstone marks the grave of John Eager. He was an ancestor of the Howard family of Baltimore and his name is perpetuated in Eager street crossing what was once one of the Howard estates. The old Eager place belonged to Col. John Eager Howard in 1821. A large stone on the roadside marks the boundary between his land and that of Thos. Shaw. The inscription on his tombstone is:

Here lyes the body of Mr. John Eager who departed this life 11 of April 1722 aged 28 years and 2 months.

To the right of Sparrows Point road, going from the Point towards the North Point road, is a neglected graveyard covered with periwinkle mingled with weeds, and surrounded by a thicket. The only stone that could be examined, bore this legend:

In Memory of Elizabeth Jones who departed this life April 12, 1848 in the 93rd of her age.

Probably Jones and Todd are among the oldest names, surviving from the days of the early Patapsco settlements. Near the Eager place, is a Todd homestead with its well-kept graveyard, though with no family tombs of eighteenth century date. In fact there is a gap of nearly a hundred years between their earliest monument and that of Elizabeth Conn, laid here with her infant in 1717. The name is an unusual one in our records and the story told is that she was the wife of Hugh Conn, a "minister," who had settled in Baltimore. Taking her infant with her to visit her parents in England, they both died on the return passage when almost in sight of home. Their bodies were landed and buried here. Afterwards a fine slab was placed over the grave, inscribed:

Here lyeth the Body of Elizabeth Conn late wife of Hugh Conn who departed this life . . . 1717 in ye 27th year of her Age . . . . Daughter E . . . Conn . . . this life . . . 22 . . . 1 year and 12 days.

The graves of members of the Todd family are thus inscribed:

Thos. J. Todd Died March 26, 1843 Aged 38 years.

Bernard Todd Died Sept 13, 1816 In his 50th year.

Geo. W. Todd Died Feb. 7, 1830 In his 23rd year.

Rachel R. Consort of Vincent Green Died January 24, 1847 Aged 28 years 2 mos. and 15 days Also her son William.

Elizabeth wife of Lancelot Rockwell Died Oct. 8, 1850 Aged 35 years.

There are also stones to Frances C. and Amelia L., children of above:

Richard Shaw Died June 30th, 1831 In his 43rd year.

Mary Shaw Died May 7th, 1835 In her 56th year.

CHAPTER VI

BESIDES the inhabitants along the water front, Baltimore county had sturdy pioneers also, in the heart of its forests. These, however, were subject to the incursions of unfriendly Indians, and in order to insure protection, forts were ordered built at intervals on the outposts. One of these, known as the "Garrison," gave its name to all the region there about. Ten years after the erection of St. Paul's church in Baltimore town, it was found necessary to build a chapel-of-ease for the "Forest Inhabitants." This was finished in 1743, and was known from the first as the "Garrison Forest Church." In 1745 it was erected into a separate parish under the name of St. Thomas, and the old churchyard preserves interesting memorials that the parent parish, through the frequent disturbance of its dead, cannot boast of.

> Here lieth Thos. Cradock
> (first rector of St. Thomas'
> Parish), who died May 7th 1770,
> in the 51st year of his age.

Here lieth Arthur, son of the Rev'd Thomas Cradock and Katherine, his wife, who died the 22d February 1769, In the 22d year of his Age.

> "Peace to thy gentle shade, O youth divine
> Our tears will flow when we approach thy shrine
> If spotless virtue, happiness, can claim
> If Godlike deeds are e'er preferred to fame
> Thy soul is wafted to immortal joys
> A life well spent deserves ye heavenly prize
> Stop pensive reader, think how time has past
> And live each day as it was thy last."

And By Desire Here lieth his brother Dr. Thomas Cradock, who died on the 19th of October 1821, in the 70th year of his age.

Dr. Cradock was an active physician for forty-five years.

Here lieth the body of Dr. John Cradock second son of the Reverend

Thomas Cradock and Katherine his wife who departed this life on the 4th day of October 1794, in the 45th year of his age.

Here lieth the body of Ann, relict of Dr. John Cradock Who departed this life on the 22d day of Feb. 1809 in the 49th year of her age.

Ann Cradock was the daughter of John Worthington, who was the great-grandson of Capt. John Worthington (whose tomb can now be seen opposite Annapolis), and Sarah Howard, daughter of Matthew Howard, one of the "Men of Severn," a most extensive landowner and planter. His name appears on record at Annapolis as far back as 1650.

To the memory of Katherine Cradock Relict of the Reverend Thos. Cradock Who departed this life on the 20th August 1795 Aged 67 years.

Charles Walker and his wife Ann Daughter of the Revd Thomas Cradock.

In the church records, the dates omitted above are given as follows: Charles Walker departed this transitory life, November 15, 1825, and was buried in the same grave with his wife.

In memory of Charles Arthur A.B. Son of Charles and Ann Walker who departed this life Oct 27th 1815 in the 20th year of his age.

                The paths of Virtue
                And of Silence trod
                Resigned his Soul
                To the Almighty God.

Dr. Thomas C. Walker Died May 31st 1860 In the 87 year of his age.

To the Memory of Arthur son of Dr. John Cradock and Ann his wife Who died on the — day of October 1821 in the 39th year of his age.

                A Memorial
                      of
                John N. Renell
          a native of Great Britain
      He was born at Topsham in Devonshire
               in April 1776,
          and died at Baltimore
       on the 5th of December 1818.
         Amiable in disposition
          Upright in character
                 and
         Sincere in friendship
he enjoyed the respect and esteem
     of a select acquaintance.

Christopher Carnan,
Who Lived and Died an Honest Man,
On the 30th of December, 1769.
Aged 39 Years.

He was the brother of Cecil Carnan, the first wife of Gen. Mordecai Gist, and probably of John Carnan, from whom the Ridgelys of "Hampton" are descended.

Cecil Carnan's epitaph reads:

To the Memory of
Cecil Gist,
Daughter of Charles and Prudence Carnan,
of London,
Who Departed this Life
The 1st Day of July, 1770.
Aged 28.

Friendly stranger, stop, gaze on this silent tomb,
The end of Nature in the prime of youthful bloom.
Lost from the soft endearing ties of Life,
And tender name of daughter, sister, mother, wife.
Ye blooming fair, in her your fading charms survey;
She was whate'er your tender hearts can say,
More than exceeds ye muses noblest point of thought
Or Pope or Milton's verses ever taught.
Farewell, lamented shade I can proceed no more;
Too fast thy memory prompts the tear to flow.
Such was ye will of fate, nor must we murmur at ye rod,
Nor allwise dispensations of our God.
Here in hope we trust, here let our sorrows rest;
The good and virtuous dead are ever blest.

Joseph West, a native of Rhode Island, Who departed this life Dec. 6th 1840, 85 years of Age.

Mrs. Violetta West, b. 22nd Sept. 1759, d. 21st Feb. 1844.

Wm. Stacey died Jan 1794.

Affliction sore long time I bore
Physicians were in vain
Till God did please and death did cease
To ease me of my pain.

It is thought that this last was a bit of grim humor on the stonecutter's part.

Sacred to the Memory of Sarah, wife of Nelson Norris, died June 19th 1814. With Christian piety and resignation and the full hope of a glorious

Baltimore County

and triumphant resurrection thro' merits of her Saviour, resigned her soul into the hands of her maker.

>Say! what is death, for when the Christian dies
>'Tis but a joyful journey to the skies
>The hour when choirs of angels hover around
>With wreaths of never fading glory crowned
>To guide the spirit to the realms above
>And sing the transports of redeeming love
>The hour the Christian bursts the sleep of clay
>To hail the morn of an eternal day.

Maria North Simkins, daughter of Robt. North Carnan, born 1792, died 1872.

To the Memory of Sarah White died Sept. 4th 1807.
>Young and old as you pass by
>As you are so once was I
>And as I am so you will be
>So prepare for death and eternity.

In Memory of Mrs. Elizabeth Hulse, who died 1801, universally esteemed.

Other inscriptions are:

Emily Hollingsworth, daughter of Mr. Horatio Hollingsworth, died 1841.

Thomas Henry Carroll, brother of John and Nicholas Carroll of the Caves, born 1796 died 1849.
>Oh! gone forever take this last adieu.

Molly Hance died 5th Dec. 1820.

Major Robert Lyon died 1842. He was a volunteer in the army of the Revolution and participated in several engagements. "May he rest in peace."

Joseph Lyon born 1796.

Brian Philpot of Stamford, Baltimore County, born Aug 9th 1750; died April 11th 1812.

Elizabeth, wife of Brian Philpot born March 4th 1768; died July 26 1853.

Rev. Charles Austin died 1849, 29th year of his Ministry of St. Thomas's Parish.

Wm. Fell Johnston born 1798; died 1862.

Elizabeth Johnston, wife of Samuel Johnston, died Dec 3rd 1805. A most affectionate wife and parent Prudent, sincere, charitable and Pius, Faithfully endeavoring through life to discharge the various duties of a christian.

Capt. Robt. North died 24th of March 1748.

Frances North, wife of Capt. Robt. North, died July 25th 1745.

Ellin, daughter of Capt. Robt. North, and wife of John Moale 2nd. died 1825.
Many daughters have done virtuously but thou excellest them all.
John Moale 2nd. died July 5th 1798.

Mr. John Moale, son of Richard and Elizabeth Moale, born in Kenton Parish, Devonshire England, Oct 30th 1697, emigrated to America 1719, married Rachel daughter of Genl John Hammond of Severn River April 17th 1723, died March 10th 1740, and was interred in the family burying ground on Moale's point, from whence his remains were removed to St. Thomas's by his descendants, Sept 2nd 1826.

Elizabeth, wife of Richard Curzon, daughter of John and Ellin Moale died 1822.

Rebecca, wife of Thomas Russell and daughter of John and Ellin Moale died 1840.

Richard, son of John and Ellin Moale died 1763.

There are several vaults, one bears the name of Samuel Ownings, 1839. In another lies Richard H. Moale, who was born in 1802 and died in 1848, also Randle H. Moale.

The first interment of which there is any record was made here in 1752, and a broken bit of stone indicates the spot where Mistress Gosnell was at that time laid to rest.

When the church was enlarged some years ago it was built over a portion of the old graveyard. Beneath the chancel lie the remains of Joseph Risteau, son of John Risteau, High Sheriff of the county, and a slab laid in the brick pavement of the aisle shows where the body of Maj. David Hopkins was deposited. Among the most prominent of the old burying lots are the Cradocks, the Walkers, the Moales, the Gists, the Carnans, the Johnsons, the Lyons, the Carrolls, the Philpots, and the Hollingsworths. Many of the bodies in the Moale lot were transferred here from the family burying ground on Moale's Point when the land was needed for city lots.

With the name of Mrs. Ellin North Moale is associated much of the local history of that part of the county. Greenspring, the estate inherited by her from her father, Capt.

ST. THOMAS CHURCH, GARRISON FOREST
Showing the graveyard at the north side. The church was built in 1743

Robert North, has given its name to the valley, which of late years has become so popular as a place of summer residence.

At the Baptist meetinghouse, known as Sater's, a broken stone with the name "Henry Sater," roughly carved, probably marks the resting place of the Founder, who came from England in 1709. He settled at Chestnut Ridge, and organized the first Baptist congregation of fifty-seven members, in 1742. Some inscriptions here are:

In memory of Henry Sater, Who Departed this Life March 8th 1788, In the 44 year of his Age.

In memory of George Sater, Who Departed this Life September 15th 1798, Aged 28 years.

In memory of [C]apt John Cock[ey] who departed this life February 8th 1808, Aged 84 years, 8 months and 24 days.

SACRED to the Memory of Ann, Wife of Philn. Towson, who departed this life June 5th 1809, Aged 38 years, 10 Months and Six days.

In Memory of Elder Geo. Grice, A preacher of the everlasting Gospel and a sinner saved by Grace, Who departed this life June 24th 1825, Aged 65 years.

    Come Saints and drop a tear or two
    For him who labored here for you.

In memory of Sarah Grice, Consort of Elder George Grice, who departed this life January 4th 1836, aged 79 years.

    Her trust in God, she did declare
    We hope his mercy she did share.

To the memory of Edward Grice, Departed this life November the 8, 1844. Aged 53 years 4 months and 28 days.

In memory of Susanna, Consort of John A. Rennons, and daughter of George and Sarah Grice, who departed this life Sept. 19th 1842, Aged 45 years 10 months and 15 days.

    Blessed are the dead
    Which die in the Lord.
    Blessed is she in realms of peace
    Where all earthly sorrows cease.

In memory of Morgeanna, daughter of John and Susanna Rennons, who departed this life October the 20th 1849, aged 22 years 4 months and 6 days.

    In Jesus Christ she had her trust
    And was resigned to return to dust.
    Though the body is beneath the sod,
    The soul hath flown to meet its God.

In memory of Avarilla Grice, who departed this life Sept 24th 1841, In the 57th year of her age.

In memory of George Grice, who departed this life Aug. 8th 1843, In the 55th year of his age.

     Held up & cheered by Jesus' Grace
     He sweetly fell asleep.

To my sister Mary Grice, Born 14th Feb. 1815; Died 3rd Jun 1855.

These three stones are enclosed in a lot with members of the Oler family of a later generation. They stand on the far side of the church.

Hier ruhet in Gott Iohannes Meyer Gebohren den 22ten August 1790, und Gestorben den 22ten August 1812, Seines Alters 24 Iahr.

In memory of Iohn meYrs, who was born the 22 of August 1790 and died the 22 of december 1812.

The two dates are as here given. The last version was cut by a rough tool.

. . . Iron Mattison . . . of Joseph, died May, 30th 1823 in the 85th year of his age.

In Memory of Notty, wife of John E. Merryman, Born March 21st 1813; Died Nov. 6th 1856, Aged 41 yrs. 8 mos. 6 days.

In Memory of Mary Merryman, who departed this life Feb. 24th 1809, Aged 28 years, 1 month and 10 days.

In memory of Arrementa Sullivan, who departed this life on the 11th of Sept 1809, Aged 59 years.

     Death from all Death has set her free
     And will her gain forever be
     Death loosed the massy chain of woe
     To let the mournful Prisoner go.
     Oh!!! Poor Menta.

To the memory of Samuel S. Burnham, who departed this life, November the 13th 1842, Aged 23 years.

     Stop Gentle friend and view this
     Sacred spot,
     Consider well, his fate will be thy lot.
     Cut off in manhood's prime a
     stranger here,
     Oh, drop the tribute of a brother's tear.
     Be this our prayer, a mark of
     Odd Fellow's love:
     Jesus admit him to thy Lodge above.

THE JOHN EAGER HOWARD STATUE
In Washington Square, Baltimore. Erected in 1904
by the Municipal Art Society

Baltimore County

In Memory of Edward Burnham, who departed this life 30th of March 1878, aged 100 years 6 months and 18 days.
> Fearless he entered Death's cold flood;
> In peace of Conscience closed his eyes;
> His only hope was Jesus blood,
> In sure and certain hope to rise.

In Memory of Elizabeth, consort of Edw'd Burnham, who departed this life February 9th 1843 in the 60th year of her Age.
> Confessed to me her willingness to die
> And took her flight to joys above the sky.

Henry R. Scott Born Dec 20 1828; Died July 16 1850.

In Memory of John Jones who departed this life April the 22nd In the year of our Lord 1814 aged 52 years. A preacher of the Everlasting Gospel.

In Memory of Joseph Boswell who departed this life August 15th 1813 Aged 32 years.

In memory of Ann Wife of Greenbury Cook and daughter of Joseph and Rachel Baysman Died Aug 26 1844 Aged 39 years 2 Mos and 24 Dys.

Standing to the right of the church, are two well preserved altar tombs inscribed as follows:

Sacred to the Memory of Thomas Walker who was born September 1742 & Died 18th October 1818 Aged 76 years and 1 month.

Sacred To the Memory of Discretion Walker Relict of Thomas Walker who departed this life December 7th 1823 aged 76 years.

On a farm near Hunt's meetinghouse, to the right of the road going to Rockland, is the Job Hunt burying ground, in which the following inscriptions are found:

In memory of Samuel, son of Job and Margaret Hunt, born Jan. 1st, 1772; departed this life Feb. 10th, 1779.

In memory of John Hunt, who departed this life 18th, day of Feb. 1809, in 62 year of his age.

Margaret Hunt died Feb. 26th, 1794, in 47 year of her age. A loving industrious wife, a Tender mother and Endulgent Mistress.

Eliza Hunt, was born Aug 11th, and departed this life Jan. 1784.

Samuel Hunt born Sept. 5th, 1781, departed this life Oct. 5th, 1782.

In memory of Rachel Anderson, who departed this life April 29, 1817, aged 54 years 5 months and four days.

In memory of Susan Hunt, consort of J. H. Hunt, departed this life Dec. 30th, 1833, in the 45 year of her age.

Sacred to the memory of Elizabeth Chew Haubert, who departed this life Oct. 27th, 1846, aged 69 years.

Capt. Lewis Beard, died Jan. 31st, 1853, Aged 46 years.

Another Hunt graveyard is on a farm near the Falls Road not far from Brooklandwood farm, now rented by Mr. Fouck.

In memory of Walter Smith, who departed this life Feb. 18th, 1772, aged 33 years 1 month and 15 days.

In memory of Elizabeth Bond, who departed this life 29th, August, 1806, in 86 year of her age.

In memory of Susannah Hunt, who departed this life 28th of December 1792, in 49th year of her age.

Here rests all that was mortal of Phineas Hunt, born Nov. 2, 1751, Died Feb. 6th, 1837 in 86 year of his age.

In memory of Susannah Hunt who died Jan. 28th, 1847, aged 83 years.

In memory of Benedict Hunt born April 17th, 1783 died Sept. 11th, 1825.

To my mother Prudence Hunt, born Jun 1790, died Aug. 2nd, 1867.

At Rockland, the farm of Wm. Johnson, is the grave of Thomas Johnson, M. D., who died in 1831, aged 65 years.

At Sudbrook, the McHenry place near Pikesville, in a good state of preservation, is the lonely tomb of a young soldier of Revolutionary times, the uncle of Wm. F. Johnson of Rockland.

In Memory of Captain Caecilius Johnson son of Thomas and Ann Johnson of Baltimore County who departed this Life September 26th, 1797 Aged 26 years and 1 month.

In the Howard graveyard at Grayrock, near Pikesville, are the following:

Sacred to the Memory of Mr. Cornelius Howard who departed this life on the 14th of June 1777, Ætat 70. He was a Tobacco Planter in the County of Baltimore, Province of Maryland. He lived much esteemed and died regarded of all.

In Memory of Cornelius Howard son of Cornelius and Ruth Howard who departed this life Feb. 12, A. D. 1844 in the 90th year of his age. Mich. 6th Chap. 8 verse.

In Memory of Ruth wife of Charles Elder who departed this life Sept. 1st, 1827 aged 79 years.

On the first of these three stones is a finely carved coat of arms, on the second, a rough imitation of the former.

Amongst the graves of the settlers of the fourth district is that of Adam Goose, on the property which he conveyed in 1760 to Michael Gore, and still owned by representatives of the Gore family. It is supposed that Michael Gore is buried in another grave on the property, with nothing to mark its position. Some of the Gore family have been removed to the Methodist burying ground at Reisterstown. An old family servant of Michael Gore, aged 90 years, said the old Gores were all Tories.

Near Reisterstown, in the same district, are the Richards' graves, 1770 and 1776; James Mannon's, 1789; graves of the Parrish family; of James Hannah on the Cherry Hill road, at Cedar Grove; on Frank Lowe's place, "Delight," and John Ford's place, farmed by Conrad Fox.

In an unmarked grave at "Pomona," once the home of Robert Riddell, lies the body of the Rev. George Ralph, a native of England. He started as a teacher in Baltimore, in 1790, was ordained by Bishop White, of Pennsylvania, in 1791, and held the position as rector of several country churches, with which the duties of school teacher were in most cases attached. He was for several years principal of Charlotte Hall school, in St. Mary's county, entering upon his duties there in 1801. A quaint building, still standing on the ground and called the "White House," was built by him. This is his only monument. He was of Irish descent, and had the proverbial eloquence of his race. He married Miss De Butts, niece of Dr. Butts, of Mt. Welby, Prince George's county, and left two children, a son and a daughter. He died in May, 1813.

Upon his death the youngsters of the neighborhood thought that some rites of their own were necessary in order to exorcise so indomitable a spirit. Therefore, with much labor they deposited a huge stone over his grave to keep him from rising again. Another story is told of him, in reference to an altercation he had with Mr. Key, while he was principal of the Charlotte Hall school. The latter exclaimed in his wrath, "Were it not for your cloth I should fight you," whereupon the reverend gentleman took off his coat and threw it on the ground saying, "Lie there divinity while I chastise rascality."

The Croxall graveyard, on the farm of Mr. Charles T. Cockey, contains many graves; the headstones of some are gone, but the footstones still remain. Near these, on the slope of the hill, are interred the bodies of the slaves. Although there are many inscriptions extant, which are given below, the graves themselves are in a dilapidated condition and need attention. This graveyard is still in the custody of the heirs, Mr. Cockey having no control of it. Most of the following inscriptions are taken from flat slabs raised on brick foundations in different stages of decay.

Here lies interred the body of Elizabeth Rogers. Departed this life on the twenty-eight day of February 1777, in the sixty second year of her age.

In memory of Richard Croxall, who departed this life on the eleventh day of May in the sixty seventh year of his age.

Also to Mrs. Rebecca Croxall, his wife, who departed this life November twenty seventh 1766. Age sixty seven years and nine months.

In memory of Thomas Gittings, who died on the twenty second day of September 1800, in the forty-third year of his age.

Enclosed within a plain iron fence, at Druid Hill Park, amidst the shade of stately pines, and near the upper reservoir, is the burial lot of the Rogers and Buchanan family.

The oldest stones are those of Dr. George Buchanan, who departed this life on the 25th day of April, 1750, aged fifty-two years, " and of Eleanor, his wife, who died August 26, 1758, aged 35 years."

Mrs. Buchanan was a Rogers.

In memory of ANDREW BUCHANAN who departed this Life On the 12th day of March 1785 in the 53rd year of his Age.

He was during the Contest that secured the Independence of America Lieutenant of this Country And served with Great Repute for many Years As Chief Judge of the Court. He was An Affectionate Husband A tender Parent An Honest Man. In short Endowed with Every Virtue That could Complete any Excellent Character.

And beside him lie the remains of his wife, "Susan," who died August 26, 1798, aged 55 years.

Nearby is the grave of Mrs. Rogers, who was born on January 19, 1797, and died August 10, 1822; also of Nicholas Rogers:

Here lies the remains of Nicholas Rogers, To the memory of a most affectionate parent this tablet is erected. Born October 7, 1753, died July 2d, 1822.

Close by this grave is another, the slab of which bears the following:

Eleanor, who died Jan. 1, 1812; born Aug. 25, 1757.

Here lies all that was mortal of Lloyd Nicholas Rogers A ripe scholar and an accomplished gentleman who died November 12th 1860 aged 73.

The Park of Druid Hill which he inherited from the original patentee to whom it was granted by the Colony of Maryland in 1760 and which he conveyed in 1860 to the City of Baltimore, surrounds this spot, a part of the original grant, and he sleeps as was his wish, with his ancestors and those whom he loved.

At Evergreen, the Buckler place on W. North Avenue, in a grove to the left of a path going to the house, is a single grave marked by a stone inscribed as follows:

Elizabeth Hepburn Born at Port Royal, Va.; Died April 22d, 1806, Aged 52 years.

The following data gleaned from the eighth, tenth, eleventh and third districts has been furnished by Dr. Benjamin Rush Ridgely, who lives on one of the old Talbott places, near Warren. The Doctor is especially well qualified to make his report a valuable guide to future generations.

The Joshua Talbott burying ground, eighth district, is

situated on land formerly owned by the Talbott family, now by George Harryman; being and lying in the northeast angle formed by the intersection of the Overshot road and that running west from Meredith bridge to the Warren factory, about 4½ miles from Towson. In this cemetery are found the following inscriptions:

John Denmead (father of the late Adam D. Sr.) died (ab) 1835.

George Ivory Willis, died before 1840.

Frances Thwaites Willis Born Sep. 18, 1763 Died Feb. 8, 1845.

Joshua F. C. Talbott only son of Edward and Frances Thwaites Cockey Talbott Born June 9, 1796 Died Mar. 24, 1869.

Eliza (Denmead) wife of Joshua F. C. Talbott and sister of the late Adam Denmead Sr. Born April 2, 1801 Died Mar. 12, 1842.

Mary Frances daughter of Joshua and Eliza Talbott Born Feb. 24, 1824 Died Dec. 31, 1830.

Adam Denmead son of Joshua and Eliza Talbott Born Nov. 19, 1822, Died Jan. 4, 1831.

Eliza Jane daughter of Joshua and Eliza Talbott Born Oct. 23, 1830, Died Jan. 6, 1831.

Thwaites Charcilla dau of Joshua and Eliza Talbott Born May 24, 1828, Died Jan. 8, 1831.

Geo. Ivory Willis, son of Joshua and Eliza Talbott Born Nov. 6, 1825, Died Jan. 9, 1831.

Elizabeth Slade, dau of Joshua and Eliza Talbott Born July 22, 1837. Died Aug 7, 1838.

Susan Eliza, dau of Joshua and Eliza Talbott, Born Mar. 3, 1842, Died 1842.

Joshua F. C. son of Joshua and Eliza Talbott Born Jan 31 1821, Died Sep 26, 1885.

Edward Cockey son of Joshua and Ann Eliza Talbott Born July 26, 1851, Died Aug 9, 1852.

Joshua F. C., son of Joshua and Ann Eliza Talbott, Born Dec. 10, 1849; Died Aug. 12, 1852.

Annie Florence, dau of Joshua and Ann Eliza Talbott, Born April 8, 1860; Died Aug. 26, 1861.

Aquila Ridgely, son of Joshua and Ann Eliza Talbott, Born May 10, 1865; Died May 24, 1865.

Rebecca, daughter of Joshua and Ann Eliza Talbott, Born July 8, 1867; Died Mar. 4, 1869.

On the "Barretts Delight" farm, which has been in the Talbott family since 1718, is the Edward Talbott family burying ground. This farm lies in the southeast angle formed by the intersection of the Warren factory road, with that beginning at the Warren road and running east to Merediths bridge, on the pike leading from Towson to Dulaney's valley, and adjoins both roads. With few exceptions, the inscriptions given are Talbotts:

In Memory of Edward Talbott Born July 15, 1723; Died Aug. 29, 1797,

In Memory of Temperance, wife of Edward Talbott, Born Sep. 13, 1720; Died Jan. 5, 1813.

Temperance, daughter of John and Hannah Talbott, Born July 24, 1782; died June 27, 1793.

Rebecca, daughter of John and Hannah Talbott, Born November 11, 1783; Died June 24, 1793.

In Memory of Mary Edwards, born—died 20 minutes after 12 o'clock in ye morning Apr. 16, 1791.

Penelope Deye Cockey Talbott, daughter of Edward and Frances Thwaites Talbott, died july 7, 1798.

Edward Talbott, son of Edward and Temperance Talbott, Born June 26, 1764; Died Aug. 5, 1801.

In Memory of James Batson, an Englishman, died Oct. 25, 1810.

In Memory of Sarah, Consort of Benjamin Talbott, Born Sep. 27, 1749; Died Jan. 8, 1815.

"Blessed are the merciful for they shall obtain mercy."

In Memory of Benjamin Talbott, son of Edward and Temperance, Born Feb. 11, 1750; Died Jan. 5, 1816.

"Blessed are the pure in heart for they shall see God."

In Memory of Vincent, son of Edward and Temperance Talbott, Born Oct. 15, 1750; Died Dec. 26, 1819.

Elizabeth, wife of Vincent Talbott, Born . . . Died May 28, 1822.

Joshua, son of Vincent and Elizabeth Talbott, Born May 26, 1775; Died Jan. 14, 1803.

Ann, daughter of Vincent and Mary Talbott, Born Feb. 11, 1804; Died July 19, 1805.

Thomas Talbott, son of John and Mary Talbott, Born Nov. 9, 1802; Died June 27, 1806.

James H. Ridgely, son of Greenberry and Harriet Ridgely, Born Nov. 16, 1817; Died Aug. 19, 1819.

Infant son of Greenberry and Harriet Ridgely, died 1822.

Infant daughter of Greenberry and Harriet Ridgely, 1830.

John Talbott, son of Vincent and Elizabeth, Born Nov. 21, 1773; Died Oct 11, 1824.

Georgiana Poteet, daughter of Eld. Thomas and Susan Poteet, Died 1830.

Vincent Talbott, son of Vincent and Elizabeth Talbott, Born Oct. 15th, 1776; died Feb. 5, 1832.

Mary Talbott, wife of Vincent Jr. and daughter of Benj. and Susan Talbott, Born Oct. 2, 1783; Died Mar. 13, 1840.

"Blessed are the dead which die in the Lord."

Abraham Wilson, died Oct. 31, 1836.

Charles W. Ridgely Jr., son of Chas. W. and Mary L. Ridgely, Born Aug. 10, 1845; Died Sep. 4, 1845.

"The Lord gave and the Lord hath taken away blessd be the name of the Lord."

Greenberry, son of Chas. W. and Mary L. Ridgely, Born and Died Apr. 10, 1849.

Lucy Talbott, daughter of Vincent and Elizabeth Talbott, Born Apr. 3, 1785; Died May 3, 1847.

> Prepare me gracious Lord
> To stand before thy face
> Thy spirit doth the work prepare
> For it is all of Grace.

Catharine Talbott, wife of Joshua Talbott and daughter of Benj. and Sarah Talbott, Born Aug. 16, 1778; Died Nov. 1, 1853.

"May she rest in Peace."

Mary Talbott, wife of John Talbott, Died 1856.

Aquila Talbott, son of Benjamin and Mary Talbott, Born Feb. 15, 1781; Died Feb. 15, 1865.

"Blessed are the pure in heart for they shall see God."

Eleanor Talbott, daughter of Benj. and Sarah Talbott, Born Jan. 10, 1786; Died Apr. 6, 1871.

In Memory of Mrs. Harriet Ridgely, daughter of Benj. and Sarah Talbott, Born Apr. 18, 1792; Died Apr. 10, 1872.

"Blessed are the pure in heart."

"Thy Statutes have been my song in the house of my pilgrimage."

In Memory of Sarah Wilmott Talbott, daughter of Benj. and Sarah Talbott, Born Oct. 28 1788; Died July 24 1879.

"Lord I come to Thee."

There are about twelve other graves, most of which are unmarked and some are of recent date.

In the burying ground of the Merryman family are the following:

Micajah Merryman Sr., Died June 7th, 1842, Aged 92 years.

Mary Ensor, his wife, Died June 1788, Aged 35 years.

Sarah, daughter of Micajah and Mary Ensor Merryman, died, Aged 23 years, Sep. 1804.

Eleanor, daughter of Micajah and Mary Ensor Merryman, Died, aged 47 years, Sep 26, 1832.

Micajah Jr., son of Micajah and Mary Ensor Merryman, Died aged 66 years, Apr. 29, 1854.

Dr. Moses, son of Micajah and Mary Ensor Merryman, Died, aged 36 years, Nov. 19, 1819.

Clarissa Harryman, wife of Micajah Merryman Jr. and daughter of George and Rachel Harryman, Died, aged 80 years, Apr. 15, 1879.

George Harryman, son of Micajah and Clarissa Merryman, Died, aged 6 mos. and 17 days, Aug. 10, 1829.

Mary, daughter of Micajah and Clarissa Merryman, Died, aged 2 mos. and 17 days, Sept. 26, 1830.

Laura Virginia, daughter of Micajah and Clarissa Merryman, Born July 1, 1841; Died Oct. 3, 1870.

Mary [Todd], widow of Benjamin Bucknell and daughter of Micajah and Mary Ensor Merryman, Died, aged 42 years, Jan. 2, 1829.

Eleanor, daughter of George and Mary Todd, Died, aged 30 years June 7, 1835.

Hannah Lemmon, Departed this life, agd 38 years, Aug. 31, 1840.
> By long experience I have known Thy sovereign
> power to save
> At thy command I venture down securely to the grave.

Micajah, son of George and Mary Merryman, Born Dec. 31, 1860; Died Jan. 5, 1861.

Andrew Lowndes, son of George and Mary Merryman, Born Dec. 11, 1864; Died Jan. 19, 1868.

Rev. Charles Gorsuch, son of George and Mary (Gorsuch) Merryman, Died in his 34 year July 3, 1894.

The Lord is my Shepherd.

A commission as lieutenant colonel was issued to Micajah Merryman, Sr., October 12, 1776, and later, one as colonel.

Micajah Merryman, Jr., was first lieutenant in a troop in 1812. When the troops were ordered to North Point, it was found that the privates were few in number, in comparison with the officers, and this troop and another were combined into one, the supernumerary officers being permitted to go to their homes. Lieutenant Merryman was one of those whose services were not needed. When, however, it was known that the British were about to land, Lieutenant Merryman went to the front, took a place in the ranks as a private and served to the end.

Micajah and Rev. Charles G. Merryman were twins, born December 31, 1860.

Situated on the tract called "Cumberland," for many years owned by the Harryman family, now by Thos. Todd, on the northwest side of the Overshot road, half a mile north of the point where this is intersected by the road running from the Warren road to Meredith's bridge, is George Harryman's burying ground. The Harryman inscriptions are:

George Harryman, died in Dec. 1794.

Sarah Harryman, died in Nov. 1799.

Sacred to the Memory of Rachel Harryman who died in the 76th year of her age June 21, 1837.

In Memory of George Harryman, born Apr. 10, 1768; died Nov. 27, 1854.

George Harryman was a member of the House of Delegates of Maryland, also a quartermaster in the war of 1812.

Ann Plat died in 1808.

Sacred to the Memory of John Gorsuch of Thomas, who departed this life July 1, 1833, in the 64th year of his age.

Sacred to the Memory of Sarah Gorsuch, who departed this life Dec. 2, 1851, in the 85 year of her age.

Sacred to the Memory of Harriet, wife of John Harryman, Departed this life aged 40 years, July 3, 1841.

In Memory of John Harryman, Born Nov. 6, 1788; Died Aug. 27, 1854.

There are eight graves containing unknown children buried

before 1830, and also those of four grown persons and one child, buried recently.

The wife of George Harryman, Sr., was Mrs. Sarah (Glenn) Merryman, and the wife of George Harryman, Jr., was Rachel Bond. Mrs. Harriet Harryman was the daughter of John and Sarah Gorsuch.

There is on this farm a stone building formerly used as quarters for blacks, in the wall of which, by the side of the door, is a stone marked "G. H. 1781."

On the property called "Montrose," owned for many years by the Nisbet family, lying on the York turnpike at the twelfth mile stone is the Nisbet burying ground, where we find the following stones:

Alexander Nisbet born at Montrose, Scotland, June 26, 1777, Came to the United States in 1784; Died Nov. 22, 1857. Judge of the Baltimore City Court, President of the St. Andrew's Society for 26 years. As a husband and father devoted and affectionate; As a friend confiding and faithful; As a judge upright and impartial.

"Blessed are the peacemakers: for they shall be called the children of God." Mattw 5-9.

Departed this life Aug, 30, 1854, Mary C. Nisbet, wife of Alexander Nisbet and daughter of John C. Owings.

"Blessed are the pure in heart for they shall see God."

Sacred to the Memory of Charles Thomas and John Nisbet, infant sons of Alexander and Mary Nisbet, This Monument is erected in testimony of the affection of their bereaved Parents, who sorrow, not as those who sorrow without hope, for Jesus called them unto him and said "Suffer the children to come unto me and forbid them not for such is the kingdom of Heaven."

Charles Nisbet born May 21, 1810; Died Dec. 13, 1813.

Thomas Deye Nisbet, born Sep 21, 1811; Died July 23, 1812.

John Owings Nisbet born Sep 9, 1819; Died Feb. 1, 1828.

Elizabeth Turnbull, daughter of C. and Anna C. Turnbull, born Apr. 30, 1840; Died June 19, 1843.

Jesus said: "Little children come unto me and forbid them not."

"Taylor's Hall," owned for many years by Col. Thomas Cockey (a son of William the emigrant), Capt. Thomas Cockey Deye and others of his family, and of late years by

Mr. Padian, has a burying ground in which are found several inscriptions of the Deye and Cockey families:

Captain Thomas Cockey Deye, Born Jan. 27, 1728; Died May 17, 1807. He was a member of the Legislature of Maryland for many years.

Sacred to the Memory of Joshua F. Cockey, who departed this transitory life Oct. 9, 1821, Aged 56 years.

Sacred to the Memory of Elizabeth, Consort of Joshua F. Cockey, aged 55 years. Died Feb. 18, 1834.

"Blessed are the merciful for they shall obtain mercy," and this saith the Lord.

Her kindness and her charity have won for her this sure reward.

In Memory of Mary S. F. Cockey, daughter of Joshua F. and Eliza Cockey, Born May 26, 1817; Died June 18, 1828.

In Memory of Wm. F. Cockey, son of Joshua F. and Eliza Cockey, Born Apr. 20, 1822; Died Apr. 26, 1822.

I. H. S. Gist I. Cockey, son of Thomas D. and Harriet Cockey, aged 1 year and 4 months; Died July 7, 1839.

I. H. S. Sacred to the Memory of Ann dau of T. D. and Harriet Cockey Born Aug. 22, 1840; Died June 20, 1841.

Rachel Cockey.
(The tombstone has fallen, with the inscription down.)

Nicholson Lux Cockey, Dutiful son of Thos. Deye Cockey, of Thomas, and Sarah Cockey, Born Aug. 17, 1839; Died Feb. 11, 1883.

Rest. Erected by his fond brother Colegate.

Sacred to the Memory of Sarah Stewart Cockey, Beloved wife of Thomas Deye Cockey, and daughter of Darby and Mary Nicholson Lux, Born Sep 13, 1807; Died June 8, 1874.

Rest. Erected to the memory of his mother by her son Colegate.

The Parks burying ground is on Chestnut-ridge, on land long owned by Peter Parks and his descendants, lying on the road leading from the York turnpike and passing through Texas to the Falls road. Three inscriptions here are:

In Memory of Peter Parks, departed this life Oct. 5, 1854, Aged 90 years.

In Memory of William Parks, Aged 37, died Sep. 14, 1849.

Died May 3, 1851, In the 11th year of his age, David, son of John and Margaret Parks.

> He died to sin, he died to cares,
> But for a moment felt the rod.
> Oh! mourner, such the Lord declares
> Are the dear children of our God.

Baltimore County 135

In Memory of Joseph B. son of William and Mary Ann Parks, aged 16 years 3, 7, died Apr. 28, 1855.

The property known as "Vauxhall" has been in the Jessop family for generations. It is on the county road starting from the York turnpike, near the fourteenth milestone, and running east towards "Sweet Air," about one mile from the York pike. Here are buried many of the Jessop family and we give some of the inscriptions:

Sacred to the memory of Charles Jessop aged 68; Died Apr. 2, 1828.

Sacred to the memory of Mary, Consort of Charles Jessop Sr., aged 64; Died July 29 1832.

Sacred to the memory of Jemima Barry, aged 61; Died Aug. 31, 1830.

David, son of Charles and Mary Jessop, Born Mar. 24, 1787; Died July 10, 1788.

David Gorsuch, son of Charles and Mary Jessop, Born Nov. 17, 1788; Died May 23, 1812.

Charles, son of Charles and Mary Jessop, Born Dec. 18, 1790; Died July 19, 1882.

In God we trust.

Elizabeth, daughter of Charles and Mary Jessop, born Jan. 28, 1793; died Sep. 20, 1794.

Abraham, son of Charles and Mary Jessop, Born Dec. 19, 1796; Died Dec. 19, 1800.

James, son of Charles and Mary Jessop, Born Jan. 26, 1799; Died Jan. 26, 1836.

Dr Abraham, son of Charles and Mary Jessop, aged 25 years, Born Dec. 1801; Died Nov. 17, 1827.

George, son of Charles and Mary Jessop, Born July 6, 1803; Died Apr. 3, 1887.

Mary, wife of Levi Merryman, and daughter of Charles and Mary Jessop, aged 49 years, Died Nov. 14, 1854.

William, son of Charles and Mary Jessop, Born Apr. 5, 1805; Died Jan. 23, 1866.

I shall be satisfied when I awaken with thy likeness.

To my dear husband Joshua, son of Charles and Mary Jessop, aged 63 years, 2 months and 21 days, Died Aug. 25, 1869.

Jemima, dau. of Charles and Mary Jessop, born Nov. 12, 1807; died Nov. 2, 1822, aged 15 years.

Harriet Ward, dau. of Charles and Mary Jessop, born Nov. 23, 1808; died Aug. 27, 1839.

In Memory of Elizabeth Ann, daughter of Charles and Mary Jessop, born Oct. 11, 1811; died Jan. 21, 1888.

In Memory of Cecilia, wife of Wm. Jessop, aged 39 years, died June 4, 1840.

Sacred to the Memory of the 1st born of William and Cecilia Jessop.

Mary, 2nd wife of William Jessop, Born Apr. 17, 1815; Died Jan. 27, 1883.

Ann M., wife of James Jessop, Born Apr. 17, 1796; Died July 5, 1832.

Our Mother Ann C., wife of Joshua Jessop, aged 71 years, 10 months and 22 days, died Mar. 19, 1878.

Sacred to the Memory of twins, children of Joshua and Ann C. Jessop, Born and died Mar. 4, 1843.

In Memory of Jemima G. (Buck), wife of Charles Jessop, aged 39 years, Died Apr. 24, 1833.

Jemima, daughter of Charles and Jemima Jessop, aged 34 years, Died June 1858.

Edward, son of Charles and Jemima Jessop, aged 40 years, 2 mos. and 29 days, Died July 28, 1884.

Mary G. (Buck), Consort of Charles Jessop, aged 62 years, Died May 26, 1865.

Elizabeth, wife of George Jessop and daughter of Joseph and Elizabeth Ashton, aged 35, Died May 5, 1854.

Emma, dau. of George and Elizabeth Jessop, Born Apr. 23, 1854; Died Feb. 2, 1876.

Dr. Charles Ashton, son of George and Ellen Jessop (second wife), born Nov. 14, 1859; died Oct. 19, 1889.

Abraham, son of Dr. Abraham and Mary B. Jessop, aged 45 years, Died Dec. 7, 1872.

In Memory of Charles, son of Levi and M. Merryman, aged 2 years. Died June 4, 1829.

In Memory of Clara A., daughter of Levi and Mary Merryman, Aged 21 years, Died Aug. 4, 1853.

In Memory of Joseph R., son of Levi and Mary Merryman, aged 22 years, Died Jan. 16, 1866.

Though closed in death, to memory still is dear.

Gussie V., dau of Levi and Mary Merryman, born Feb. 14, 1845; died Mar. 5, 1871.

He giveth his beloved sleep.

Mother Cecilia P., wife of the late Charles W. Johnson, aged 52, 2, 15, Died Oct. 22, 1892.

Harriet Ward, daughter of James P. and Arietta J. Bailey, Born Oct. 25, 1857; Died Aug. 10, 1858.

In Memory of Amanda C., wife of Henry V. Marshall, Born Apr. 5, 1835; Died Sep. 7, 1885.

The Marsh burying ground in the tenth district is located on the property owned for many years by the Marsh family, lying about one mile from the bridge on the turnpike leading from Meredith's bridge to "Sweet Air." Inscriptions here are:

Joshua Marsh, died in his 68 year on Nov. 5, 1825.

Temperance, wife of Joshua Marsh, died aged 80 years Apr. 29, 1856.

Stephen, son of Joshua and Temperance Marsh, died in the 43 year of his age, on Sep. 15, 1829.

Nelson, son of Joshua and Temperance Marsh, died in the 20th year of his age, on Feb. 20th, 1826.

Dennis, son of Joshua and Temperance Marsh, Born Aug. 13, 1795; Died Oct. 15, 1831.

Elijah, son of Joshua and Temperance Marsh, Born Oct. 12, 1790; Died Apr. 11, 1857.

In Memory of Joshua, son of Joshua and Temperance Marsh, Born July 8, 1801; Died Oct. 11, 1875.

Beale Marsh, son of Joshua and Temperance, Born Aug. 13, 1803; Died May 25, 1880.

Amos Matthews, son of Mordecai, Born Apr. 17, 1800; Died June 26, 1874.

Ellen Matthews, relict of Amos Matthews, and daughter of Joshua and Temperance Marsh, Born Aug. 17, 1799; Died Jan. 13, 1883.

Blessed are the dead who die in the Lord.

Joshua Marsh was captain of the militia during the Revolutionary war.

Royston inscriptions, found in the Wesley Royston burying ground, on land owned by the Royston family for many years, on the road running east from Phœnix factory to the York turnpike, near the fourteenth milestone are:

In Memory of John Royston, aged 59, Died Sep. 11, 1822.

In Memory of Ruth, wife of John Royston, . . . 78 . . . Died Feb. 10, 1839.

In Memory of Thomas Royston, 36 years, 5, 11 days, Died Oct. 6. 1823.

In Memory of William Royston, 56 years, Died Aug. 26, 1827.

In Memory of Elizabeth, wife of Wm. Royston, . . . 69, . . . Died Feb. 26, 1870.

In Memory of Georgie B., daughter of Wm. and E. Royston, Died Aug. 4, 1842.

In Memory of John Royston, son of Wm. and E. Royston, . . . M. L. R. . . . S. G. 1834.

In Memory of our father, Wesley Royston, Born Jan. 15, 1804; Died Dec. 17, 1892.

Precious in the sight of the Lord is the death of his saints.

In Memory of Mary A., wife of Wesley Royston, . . . 64 . . . Died Jan. 5, 1873.

And I heard a voice from Heaven saying unto me: "Write, Blessed are the dead which die in the Lord from henceforth; yea, saith the spirit, that they may rest from their labours and their works do follow them."

In Memory of Emma, dau. of Wesley and Mary Royston, 4 years, Died May 24th 1849.

In Memory of Clara W., wife of Eli. Matthews, and dau. of Wesley and Mary A. Royston, aged 30; Died Aug. 6, 1865.

> We have laid her in the silent grave
> Beside her children dear to rest.
> We know her happy spirit, now,
> Is numbered with the blest.

In mem. of Caleb Royston, aged 62 years, Died June 24, 1860.

In Mem. of Mary, wife of Caleb Royston, . . . 38 . . . Died June 5, 1845.

In Memory of Ariel Royston, Aged 24, Died June 5, 1824.

In Mem. of Edmund S. Royston, 24 years, Died Oct. 7, 1859.

> Dear wife, weep not for me;
> For all your tears are vain.
> Prepare to meet your God
> That we may meet again.

In Memory of Sarah A., wife of Wm. T. Royston, 76 years, Died Aug. 2, 1894.

In Mem. of Mary Ellen, dau of Wm. T. and S. Royston, Died Aug 21, 1853.

In Mem. of Mary E. Royston, 27 years, Died Feb. 17, 1871.
The Lord is my light and my salvation, whom shall I fear?

Margaret E., Beloved wife of Geo. R. Royston, Born Oct. 16, 1834; Died July 16, 1879.

One stone is marked "S. R." and here are seven graves, unmarked.

The Peerce family burying ground in the eleventh district is on land which has been in the possession of the family for probably a century, lying on the east side of Dulaney's valley pike, near the head of the valley.

It is said that the farm came into the possession of the family in the following way: Mr. Peerce owned a farm where Washington city now stands, and Mr. Hanson, husband of the widow Addison, née Dulany, owned that in Dulany's valley. Mr. Peerce had seen the latter farm and had tried to make an exchange, but unsuccessfully. At last Mr. Hanson heard that the location for the future city had been decided upon and he immediately went to Mr. Peerce and offered to make the exchange. As the property in Dulaney's valley was worth twice as much for farming purposes, Mr. Peerce, in his ignorance of the state of affairs then existing, closed at once with the offer and soon found that he had been " sold."

To show that Mr. Hanson was not without generosity, he deeded some choice lots back to Mr. Peerce.

The inscriptions found in this burying ground are:

Sacred to the Memory of Edward Peerce, who departed this life Apr. 27, 1823; aged 68 years.

In Memory of Anna, Consort of Edward Peerce, born Nov. 17, 1771, and departed this life Jan. 1, 1831. Aged 59 years and 46 days.

Sacred to the Memory of James Peerce, who departed this life in Aug. 1797, Aged 2 years and 6 months.

Our Father William F. Peerce, born Sep. 4, 1790; Died Jan. 1, 1878.

Our Mother Louisa, Wife of William F. Peerce, born Apr. 13, 1800; died Nov. 4, 1865.

Blessed are the pure in heart for they shall see God.

Our Brother, Henry Peerce, born Sep. 10, 1838; died Aug. 5, 1840.

Suffer little children to come unto me and forbid them not for such is the Kingdom of Heaven.

Our Aunt, Susan Smith, born June 16, 1789; died Aug. 4, 1868.
Blessed are the dead who die in the Lord.

In Memory of Elizabeth, Consort of William Ferguson Sr., who departed this life in Sept 1830. Aged 84 years.

In Memory of Mary, Consort of David B. Ferguson, who was born on July 25, 1785, and departed this life Aug. 10, 1835.

In Memory of David B. Ferguson, born Jan. 1, 1784, and died Dec. 29, 1863.

Blessed are the dead which die in the Lord from henceforth, Yea saith the spirit, that they may rest from their labours and their works do follow them.

In Memory of Levi Ferguson Sr., born Mar. 4, 1777; died 1843, Aged 66 years and 11 months.

In Memory of Elizabeth Ferguson, Consort of Rev. Levi Ferguson, born July 15, 1788; died Sept. 27, 1870.
Blessed are they that Die in the Lord.

There are two graves marked with dark sandstone, and the graves of one adult and two children, recently buried.

Mrs. Wm. F. Peerce was a Smith, a sister of Larkin Smith.

The original burying ground of the Cockey family is located on land owned in 1728 by John Cockey, son of William, the immigrant, and now belonging to the Browns of Brooklynwood. It is in the third district, lying and bounding on the road running up the north side of Green Spring valley, from the Falls road at Cockey's old tavern. The cemetery is on the top of a slight hill in a meadow-like field about three hundred yards from the Falls road and about the same distance from the farm buildings of George Brown.

John Cockey, one of the Justices of Baltimore county, and also one of the Commissioners appointed in 1732, to lay off ten acres east of the falls as an addition to Baltimore city, is buried here. His tomb is inscribed:

In Memory of John Cockey, son of William the immigrant, aged 66 years, Died Aug. 15th 1746.

Other inscriptions are:

Elizabeth Baker, wife of Rev. Charles Baker, and formerly wife of John Cockey, aged 95, died Aug. 5th, 1780.

W. Cockey, son of John and Elizabeth, born 1718, died —— 1756.

Wm. Cockey, aged 9 years, 1782.

Richard Owens aged 17 months and 20 days, Oct. 12, 1787.

Elizabeth Baker's maiden name was Slade. W. Cockey married Constant Ashman.

In writing of this old burial ground in 1855, Dr. John Paul Cockey states, among other things, that the brick wall which his grandfather, Capt. John Cockey, placed around it has been almost entirely removed by repeated robbery of its materials, notwithstanding the reservation of the burial ground, with its privileges, when Capt. John Cockey sold the adjacent lands. The robbery has been continued until there is no trace that there ever was a brick in the vicinity, and some of the stone foundation has also been taken away. The gravestones, too, have been taken up and thrown under an ash tree growing upon the lot and some of them are broken; two only remained standing in 1898. It is not probable that the number of graves here was ever large.

There is another old graveyard in this vicinity, in the eighth district, on land formerly owned by Caleb Cockey, now by Mr. Edward T. Hamilton. Here the stones have been buried, it is said, sufficiently deep not to be disturbed by the plow, and the land is worked over like other portions of the field. So far there has been no way or ascertaining the number of persons buried there or their names.

The family burying ground of John Cockey, Jr., is situated on the old tavern property of Stephen Cockey, on the east side of the Falls road where it crosses Green Spring valley, to the right of the field road beyond the orchard. Inscriptions found here are:

In Memory of John Cockey, son of Thomas and Prudence Cockey, was born December 20th 1758, departed this life October 22d 1824, Aged 65 years 10 months and 2 days.

In Memory of Thomas Cockey, Son of John and Mary Cockey, was born February 5th 1787, departed this life December 30th 1816, aged 29 years 10 months and 25 days.

John Cockey Born Nov. 5, 1788, Died May 4, 1873.

Mary Beloved wife of John Cockey, Born Aug 13, 1792, Died Oct. 13, 1846.

John Cockey Born Oct 3d, 1827, Died Dec 19, 1877, Aged 51 years.

Thomas Cockey married Prudence Gill; his son, John, married Mary Coale. John, the son of John and Mary (Coale), married Mary Fishpaw, and their son, the fourth John, first married Harriet Parks, and secondly Emma Hall.

Charles O. Cockey, son of John and Mary Cockey, Born April 6, 1830, Died Nov. 24, 1896.

Nimrod Skipper, son of John and Sarah Skipper, born 2d Jan. 1819, died 6 March 1852.

Elizabeth, widow of Nimrod Skipper and wife of John H. and daughter of John and Mary Cockey, born June 27, 1820, died Dec. 30, 1887.

In Memory of Mary Ann, Consort of Henry C. Collings and daughter of Nimrod and Elizabeth Skipper, Born Dec. 2, 1842, Died June 2, 1866.

In Memory of Harriet, wife of John Cockey Jr., Born Sept 3d, 1832, Died Oct. 25th, 1861, Aged 29 years 1 month and 22 days.

In Memory of Harah May, son of John and Harriet Cockey, Born May 2d, 1860, Died 6, 1861.

Stones are found to the following children of John and Emma Cockey: Powell, aged 18 years, died June 28, 1885; Clarence Hael, aged 11 years, died October 9, 1876; "Our little Hattie," aged 5 years and 8 months, died 1876.

"Our little Sallie," daughter of Samuel B. and Laura Cockey, born November 12, 1876, and died November 7, 1878.

John F. Cockey, born July 6, 1851, died Feb. 21, 1878.

In memory of George Joice Sr., who died 2, Jan 1856, Aged 65 years.

John Edmund, son of S. J and Mary Read, born July 23, 1855, Died Aug 19, 1856.

To the left of the field road beyond the orchard we find:

Fell asleep in Jesus October 4th, 1864 Julia Ann Beloved wife of Thomas Armacost, In the 57th year of her age.

None know her but to love her
None named her but to praise.
Farewell Mother, we thy loss deplore
The time was short the pain was great thou bore
But Jesus sent his Angels from the skies
And bore thy spirit up where pleasure never dies.

To our Mother Susan, wife of Michael G. Elsroad of Balto. co., Born June 19, 1805, Died May 9th, 1861.

She has gone Wife and Mother at once.

In Memory of Henry Smith, who departed this Life 7th Feb. 1862, in the 77th year of his age.

Rest dear Husband, rest in peace,
The mortal pang is past.
Jesus has come and borne thee home
Beyond the stormy blast.

In memory of Robt. W. Smith of Co. B. 1st Md. V. I., son of Henry and Teresa Smith, who departed this Life 1st Feb. 1864, Aged 22 years.

Rest Soldier, rest, thy warefare o'er,
The battle roll thou'llt hear no more.
The duty bravely, nobly done
The conflict past, the victory won.

The following inscriptions, found in St. John's churchyard, in Western Run parish, are contributed by Mrs. Monte Griffith. St. John's church, Worthington valley, is one of the offshoots of St. Thomas' parish. In the churchyard are numerous graves, the occupants of some of which have been brought here from private burying grounds. Among the latter are Samuel Worthington, his two wives and a son. They were removed from the burial lot of Samuel Worthington, which was located upon "Bloomfield," his home place. It contained an acre of ground inclosed with a stone wall, and was entailed by him for all time, for such of his descendants as might wish to be buried there. Some years after the bodies had been removed the place was sold, and the present owner at his own risk has destroyed all trace of the graveyard.

Here lies the body of Samuel Worthington, who departed this life 9th day of April 1815, Aged 81 years.

"He is not dead but sleepeth in Christ."

He was the grandson of Capt. John Worthington, who lies buried, on what was his home place, opposite Annapolis. From his father, John Worthington, the eldest son of Captain John, Samuel Worthington inherited 1,000 acres, part of a tract of land called "Welches Cradle." He added largely to his possessions and was a pioneer in the valley which now bears his name. On the stone of Mrs. Worthington appears:

In honor of Mrs Mary Worthington, wife of Samuel Worthington, who was born 21st day of March 1744, and departed this life the first day of October 1777, Aged 37 years and 6 months, leaving a disconsolate husband and 11 weeping children to lament their irreparable loss.

This Amiable woman lived beloved and died lamented by both rich and poor.

>And her soul is gone to heaven above
>enjoying her dear redeemers love;
>While time shall roll and never end
>A blest eternity to spend.

Mrs. Worthington's maiden name was Mary Tolly. I was present when her remains were disinterred for removal to St. Johns. She had been buried ninety-two years, but every one of her fine teeth had remained intact, although some of them fell out when the skull was moved.

Another inscription reads:

Martha Garretson, Second wife of Samuel Worthington, born August 13th 1753; died Dec. 31st 1831. Mother of 11 children 10 of whom survived her.

When the remains of this lady were removed her long gray hair was still wound about her head, and held in place by a comb which was intact.

Here lies the body of Samuel Worthington Jr., who departed this life The 7th day of Dec. 1811, Aged 36 years.

>Remember me as you pass by
>As you are now so once was I
>As I am now so must you be
>prepare for death and follow me
>Not lost, blest hope, but gone before
>to joy and peace forever more.

The names of the brothers, sons and grandsons of Samuel Worthington appear in the parish registers and vestry proceedings of St. Thomas' and St. John's, down to the present time. He was a member of the Committee of Safety during the Revolution, but in spite of this undoubted fact, I have heard him accounted a "tory." His eldest son, John Tolly Worthington, familiarly known as "The Old Squire," lies buried on the lawn of "Montmorenci," where he lived and died, and which place adjoins that of his father, "Bloomfield."

His monument is a shaft and on the four sides appear the following:

Sacred To the memory of John Tolly Worthington, Born Sept 29th A. D. 1760; Died Sept 8th A. D. 1834, Ætatis 74. This Monument has been erected as a tribute of respect to the memory of a beloved Grandfather.
Sweet is the memory of the just
While he sleepeth in the dust.

Polly Worthington was the wife of John Tolly Worthington, and daughter of Brice Thomas Beale Worthington of Annapolis, being a cousin of her husband. Her epitaph is:

Polly Worthington Born August 19th 1768; Died Feb 9th 1839, Aged 70 years.

Other Worthington stones are:

Sacred To the memory of Mary Tolly Worthington, daughter of John T. and Polly Worthington and wife of John T. H. Worthington, Born March 25th A. D. 1770; Died Dec 1st A. D. 1840. Also John T. H. Worthington, Born Nov 1st A. D. 1788; Died April 27th A. D. 1849.

In Memory of Charles Worthington, Born September 22nd 1770; Died July 15th 1847.

Charles Worthington was the son of Samuel Worthington, and lived and died at "Belmont," a place adjoining his father's. He married Susan Johns, daughter of Col. Richard Johns.

In Memory of Susan Worthington, Consort of Charles Worthington, Born January 11th 1781; Died March 10th 1843.

Kensey J., son of Charles and Susan Worthington, Born April 16th 1814; Died January 4th 1863.

Richard J. Worthington Born Sept 7th 1807; Died March 13th, 1870.

Rosetta W. Worthington, Daughter of Charles and Susan Worthington, Born October 29th 1818; Died March 1st 1840.

Mary Johns Tolly Semmes, Relict of Robert Semmes and daughter of Charles and Susan Worthington, Born Jan. 8th 1804; Died Oct. 19th 1885.

Edward Worthington, son of Charles and Susan Worthington, lies buried here, but as yet no stone marks his grave. Mrs. Sarah Weems Carter is also buried here, but no stone marks the spot. She was a daughter of Charles and Susan Worthington. Buried October 31, 1880.

Other inscriptions may be found as follows:

Sacred To the memory of Samuel Worthington of John, Born Dec. 4th A. D. 1825; Died May 31st A. D. 1860.

Sacred To the memory of Kinsey Johns, son of Richard and Ann R. Johns, born Jan 6th 1825; died August 5th 1827.

John Johns, Born March 24th 1779; Died December 31st 1857.

A generous benefactor of this Parish and of various public institutions.

In memory of Kensey Johns, Departed this life on the 4th of April 1846, In the 70th year of his age.

Sacred to the memory of Richard Johns, Born Dec. 12th 1790; Died Feb. 2nd 1887.

In Memory of Hickman Johnson, Born Feb. 22nd 1771; Died Oct. 16th 1825.

> I know that my Redeemer liveth.
> The just shall live forevermore.

In Memory of Heith H. Johnson, Born May 7th 1803; Died Feby 24th 1831.

Elisha S. Johnson, Born Feb. 10th 1791; Died Dec. 9th 1866.

Into thy hands I commend my spirit for thou hast redeemed me. O Lord thou God of hosts. Psalm XXXI ch 5 v. 1.

In Memory of Eleanor Caroline Johnson, Consort of Edward Gill, who died March 31st 1835, Aged 37 years, 1 month and 23 days.

> Death snatched away the parent bird
> When the little ones most needed her care.

In Memory of Edward Gill Sr., who departed this life Oct 7th 1818, Aged 71 years, 3 months and 5 days.

> A man sedate of sober mind
> to wife and children ever kind;
> But this great merit many have.
> Death snatches all men to the grave.

Also Mary his wife, Born June 22nd 1762; Died Dec. 16th 1839.
Blessed are the dead who die in the Lord.

Sacred To the Memory of William C. Hood, Born March 20th A. D. 1811; died July 31st A. D. 1852.

Sacred To The Memory of Richard Johns, who departed this life on the 6th day of January 1806, Aged 62 years 4 months and 23 days.

Sacred To The Memory of Sarah Johns, who departed this life on the 21st of January 1795.

Sarah Johns was the daughter of Col. John A. Weems of Anne Arundel county.

Sacred to the memory of Ann Ridgely Johns, Consort of Richard Johns, Born Dec. 7, 1794; Died May 17 1825.

Sacred To the memory of James Hood, Born 19th Feb'y 1775; Died 25th April 1838.

Sacred To the Memory of Sarah S. Hood, Born 20th Oct. 1780; Died 20th Nov. 1849.

In Memory of Ann Johnson, Born 1758; Died July 23rd 1821.

Kezia Murray, Born Nov. 24th 1771; Died Feb. 19th 1847.

Eleanor C. Orrick, Born July 12th 1827, Departed this life . . . 30th 1848.

Among the well-known names of a later generation are those of Semmes, Morehead, Griffith, Rogers, Orrick, Gill and Johnson.

In the family vault at "Hampton," built of marble and brick, repose six and possibly seven generations of Ridgelys. Capt. Charles Ridgely, born in 1733; died June 28, 1790, made provisions in his will for the building of this vault. Tradition says that his remains, with those of his father, Col. Charles Ridgely, and other members of his family, were placed here when the city of Baltimore ran its streets through the Spring Garden property, owned by the Ridgelys, and obliterated all traces of an earlier burying ground. A complete record of those buried at Hampton begins, however, with the succeeding generation, and as one looks through the iron grating of the doorway, one sees a wall of marble slabs duly inscribed with the names of the dead. This final touch, by which a charnel house was transformed into a worthy monument to her race, was given by the late Mrs. Charles Ridgely, a granddaughter of Governor Charles Ridgely with whom the record begins. The inscriptions are:

Governor Charles Ridgely, born Dec. 6, 1760; died July 17, 1829.

Priscilla, wife of Gov. Ridgely, died April 30th, 1814.

Charles Ridgely Jr., eldest son of Gov. Ridgely & Priscilla his wife, born August 26, 1783; died July 19, 1819.

Rebecca D. Hanson, wife of Charles W. Hanson and daughter of Governor Ridgely, born March 5, 1786; died Sept. 1837.

Chas. W. Hanson, died Dec. 8th, 1853, in the 70th year of his age.

Sophia Gough Howard, wife of James Howard & daughter of Governor Ridgely, b. July 3, 1800; d. April 18, 1828.

Priscilla Hill White, wife of Stevenson White & daughter of Governor Ridgely, born March 17, 1796, died April 10, 1820.

David Latimer Ridgely, 3rd son of Gov. Ridgely, b. Nov. 19th 1798; died 1846.

Mary Louisa, widow of David L. Ridgely, born July 4th, 1808; d. Nov. 8, 1863.

Eight children of D. L. & M. L. Ridgely.

John Ridgely of H., son of Gov. Ridgely, b. at Hampton Jan 9th, 1790; died at H. July 17, 1867.

Eliza E., wife of John Ridgely of H., b. Feb. 10, 1803; d. Dec. 20, 1867. 3 infant children of John & Eliza E. Ridgely.

Mr. & Mrs. Nicholas G. Ridgely, the parents of Mrs John Ridgely, and John Clemm, son of Daniel & Johanna Ridgely, a young cousin who died Sept. 26, 1839.

Charles Ridgely of H., son of John & Eliza E. Ridgely, born March 22, 1838, died at Rome, Italy, on Good Friday, March 29, 1872.

Margaretta S. Ridgely, widow of Charles Ridgely of H., b. Sept. 24, 1824, died March 31st. 1904.

Rev. Charles Ridgely Howard and John Eager Howard, brothers of Mrs. Margaretta Ridgely, her son Charles and her grandsons John Stewart and Charles, complete the number.

The vault yard, inclosed by a high brick wall and entered through an iron gateway, also shelters the dead. Here in one corner is the tomb of Julianna Howard, a sister of the late

The Vault Yard at "Hampton," Baltimore County

Mrs. Ridgely and a granddaughter of Governor Ridgely. She was born August 25, 1821; died May 22, 1853.

A Celtic cross marks the grave of Eliza Buckler, daughter of John and Eliza Ridgely, and the body of her first husband, John Campbell White, reposes beside her. She was born October 28, 1828; died March 3, 1894.

John Campbell White, departed this life February 6, 1853, in the 28th year of his age. Near him is the grave of an infant son. An antique altar tomb is inscribed:

> To the Memory of Eliza Ridgely, wife of N. G. Ridgely and daughter of M. and E. Eichelberger, Departed this life the 10th of February, 1803, A few hours after the birth of an only Daughter, aged 19 years and 2 months.

On the opposite side of the inclosure is a modern marble cross to the memory of Howard Ridgely, the third son of Charles and Margaretta S. Ridgely, born January 7, 1855; died September 28, 1900.

There are also several unmarked graves level with the ground. Periwinkle overruns the whole inclosure and, with the ancient ivy on the walls, enables the spot to retain its beauty throughout the changing seasons of the year.

At Taylor's Meetinghouse, on the Hillen road, in the ninth district, are the graves of its founders, Joseph and Sarah Taylor, inscribed as follows:

> Sacred to the memory of Sarah, Consort of Joseph Taylor, who departed this life September 23rd 1843, In the 84 year of her age.
> For we must all appear before the judgment seat of Christ. 2nd Cor. 5 Chap. 10 verse.
>
> Sacred to the memory of Joseph Taylor, who departed this life the 21st of March 1850, In the 66th year of his age.
> Blessed are the dead which die in the Lord. Rev. 14 Chap 13 v.
>
> In memory of Hannah, wife of William Scharf, who departed this life August 7th 1829, In the 50th year of her age.
>
> In memory of William Scharf, who departed this life May 5th 1840, In the 71st year of his age.
>
> Sacred to the memory of Capt. George Pollard, who departed this life December 10th 1834, In the 66 year of his age.

Sacred to the memory of Hannah Dodd, who departed this Life May the 1st A. D. 1836, Aged 45 years and 5 months.

She was a kind and affectionate wife, a tender and indulgent mother. She lived and died a humble Christian.

Sacred to the memory of Hannah Welch, Daughter of Luke & Catherine Stansbury, who departed this life November 11th 1821, In the 44th year of her age.

She was an affectionate Mother, a sincere friend and beloved by all who knew her. May her soul rest in peace.

William Dorsey, Son of Isaac and Elizabeth Anderson, who departed this life September 27th 1847, In the 20th year of his age.

> Weep not for me oh parents dear
> But to thy Saviour look
> 'Twas he who led my spirit here
> My name is in his book.

Other names represented, of a later date, are: Holloway, Wild, Anderson, Hiss, Woodward and Purviance.

About two miles from Towson, between the Joppa and Hillen roads, is "Union Hall," one of the old Stansbury places, where are found the following inscriptions:

In memory of William Stansbury, who was born Janry 20th 1716 and departed this life Nov. 3rd 1788, In the 73rd year of his age.

An honest man the noblest work of GOD.

In memory of Elizabeth Stansbury, wife of William Stansbury, who was born July 12th 1721 and departed this life Sept 10th 1799, in the 79th year of her age.

Her life a pattern to . . .

The rest of the inscription is hidden by the earth. This stone is very gritty and hard to decipher.

Dedicated to the memory of Jacob Stansbury, who was born on the 14th March 1755. And died on the 22d of February 1812, Universally respected.

In Memory of William Stansbury, who was born April 4th 1746, and departd this life in the 80th year of his Age.

An honest man the noblest work of GOD.

In Memory of Belenda Stansbury, wife of Wm. Stansbury, who departed this life April 7th 1830, upward of 80 years old.

A dutiful wife and an affectionate mother.

In Memory of Mary Stansbury, wife of John E. Stansbury, who departed this life 5th Dec. 1800, In the 23rd year of her age.

In memory of Ann Stansbury, wife of Jn E. Stansbury, who departed this life the 1st of April 1815. In the 32nd year of her age.

Sacred To the memory of our dear father John E. Stansbury, who departed this life April 30th 1841, Aged 81 years and 11 months.
He lived beloved and died regretted. May our end be like his peace.
> O what are all my sufferings here
> If Lord thou count me meet
> With that enraptured host to appear
> And worship at thy feet.

Isaac Stansbury, who was born July 2nd 1752, and departed this life October 1792, in the 41st year of his age. A man of Sympathy.

Mary E. Stansbury, Dec. 21st 1846; June 13th 1887.

William E. Stansbury, Son of John E. Stansbury, April 14th 1811; March 27th 1878.

Sarah A. Stansbury, Jan 15th 1850, Aged 4 years and 11 months.

In Memory of Sarah Brown, Consort of Josiah Brown and daughter of William Stansbury, who departed this life August 7th 1834, aged 51 years and 6 months.

Sacred to the memory of Solomon C. Wallace, who departed this life May the 7th 1840, in the 52nd year of his age.

Sacred to the memory of Mary E. Wallace, born August 9th 1824, and died December 16th 1829.
She was her parents only joy. They had but one darling child.

John Wallace, 1832, aged six months, an Infant Martha.

In memory of Benjamin Brady, who was born Nov 29th 1760, and departed this life Dec. 18 1839.
He was for 50 years a pious member of the Methodist Church.
> Happy soul thy days are ended
> All thy mourning days below
> Go by angel guards attended
> To the sight of Jesus go.

Samuel Beady, Born Oct. 5 1801; Died Dec. 28 1871.
> Rest loved one in blissful sleeping
> Angels guard thy dreamless rest
> God holds thee in sacred keeping
> 'Mid his chosen ones, the blest.

The old burial ground of the Hillen family, situated on the Hillen road, about two and one-half miles southeast of Towson, has been obliterated and the stones from the graves removed to Prospect Hill cemetery. The following is a synopsis of the inscriptions:

Solomon Hillen, born October 22d, 1737; died March 27th, 1801.
Martha Hillen, relict of Solomon Hillen, died January 10th, 1769.
Martha Hillen, second relict of Solomon Hillen, died October 3d, 1777.
Thomas Hillen, died December 31st, 1847, aged 88 years.
John Hillen, born October 6th, 1761; died August 12th, 1840.
Solomon Hillen, born April 1st, 1770; died July 29th, 1811.
Catharine Hillen, relict of John Hillen, died August 13th, 1820.
Elizabeth Hillen, born March 1st, 1764; died March 27th, 1784.
Thomas J. Hillen, born July 6th, 1798; died January 22d, 1847.
John Francis Hillen, born July 8th, 1801; died February 15th, 1834.
John Hunter, died November 15th, 1834.
Martha Hunter, relict of John Hunter, died October 3d, 1825, in her 54th year.
Henry Hunter, died August 12th, 1837, in his 23d year.
Edmund Hunter, born October 22d, 1828; died January, 1829, aged 3 months.
Robina Ann Hunter, born July 28th 1826; died January 27th, 1840, aged 14 years and 6 months.
Elizabeth Rusk, died July 8th, 1814, and John Hillen, Jr., died at New Orleans, August.30th, 1811, aged 16 years, 6 months and 11 days.
Janet Wells, died March 4th, 1825, aged 82 years.
Lydia Wilson, died March 4th, 1846, aged 68 years.
Mary Armour, relict of David Armour, born February 24th, 1722; died August 10th, 1802.
Mary Rutter, died April 23d, 1820.

The first interment was that of Solomon Hillen's wife, which occurred in January, 1769, and the last was that of Thomas Hillen, January, 1848.

William Buchanan, son of George and father of James M. and Charles Buchanan; also stepfather of David Perine, died in 1828 and is buried at Homeland on Charles Street Avenue, now owned by the Perines.

On a section of the old Drumquhasel tract, known as "Aneslie," and owned by the late F. H. McE. Birckhead, is a burial lot containing thirteen graves. Among them is that of James Govane, after whom Govanstown was named, who died in 1783; also James Govane Howard, born in 1777 and died November 19, 1819.

At "Cowpens," a Howard estate, whose present owner is Frederick von Kapff, there is but one stone preserved:

David Amos, Son of James and Catherine Amos, Born September 28th 1779; Died September 22, 1799.

In the burying ground on the Jenifer place are the following inscriptions:

Wm. M. Risteau, Born Feb. 18, 1791; Died June 21, 1853, In his 63d year.

Susan Risteau, wife of Wm. M. Risteau, Born April 7, 1791; Died Nov 2, 1850, In her 60th year.

Dr. Thos. C. Risteau, Departed this life Feb. 3d 1865, in his 71st year.

Ann Boyd, wife of Dr. Thos. C. Risteau, Born Feb. 17, 1792; Died June 5, 1878.

A Rest with God, a life that cannot die.

Daniel Jenifer, Born Sept 27, 1815; Died Aug 5, 1890.
Blessed are the pure in heart, for they shall see God.

Near the old Friends' Meetinghouse on an elevation above Ellicott City in Howard county is the Ellicott family burying ground. It is well kept, has a stone wall around it and the graves are so arranged that members of the different branches of the family lie together. A walk through the middle leads to the monuments of Andrew and John Ellicott, which give an epitome of the family history. The inscriptions are:

Andrew Ellicott was born in Buck's Co., Pennsylvania, 1st. month 22d., 1733, To which place his grandfather emigrated from Falmouth, England, about the year 1700, Soon after his marriage to Mary Fox. Andrew removed from his mills in Buck's Co., 5th month, 16th, 1771, and became interested with his Brother John In the settlement and improvement of this place. He died 6th month, 20th 1809, Aged 76 years.

Esther Ellicott, 1827, wife of Andrew Ellicott.

John Ellicott, 3rd. brother of Andrew, born in Buck's Co., Pennsylvania, 12th month 28th, 1739, And removed with his brother Andrew from their mills in Buck's Co. 5th month, 16th 1771. He died 12th 28th, 1794, Aged 55 years.

Andrew Ellicott's first wife Elizabeth Brown was a first cousin of his second. She is also buried in this graveyard.

In the Cook graveyard, on the farm of Mr. John Owings, are stones with the following inscriptions:

Elizabeth Powell died on the 6th of April, 1845, aged 25.

Mary C. Cook, died 1848, aged 16 years.

Eleanor A. Cook, born Nov. 5th, 1795; died February 22nd, 1853, aged 57 years.

George Cook died on the 7th October, 1849, aged 57.

Margaret Mace, died December 19th, 1842-7.

W. H. Worthington, died 18th June, 1849, aged 7 months.

On the farm of the late Reuben Johnson and inclosed with a substantial stone wall, is a Dorsey graveyard in good condition, where the following stones are found:

Sacred to the memory of Caleb Dorsey of Thomas, who was born 1749, and died 14th April, 1837.

Sacred to the memory Elizabeth, wife of the opposite Caleb Dorsey of Thos., who was born April 22nd, 1758, and died May 9th, 1840, aged 82 years.

Caleb Dorsey of Thos. was the great grandson of Col. John Dorsey.

Sacred to the memory of Thomas Beale Dorsey of Thomas, who departed this life 6th, Sept 1828, in the 60th year of his age.

Sacred to the memory of Achsah, wife of Thomas Beale Dorsey, who departed this life Sept 31st, 1837 aged 51 yrs. 2 months and 9 days.

Sacred to the memory of John W. Dorsey who departed this life in the 50th year of his age.

Sacred to the memory of Ann W. Dorsey eldest child of Caleb & Elizabeth Dorsey born March 28, 1773; died Nov, 6th, 1836.

The Christians tomb: Here sleepeth in sure and certain hope of the resurrection of eternal life. Susannah Brookes, second daughter of Caleb Dorsey of Thos. & Elizabeth, who was born the 6th day of Feb, 1774, and departed this life 1848.

Sacred to the memory of Thomas Beale Dorsey, eldest son of Caleb Dorsey of Thos. born 16 Dec, 1776; died 10 Feb, 1809.

Sacred to the memory of Margaret R. Howard, niece of Caleb and Ann H. Dorsey born Oct 13th, 1836; died Feb 19th, 1855.

On the Thomas M. Johnson farm, once the home of John Worthington Dorsey, are found the following:

John Worthington Dorsey, who was born on the 8th of October, 1750, and died on the 13th of May, 1823, in the 73rd. year of his age, Respected and esteemed by all who knew him.

Here Lie the remains of Comfort Dorsey, Widow of John W. Dorsey, who departed this life on the 23rd day of July, 1837, in the 78th year of her age.

At losing such a mother, children well might grieve.

Milcah Goodwin Dorsey died Sept. 25, 1850, In the 68th year of her age.

Priscilla R. Dorsey, daughter of Chals. W. & Mary P. Dorsey, Born Jan'y 7, 1829, Died March 12th, 1847, Aged 18 years.

Rebecca Goodwin, a member of the Society of Friends & oldest daughter of Wm. and Milcah Goodwin of Baltimore, who died April 8th, 1846, aged 72 years.

Full of Faith, Hope and Charity her days were spent in devotion to God, & debts of benevolence to her fellow mortals.

Here rest the remains of Samuel Worthington Dorsey, Born on the 25th of Nov, 1782, and deceased on the 22nd. October 1808.

A noble spirit hath departed hence.

In memory of My Mother Mary Campbell, wife of John T. B. Dorsey, Died Feb'y 16, 1852, Aged 32 years.

Elizabeth Rebecca Dorsey, daughter of Judge Thos. B. & Milcah Dorsey, who died Sept. 7th, 1845, in the 23rd year of her age.

> All is not here of our beloved and blessed;
> Leave ye the sleeper with her God to rest.

Charles S. W. Dorsey, Attorney at law and youngest son of John W. & Comfort Dorsey, who died July 9th, 1845, in the 49th year of his age.

Sacred to the memory of Mary Tolly Dorsey, only daughter of John W. & Comfort Dorsey, Born on the 22nd. of Jan. 1790; she resigned her earthly spirit on the 5th of Jan'y 1793, aged 2 years 11 months and 14 days.

In memory of Samuel W. Dorsey, son of Edward and Martha Ridgely, died on the 15th day of April 1797, aged 10 months and 15 days.

> Here lies a widowed mother's darling son
> Whose life was ended ere his cares begun
> From Earthly pleasures he withdrew in haste
> To joy eternal 'round a throne of grace.

Sacred to the memory of Rebecca Comfort, wife of Allen Bowie Davis and eldest child of Thomas Beale and Milcah Dorsey. Born on the 16th of Feb. 1809, and died on the 8th of July 1836, in the 28th year of her age.

She departed this life in perfect resignation to the will of God and in the blessed hope of a glorious resurrection through the merits and death of the Saviour in whom she trusted.

May my latter end be like hers.

At "Belmont," another Dorsey homestead, there is also a graveyard. It contains fine old slabs of the tabular kind, but so overrun with honeysuckle and periwinkle that it has been found impossible to copy them. Here lie the remains of Caleb Dorsey, who in 1738 built "Belmont" as a home for his bride, Priscilla Hill. He was born July 18, 1710; died June 28, 1772. His widow died March 8, 1781, in the 63d year of her age. Beside them repose their descendants up to the fourth and fifth generation.

The historic church of Howard county is Christ Church, Queen Caroline parish. It was built in 1809, and the site on which it stands was given by Caleb Dorsey the elder, some years before the parish was organized, for a chapel of ease, with the understanding that the title of the two acres on which it stood should be confirmed to the vestrymen of a new parish, whenever it should be laid off. This bit of land, however, was a part of an estate entailed upon Caleb's son John, and his heirs. John released his right, and by a petition to the General Assembly, who granted it, the title was made good to the parish, Governor Ogle having put his signature to the Act.

On September 27, 1727, the freeholders of Queen Caroline parish, then a part of Anne Arundel county, met at the parish church and "made choice" of Henry Ridgely and John Howard as churchwardens; Thomas Wainright, John Dorsey son of Edward, John Hammond son of Charles, Orlando Griffith, Richard Davis and Robert Shipley as vestrymen. As most of these worthies were landowners in this section and consequently had their own private graveyards, we find no

CHRIST CHURCH, QUEEN CAROLINE PARISH, HOWARD COUNTY
Built in 1809 and still standing in 1908

memorials to them in the old churchyard. However, a few years ago, some tablets to them or their descendants were seen preserved in the gallery of the church.

There were two rectors of this parish who cannot be passed by without especial mention. The first, Rev. James Macgill, was appointed in 1730 as its first rector, an office he held for nearly fifty years, terminating with his death, December 26, 1779. The second, Rev. Thomas Claggett, a great-nephew of Caleb Dorsey the elder who gave the land for the church was consecrated in New York on September 17, 1792, as first Bishop of Maryland. The centennial celebration held at Christ church September 17, 1892, was partly in commemoration of this event and partly to celebrate the birth of the diocese of Maryland which dates from the same day.

The "managers" of the church when it was rebuilt in 1809, were Dr. R. G. Stockett, Dr. Lloyd T. Hammond, Samuel King and Samuel Brown. It is said that they contributed the services of their slaves, and a substantial brick edifice and one that has withstood the storms of nearly a century, was the result.

Governor Warfield, whose term expired in January, 1908, is from Howard county, though Warfield is a name well known in the annals of Anne Arundel and Baltimore counties also. Dr. Charles Warfield, who died in 1813, is buried at "Bushy Park," and Capt. Benjamin Warfield, who died in 1806, at "Cherry Grove," both in Howard county.

Carroll county furnishes but few mementos of the generations of the past. The manor house of Doughoregan was built about the year 1727, together with a private chapel in which the heirs of the Carroll family were buried for more than one hundred and fifty years. Though the bodies have been removed to the Bonny Brae cemetery, where the Catholics bury their dead, the tablets covering the walls remain, and here we have in perfection an example of the domiciliary chapels that served as centers of worship to the country around, in the early days when Catholics were not allowed to build churches.

Doughoregan Manor was one of the homes of Charles Carroll of Carrollton, who lived to be the last surviving "signer" of the Declaration of Independence. He was born in September, 1737—one authority giving the date as the ninth, another as the thirtieth—and died November 10, 1832, after a very remarkable and distinguished career. Maryland, proud of him as her son, chose him with unanimous accord as the one most worthy to be honored by a statue in the old Hall of Representatives at the Federal capital. His Carroll county home has probably furnished hospitality to more celebrities than any other mansion in Maryland, for it is also the home of his grandson, John Lee Carroll, who was Governor of the State in 1876.

In the Sykesville churchyard many of the members of the Warfield family are buried, though none of a very early date. The few inscriptions obtained from this spot are fragmentary in the extreme:

James Soper, died 1811.
Jesse Hollingsworth, died 1845.
George Frazer Warfield, died 1849.
Susannah Warfield, aged 93.
Rev. Dr. Piggot, aged 93; also members of the Hollingsworth family and possibly the Watkins.

CHAPTER VII

ALL SAINTS parish, with which so many of the historic names of Frederick county are identified, is older than the county itself. The metes and bounds of this parish were defined in 1742, whereas the county was not erected until 1748. The old parish church has long since disappeared, some of the bricks having been used in the construction of its successor, built on Court street about the year 1814. However, the churchyard remains. Since the civil war few interments have been made here, consequently ancient tombs predominate. They are fairly well preserved and among them are good examples of old blue stones, flat slabs on brick foundations and clear cut inscriptions in old English text. Perhaps the oldest is that of Sarah McPike, who died in 1784. Margaret, wife of Col. James Johnson, died in 1813; her daughter in 1797; Dr. Edward Eastburn in 1821; Margaret Howard in 1844 and Dr. Tyler in 1841. The latter built a beautiful house and lived where the Eichelberger homestead now stands.

The revolutionary hero, Gen. Roger Nelson, lies under a flat stone literally covered with the record of his military exploits and the names of the battles in which he fought. Dr. Philip Thomas died in 1815, and is recorded as a friend to the sick and one whose "humanity knew no distinction of rich and poor." The memorial to Elizabeth Shanks, who died in 1821, was erected by a friend. Among the names are many familiar to Marylanders, such as Dorsey, Johnson, Vernon, Hanson and Maulsby, while others are of local significance: Malambre, Bishop, Bradford and Pigman. From a member of the latter family came the property where the parsonage of the Reformed Church now stands, and Mark Bishop, who died in 1836, was a blacksmith whose smithy occupied the site now belonging to the Methodist Episcopal Church. There are many vaults, from some of which the dead have been removed to Mt. Olivet cemetery. Here again we find the names of Hanson and Johnson, besides those of Graham, McPherson and others. In one of these vaults, built entirely underground and with not enough elevation of the sod to show where it is, Thomas Johnson, the first governor of the State, is buried, with his family about him. The late Mrs. Ann Graham Ross, his great-great-granddaughter, had a pure white block of marble placed over the traditionary spot on July 4, 1894, members of the Society of the Daughters of the American Revolution taking part in the ceremonies, and the Rev. Osborne Ingle reading the service from the governor's own prayer book. The marble is inscribed as follows:

Thomas Johnson
Born November 4, 1732;
Died November 26, 1819;
First Governor of the
State of Maryland.
1777-1779.

The account of old All Saints churchyard would be incomplete without a few examples of the epitaphs. Over the grave of Sarah Neill, aged 18, we read:

Since beauty and useful acquirements could not ward off the early stroke, well may we conclude the flight of this virtuous soul for nobler purposes, than to be for years distracted on this fluctuating stage.

Of John Wolfender we are told:

He has gone to a better world.

Two infants of the name of Bradford are addressed:

Sleep soft, sweet babes; no dreams disturb your rest.

Frederick County 161

The following describes a manner of death unusual in the present day:

John Hanson Thomas gave his life for another; he contracted his death by constant attendance at the bedside of his father, who died six days before. He bore a conspicuous part in public affairs, carrying to the public service a vigorous mind, a steady, yet temperate zeal; industry guarded by prudence and great energy of character and conduct, supported by integrity and modesty, and softened by charity.

The Linganore cemetery at Unionville is kept in beautiful order by the corporation that has charge of it. Some of the oldest stones bear only the initials of the dead and the year, for instance: "B. W. 1793"; "Anddicas, 1791"; "B. D. B. 1810"; "A. D. N. H. 1797"; while one has only the date "1801," and another challenges the curious as "C. H. O. P. June 4, 1829."

Some of the inscriptions found here are:

Sacred to the Memory of Sarah, wife of Eli Dorsey, Died 1798, June.... 1797, nursed Bishop Asbury through a serious illness at her home. "Once lovely features of body and mind, but above all her triumphant death." ASBURY.

Erected in 1802 by the Trustees of Linganore Station.

In Memory of Elizabeth, Wife of John Ecker senior, who died the 8th of Sept. 1811, Aged 58 years and 2 months. Married 42 Years.

Sacred to the Memory of Matakiah Bowham, Departed this life September 15th 1811, In the 48th Year of his Age.

In Memory of John Warner, Who departed this life the 7th day of February 1825.

Sacred to the Memory of Peter Lugenbeel, Who departed this life March 8, 1832, Aged 29 yrs., 1 mo. and 24 days.

>Friendship love and youthful bloom
>And blossoms gathered for the tomb.

Also an infant daughter of the deceased, who died Feb 11th 1832.

In Memory of John L. Lindsay, Who departed this life May 1st 1840, Aged 1 year, 7 mo. and 20 days.

In Memory of Edward C., son of George W. and Barbara Dudderrar, Departed this life July 20th 1812, Aged 18 mo.

In Memory of Joseph Miller, who departed this life July the 17th, 1798, Aged 61 Year.

In Memory of Edward Lindsay, Twin Brother to Hamilton Lindsay, who Departed this life September 28 1837, Aged 3 years, 3 months and 4 days.

In Memory of Elizabeth Lookinbeal, Who Departed this life October 6th 1808, Aged 28 yrs., 10 mo. 14 d.

In the cemetery at "Pleasant Fields," the Gaither homestead, near Unionville, nineteenth district, are the following:

In Memory of Margaret Ann Gaither, Relict of William Gaither, who departed this life April 29 1844, Aged 47 yrs. 11 mo. and 7 days.

Departed this life March 11, 1849, William B., 4th son of William and Margaret A. Gaither, Aged 22 yrs. 11 mo. 3 days.

Sacred to the Memory of William Gaither, who departed this life January 1, 1834, After a few hours painfull illness.

>And has gone to a mansion of rest,
>From a region of sorrow and pain,
>To the glorious the home of the blest,
>Where none can suffer again.

Sacred to the Memory of Basil Norris. Departed this life Sept. 16 1822, Aged 26 yrs. and 26 days.

Until the year 1898, a simple headstone in Mt. Olivet cemetery, Frederick city, marked the spot where Francis Scott Key was buried, along side of his wife.

>Francis Scott Key
>Born Aug. 9, 1780
>Died Jany 11, 1843.
>
>Mary Tayloe Key
>Born May 26, 1784
>Died May 17, 1859.

At present his body reposes beneath a handsome memorial erected through the efforts of the Key Monument Association. In the family lot are buried his eldest son, Francis Scott Key, Jr., and his son-in-law, Simon Blunt.

A graveyard, until within recent years attached to the Novitiate at Frederick, was from 1763 to 1837 the churchyard of St. John's Roman Catholic church, and many distinguished members of that faith were buried there. A row of modern cottages now covers the spot, and the dead are scattered. Some we find in Mt. Olivet, but who can tell where they have laid McHugh Sweeney, who died September 21, 1794, "Whilst engaged in the service of his country against the Western Insurgents"; or who can say where Samuel Lilly lies? He died March 10, 1812, and was recorded as "Benefactor of this congregation."

Among the Jesuits who once lay in this obliterated home of the dead were many whose names and labors are still recalled with reverence and affection by surviving members of their flock.

In 1900, the grave of Roger Brooke Taney, once the principal object of interest in this graveyard, was removed with that of his mother to the Roman Catholic cemetery. The plain flat slab that marks the spot is inscribed as follows:

> Roger Brooke Taney
> Fifth Chief Justice of the Supreme Court
> of
> The United States of America
> Born in Calvert County Maryland,
> March 17th 1777;
> Died in the City of Washington,
> October 17th 1864.
>
> He was a profound and able lawyer;
> An upright and fearless judge,
> A pious and exemplary christian.
> At his own request
> He was buried in this secluded spot.
> Near the grave of his mother.
> "May he rest in peace."

The following is the inscription on his mother's tomb:

In memory of Mrs. Monica Taney, Who died in Frederick Town Novr. 29th, 1814, Aged 54 years.

Here, as is the case in most of the Catholic cemeteries, the I. H. S. appears above the inscription on each headstone, and the initials R. I. P. follow. Other inscriptions are:

In Memory of Ann, Wife of Thomas Young, who Departed this life April 24 in the year of our Lord 1812, Aged 30 years.

In Memory of Winnie Young, wife to Andrew Young, She Departed this life 30th day of May in the 32 year of age, 1786.

Sacred to the Memory of Capt. John Smith, Born Nov 9th 1754 Departed this life 26th Jan. 1805.

Sacred to the Memory of Charles Smith, Born May 1st 1788, and departed this life 16th Dec. 1809.

Here lies Catharine Smith, who died July 26th 1816, in the 24th year of her age. Amen.

Sacred to the Memory of Helena Fenwick, who died April the 26th 1817, in the 67th year of her Age.

Here lies the body of Leonard Jamison, who was born Oct. 13th 1762 and died in Va. Nov. 14th 1821.

Here lies the body of Richard Brooke, who died Mar. 8th 1815, in the 42nd year of his age. May he rest in peace.

Here lies the body of Leonard Smith, who Died March 25th, 1794, in the 60th year of his Age.

Here lies the body of Tresa Smith, who died July 3rd 1802, in the 32 year of her Age.

In Memory of Henry Jamison, who died Oct. 24th 1815, in the 72nd year.

In Memory of Mrs. Mary A. Brooke, who departed this life Dec. the 25th 1835, in the 44th year of her age. May she Rest in Peace.

In Memory of Thomas William Thompson Mason, who departed this life Oct. 11th 1822, Aged nine months, son of Thompson and Ann Mason, of Va.

In Memory of William Lee, Nat. 23rd June 1775, Obit. 8th July 1845. Req. in pace.

Francis Margetty, Born 1756, Died 1721.

Mary F. Margetty, Born 1773, Died 1847.

Emma Margetty, Born 1797, Died 1864.

In Memory of Andrew Young, who Departed this life Jan. 29th 1828, Aged 49 yrs. 7 mo. 23 days. Blessed are the dead who died in the Lord.

Roger Nelson, he was born 17th Feb. 1824, died 1832.

In the German Reformed cemetery, which lies west of the city of Frederick, the body of Whittier's heroine rests along side that of her husband. The lot is inclosed by a heavy iron railing, and the stones are inscribed:

Barbara Frietchie Died December 18th, 1862, Aged 96 years
John C. Frietchie Died Nov. 10th, 1849, Aged 69 years.

The most ancient and important tombs of the priests buried

in Mt. St. Mary's cemetery, on the hill back of the college, at Emmittsburg, are as follows:

Very Rev. J. McCloskey; J. McCaffrey; Henry S. McMurdie; John O'Brien; Thomas O'Neil, 1874; H. X. Xanpi, 1869; Leonard Oberinger, 1865; Thomas Augustine McCaffrey, 1853; Jos. Plessier, 1832; Jas. A. Lynch, 1828; Chas. Duhamel, beginning of the last century—a long epitaph nearly illegible.

Among the college students are: Tedro Morn, 1845, native of Buenos Ayres; J. B. Castilloes, 1849.

Other old tombstones are those of Edward Brawner, 1811, and Thomas Sim Lee Horsey, 1834.

Near the site of the old Elder homestead, at the Pleasant Valley Mission, is the family burying ground.

On a marble shaft erected about the year 1878, by Archbishop Elder to his ancestor, who moved hither from St. Mary's county in 1728, are the names of William, the said ancestor, and his two wives.

Wm. Elder Sr. born 1707, aged 68, died April 22, 1775.

Nearby was erected by Wm. Elder Sr. the first altar to the Living God in what is now Known as Mt. St. Mary's Emmittsburg and Mechanicstown Congregations, about the year 1745.

Ann Wheeler, first wife of Wm. Elder Sr. died August 11, 1739, aged 30 years.

Jacoba Clementina Elder, 2nd wife of Wm. Elder Sr. died Sept 12, 1807, aged 90 years.

In the cemetery are the graves of Sarah Elder, born 1760; died 1784. Elizabeth Mills, wife of Aloysius Elder, born May 9, 1767; died August 2, 1802. Aloysius Elder, 1827. Mary J. Elder, 1842; the last interment made in the old cemetery. Louis Colbert (colored), 1838, aged 104 years. His wife, 1831, aged about 60.

There is a stone, with letters nearly effaced, of an Elder who died August 22, 1786; a stone with W. A. H. 1784; one to Henry Livers, date illegible; and a large slab to Arnold Elder, born 1745, died 1812.

The oldest tombs at "Black Castle," Union Bridge, are thus inscribed:

This humble stone, the Mournful tribute of Conjugal affection, designates where lies enterred the remains of Mary, wife of Thos. Hammond, who departed this life March 23, 1847, in the 31 year of her age. Her many virtues ensured her the esteem of all who knew her; her friends were numerous her enemies unknown.

This Token of Respect is to Perpetuate The Memory of Adelia Marriott. She was one of the most indulgent Mothers, A Daughter of Charles & Elizabeth Hammond of this County; Born Oct. 20th 1812 And died in the City of Frederick July 30 1857, In the 45 year of her age.

This Stone is Raised in Memory of Vachel Hammond, who Departed this life 18th December 1821 in the 72d year of his Age.

In Memory of Majr Genl Robt Cummins, Who departed this life Nov. 14, 1825, In the 72d Year of his Age.

In the German Reformed churchyard at Hagerstown, Washington county, rests the body of Jonathan Hager, the founder of the town, and a person prominent in its history. A shaft lately erected by his descendants fitly commemorates his devotion to his people.

Here lieth the remains of Captain Jonathan Hager, Founder of Hagerstown, Born 1719, Died Nov. 6, 1775.

His only son, Jonathan Hager Jr., Proprietor of Hagerstown, Born 1775, Died Dec. 1798. Was Gott that Ist wohl gethan. Ære Perennius.

Sacred to the Memory of Gen Daniel Heister The patriot, the soldier and the statesman, Who departed this life on the 7th day of March 1804, In the 57th year of his age.

To enjoy the felicities of a happier state and to live in the memory of surviving friends.

Also Rosana Heister, Consort of Gen. Daniel Heister and daughter of Jonathan Hager, who departed this life on the 11th day of January 1810, in the 58th year of her age.

"Survey this house of Death
O soon to tenant it, soon to increase
The trophies of mortality, for hence
is no return."

The Episcopal graveyard at Hagerstown contains the following:

Sacred to the memory of Mrs. Mary Duvall, who departed this life Oct 26th 1833, In the 48th year of her age.
In token of their sorrow for her loss, and of their affection for her memory, this stone is placed at her grave by her children.
Mary Macgill, daughter of The Rev. James Macgill, first Rector of Queen Caroline's Parish, Anne Arundel County, Md., was born March 25, 1749, and Died Aug 18, 1824.
Dr. William D. Macgill, Born Jan 6, 1801. Died March 22, 1833.
Dr. N. Carroll Macgill, Born May 13, 1804; Died Sept. 14, 1839.
"Blessed are the pure in heart."
Sacred to the memory of Rebecca Gaither, who departed this life June 5 1841.
> There is a land of pure delight
> where saints and Angels dwell.

Henrietta & Matilda Gaither of later date.
Sacred to the memory of Susan Stewart Gaither, who departed this life Jan 11, 1846.
"I know that my Redeemer liveth."
Sacred to the memory of Elizabeth Gaither, who departed this life June 30, 1845, in the 83rd year of her age.
Mrs. Matilda Smoot, wife of Geo. C. Smoot, departed this life March 7, 1844, aged 68 years.

The names of Neill, Chandler, Berry, Callender, Hughes, Wharton also appear in this graveyard, but most of them are of a later date than 1850.

In the Lutheran yard is a monument to the memory of David Harry, a Revolutionary soldier, who died in 1843, at the advanced age of 93 years.

At Williamsport, in a most beautiful spot overlooking from a high hill, the Potomac river, was the shaft erected to Gen. Otho Holland Williams by the Mediary Lodge of Masons, in honor of his early connection with the order. The land for the cemetery was donated by him, and the grant confirmed by an act of the Assembly of Maryland, in 1785, so that it forms for him a most fitting resting place. The shaft bore this inscription:

Fatti Maschi; Parole Femini, Dedicated to the memory of Gen. Otho Holland Williams, Founder of Williamsport in 1787. Died in 1794, aged 45 years.

Beloved, honored and deplored. A distinguished patriot and hero in the Armies of the United States, in which he attained by merritorious service The Rank of Brig. Gen. during the war that terminated in establishing the independence of this, his native country. He was an active member of the American Lodge of the American Army.

The memory of the just is blessed, and shall live and flourish like a green bay-tree. A devoted, tender and affectionate husband, father, and brother; a refined generous, and stead-fast friend. A loyal and enlightened citizen; a virtuous, benevolent and accomplished man.

The whole cemetery, known as the "Riverview Cemetery," under the care of an association of ladies, formed in 1880, had been put in perfect order by them, and suitably inclosed by a fine iron railing. Several years ago this beautiful cemetery was desecrated by vandals who demolished about a hundred monuments and headstones. Conspicuous among these was the stately shaft erected to the memory of Gen. O. H. Williams, as above. The money loss was estimated at $25,000, and some of the monuments can never be replaced.

At Mountain View cemetery, Sharpsburg, are two inscriptions of Revolutionary officers:

In memory of Captain Alexander Thompson, An officer in the Revolution, Born A. D. 1753, Died December 24th, 1815, Aged 62 years.

Captain Joseph Chapline of the Revolutionary War, Died August 31st, 1821.

In the old Lutheran graveyard is the unmarked grave of Prof. Henry Young, a revolutionary soldier and afterwards, for thirty years, a teacher of English and German in the Sharpsburg school. He died February 26, 1829.

Within an enclosure in "Fountain Rock" cemetery at the College of St. James, are interred the remains of:

Samuel Ringgold, deceased Oct. 18, 1829, aged 60 years; Maria Ringgold, his wife, deceased Aug. 1, 1811, aged 35 years; Edward Lloyd Ringgold, fourth son of Samuel Ringgold, deceased July 28th, 1822, aged 16 years; Charles Ringgold, sixth son of Samuel Ringgold, deceased May 28th, 1817, aged 6 years; Charles Anthony Ringgold, ninth son of Samuel Ringgold, deceased Sept. 25, 1823; aged 5 years.

Benjamin Ringgold, brother of Samuel Ringgold, deceased Aug. 1798, aged 25 years; Thomas Ringgold, brother of Samuel Ringgold, died March 1818, Aged 40 years.

The above is inscribed on one slab and the inclosure is a brick wall with a shingle coping.

The Rockland house, residence of the late Col. Frisby Tilghman, in Washington county, Md., was built by him in 1796. Members of the family are buried in the graveyard. Some of the inscriptions are as follows:

Col. Frisby Tilghman, born Augt. 4th 1773, died April 14th, 1847.

Anna Maria Ringgold, wife of Col. Frisby Tilghman, born March 9th 1772, died February 21st, 1817.

Louisa Lamar, second wife of Col. Frisby Tilghman, born August 30th, 1789, died March 9th 1843.

George Tilghman, born May 11th, 1797, died August 25th, 1831.

Ann E. Lamar, wife of George Tilghman.

Dr. Frisby Tilghman, born Oct. 22nd, 1807, died Oct. 2nd, 1853.

Ann Cheston Tilghman, wife of William Hollyday, born 20th of February 1810, died 21st of January 1834.

Sarah Lamar Tilghman, infant, died when 10 days old.

James Hollyday, eldest son of James and Susanna Tilghman Hollyday of Readbourne, Queen Anne's County, Md.

Rebecca Hammond, wife of Thomas E. Tilghman.

At the "Vale," a farm near Frostburg, Alleghany county, once owned by Mrs. Sprigg, daughter of Colonel Lamar, is the following:

"In memory of Colonel William Lamar, a soldier of the Revolution. At the tap of the drum in his native state, Maryland, to the standard of his country he flew, nor left until he was acknowledged free and independant amongst the nations of the earth. At the battles of Harlem Heights, White Plains, Germantown, Monmouth, Staten Island, in the North; at Guildford Court-house, Eutaw, Camden, the capture of Forts Motte, Granby, Wateree and the siege of '96 in the South, he was present and actively engaged and by his coolness, bravery and skill he rendered most signal and important services to the army. At Guildford the desperate charge of the American troops, which turned the scale of victory in their favor, was ordered at his suggestion, which was communicated to Gen. Greene through Major Anderson and the plan of firing Fort Motte which was successfully adopted, and which occasioned the immediate surrender of the fort by the British, originated exclusively with him. In the disastrous' battle of Camden he was present in the fight and was by the side of De Kalb when that brave officer fell. In the siege of Ninety-six the immortal Kosciuszko was his fellow-soldier, and served under him for a while. The noble conduct of this brave Pole was the fond theme of his admiration and praise through life. Entering the army at the commencement of the Revolution he continued in it, engaged in active service, until the close of the war. During the contest he made but one visit home. He married early, had sons and daughters, the most of whom he lived to see begirt with glowing infancy. Possessing a heart full of kindness and a temper almost proof against anger, he was respected in all the relations of life. He was born in Frederick County, but for thirty years previous to his death, resided in Alleghany, where he died January 9, 1838, aged 83. Also sacred to the memory of Margaret Lamar, his wife. She was beloved and esteemed by all who knew her for the many virtues that adorned her character. She died universally lamented, March 17, 1821, aged 54 years."

Ninety-six, referred to here, is the name of a Post.

CHAPTER VIII

IN the upper part of Montgomery county, at Beallsville, beneath the shadow of Sugar-Loaf Mountain, is a secluded and historic spot, known as the Monocacy cemetery. A chapel of ease of All Saints parish, Frederick county, called the Monocacy chapel, stood here as early as 1747, and the parish church of St. Peter's followed in 1770, when this section fell within the borders of a new parish. Changes took place here as elsewhere. New centers sprang up and another St. Peter's was erected at Poolesville in 1849, after which the old church fell into ruins. The vestry transferred the churchyard to an association that had bought adjoining land. The latter received its charter in 1872, as "The Monocacy Cemetery Society of Montgomery County."

During the Revolutionary war, prayers for peace were offered in the old Monocacy chapel, and the churchyard became a camping ground for the American forces during the war of 1812.

The earliest gravestone bears the date 1748, but the name is lost. Another fragmentary inscription is to one who departed this life "the 52 year," in 1752. The others follow:

Revd. T. Dade, Obt. 6th F. 1822, Æt. 80 yrs.

Erected in Memory of John Douglass of Castle Steuard, Wigtonshire Scotland, who died here Nov 2. 1832, Aged 36 years.

In Memory of Mary, Born January 22nd 1815, and of Anastatia, Born March 29th 1831, Daughters of John and Mary Cross, who together departed this life August 8th 1855.

> When ardent glowed the Summer skies
> Mid burning heat and sultry weather
> Death came to them in friendly guise
> And smote them in his love together.
> In Union thus they lived and died
> And here lie buried side by side.

Robert Wilson, Born Sept 13, 1762; Died March 4, 1835.

Solomon Davis, Died July 10, 1822, Aged 48 years.

Mary White, Consort of Capt. James White, of Montgomery County.

Francis B. Austin, Died July 4, 1829, Aged 18 years.

A. M. G. Dd. Mo. 2, 1786.

Miss Mary Hilleary, Died June 20, 1816, Aged 32 years.

Mrs. Sarah Ann Gumaer, Died Oct 14th 1842, Aged 25.

John Scrimeger, died Nov. 7, 1830, Aged 23 years.

Mrs. Mary Manly, Died June 18, 1823, Aged 52 yrs.

John Manly, Died Nov. 25, 1816, Aged 64 years.

Dorcas Hammontree, Died Feb 21 1836, Aged 37 years, 11 mon. and 12 days.

Benjamin Pooll, Died Dec. 16, 1843, Aged 71 yrs.

Robert Doyne Dawson, son of Thomas and Elizabeth Dawson, Born July 10th 1758, died August 13th 1824, Aged 66 yrs. 1 mo. 3 ds.

Douglass Davis is buried between two large maple trees which measure each about 3½ or 4 feet in diameter. Age of the trees supposed to be between 100 and 125 years.

Among those of later date are:

Col. Robt. T. Dade, son of Rev. Townsend Dade, born Oct 14th, 1786; died Feb. 1873, Aged 86 yrs. 5 mon. He served in the War of 1812.

William T. Johnson, born Feb 17, 1818; died July 18, 1861, Aged 43 years, 3 m. and 1 day.

Sarah Ann, his wife, died Aug. 31st 1856, Aged 62 years, 8 mon. and 11 days.

Jane Plater, Widow of Snowden Pleasants, formerly Mrs. Elisha Williams, born March 17, 1799; died May 9, 1881.

Henry W. Talbot, born Nov. 12, 1789; died Feb. 7, 1859.

Sarah, his wife, died Jan. 25, 1883, Aged 88 years, 7 mo. and 11 ds.

William Spelton Cady, died April 28, 1861, Aged 42 years, 4 days.

Lewis B. Wynne, A minister of the Primitive Baptist Church, born in Kentucky June 30, 1815; died at College Hill, D. C., Feb. 3, 1883.

"Accounting that God was able to raise him up from the dead."

Gassaway Sellman, born Feb. 4, 1811, died April 6th, 1857, Aged 46 yr. 2 mon. and 2 da.

William Sellman, born Feb. 1st, 1786, died Dec. 31st, 1857, Aged 71 yr. 11 mon.

Ruth, wife of William Sellman, born Dec. 9th, 1786, died Mar. 19, 1862, Aged 75 years, and 3 months.

Sacred to the Memory of our mother Prudence, wife of Maj. Greenberry Griffith, Died Dec. 7th, 1881, Aged 75 years and 3 months.

Rockville cemetery has the following:

In Memory of Miss Mary Bowie who departed this life the 2nd of June 1800, in the 26th year of her Age.

In Memory of Richard Bowie who departed this life the 27th of March 1801, in the 18th year of his Age.

Allen Bowie, 1803, and Ruth Bowie, 1812.

Mrs. Sarah Johns, wife of Mr. Thomas Johns, died July 2nd 1782, Aged 32 years.

Mary Ann Grimes, Departed this life on the 18th of August 1815, Aged 9 Years, 7 Months and 27 Days.

Gassaway Perry, Born July 24th 1787, died July 26th 1834.

Addison Belt, Born Nov 11th 1789, died March 11th 1857.

John Harden, Born 1683, died 1732.

In Memory of McHenry Hilleary, who departed this life July 19th, 1792, in the 54th year of his Age.

Upton Beall, died Jan. 25th 1827, in his 57th year.

Jane Neal, Wife of Upton Beall, died Aug 2nd 1849, Aged 56 years. "God giveth His beloved Sleep."

Harriet Ann, daughter of Upton and Jane Neal Beall, died Jan 17, 1824, Aged 4 years.

Upton, only son of Upton and Jane Neal Beall, died July 1st 1820, Aged 1 day. "Of such is the Kingdom of Heaven."

Elizabeth A. O. Young, died 1842, Aged 31 years.

In Memory of our Mother Rebecca M. Young, who died in 1822, Aged 45.

Sacred to the Memory of our Father, Henry H. Young, Born September 17, 1776; Died March 9, 1854.

Anna Miller, Died March 16, 1850, Aged 7 Years, 5 Mos. and 23 days.

John O. Miller, Died July 7, 1848, Aged 1 year, 8 mos. and 23 days.

William Braddock, Died Sept. 11th 1830, Aged 41 Years, and 19 Days.

There are numerous very old and sunken graves in the cemetery without anything to identify them.

Allen Bowie lived, at the time of his death, in the fifth election district of Montgomery county; it is now the thirteenth election district. A great number of Bowies appear in the Montgomery county necrology. A sketch of the family is to be found in the *Baltimore Sunday Sun*, January 28 and February 4, 1906.

Four miles from Rockville is what was once known as the "Willow Tree" graveyard. The tree that formerly stood there and gave it its name, has long since disappeared. This graveyard is on the west side of Rock creek, amidst briars and thorns that make it a difficult task to copy the inscriptions. The following have been obtained for us, through the kindness of a gentleman living in the neighborhood:

John L. Summers, Born May the 12th, 1764, Died June 15th, 1802.

In Memory of Anne Maria Wilson, Born January the 11th, 1767, Died December the 18th, 1813.

Thomas Linstid, Born September the 27, 1761, Died April the 28, 1816.

Sacred to the Memory of Mrs. Mary Lyton Crabb, consort of Charles Henry Crabb, who departed this life August the 7th 1812, in the 17th year of her age. "Life how short; Eternity how long."

St. John's Catholic church at Forest Glen, is a successor to the one known as "Nancy Carroll" chapel, where the Rock Creek Mission was established many years ago. This chapel was built by Anne Carroll, sister of Bishop Carroll, and wife of Robert Brent. The inscription on the memorial erected to her, heads the list.

Sacred.
To the Memory of
Mrs Ann Brent relict of Robert Brent Esq
of Stafford Co. Va.
Daughter of Daniel Carroll Esq.
She was born on the 13th July A. D. 1733
Departed this life Nov. 1804
In the 72nd year of her age
This stone is placed over her grave
by her surviving children,
In testimony of their ardent and devout attachment
which they cherished for so good and examplary a mother,
as a tribute of their profound respect
to the virtue and piety
which adorned her life and character.
Requiescat in pace.

Catherine Digges, Relict of George Digges, of Warburton and daughter of Robert and Ann Brent, born in Stafford Co. Va. Died at Washington City, District of Columbia.

I. H. S. Sacred to the Memory of Mrs Eleanor Carroll, Relict of Daniel Carroll Esq. She died on the third day of February in the year 1796, Aged 92.

On the arms of a cross standing near Madam Carroll's tomb is the following:

Miss Priscilla Neale, Died Jan. 21 1858 (1853 ?). Edward, 1839.

Harriet Brent, Relict of Robert Young Brent, Oct. 10 1863, In the 64th year of her age.

In Memoriam. Robert Young Brent died . . . 1855, In the 67th year of his age.

Sarah Hayes and Caroline, daughters of above, died after 1850.

Harriet, a child, Clementina, Emily and Julia Brent seem to have a stone in common. "Even in death they were not divided."

William Cottinger Brent, died Sept. 15 1850, In the 36th year of his age.

Sacred. To the Memory of William Brent, Born at Aquia, Stafford County, Virginia; Died In Washington, D. C., Dec. 15 1848, Aged 75 years. And Elizabeth Brent, Relict of William Brent, born in Charles Co., Md., died In Washington, D. C., March 29th 1855, Aged 63 years. R. I. P.

I. H. S. To the Memory of Martin O'Connor, who was born in the year A. D. 1750, and died in the year A. D. 1829. Also Sarah O'Connor, who was born in the year A. D. 1785 (1745 ?) and died in the year A. D. 1814.

Mary Ann Fenwick, born March 8, 1779 [1799 ?]; Died in 1848 (1845 ?).

Sacred to the Memory of John O'Connor, A. D. 1832, Aged 33.

"Christian pray for his Soul, Who while he Look'd with joy And hope around Him, was suddenly Attacked and overcome by Man's Common leveller Death."

Mary Fenwick, 1787-1805; Annie Fenwick, 1793-1833; Teresa Fenwick, 1791-1820; James Fenwick, 1795-1830; John Fenwick, 1797-1862; Philip Fenwick, Dec. 12th 1789-1863.

Sacred to the Memory of John Fenwick, 1750-1820. His wife Mary Thompson Fenwick, 1762-1837.

Sacred to the Memory of Wm W. Diggs, born 1790; died Jan 17th 1830.

In Memory of Sarah Sweaney, who departed this life Jan 6th 1831; aged 80 years.

In Memory of Mary Whelan, who departed this life Dec 27th 1830, in the 60th year of her age.

In Memory of Julian Whelan, who departed this life June 25th 1832, aged 35 years.

Sacred to the Memory of George R. Carroll, who departed this life in 1858, aged 45 years.

Sacred to the Memory of G. D. Carroll, M. D., Died 1844, aged 56 years.

Sacred to the Memory of Ann Carroll, Born April 27th 1777; died July 29th 1862.

Sacred to the Memory of Elizabeth Digges Carroll, born Aug 4th 1752; died Jan. 27th 1843.

Sacred to the Memory of Daniel Carroll, Died June 19th 1790. R. I. P.

Bridget Connelly Died Dec 4th 1829 aged 52 years.

Those of a later date are:

Charles Edward Brent, 1886. Ann Maria, Relict of Dr. Ray Livingston, 1863. Theodore Mosher and his wife Mary, daughter of Robert Young Brent, 1878 and 1892; their infant son John Carroll. Henry Goodfellow "Major and Judge Advocate U. S. A.," 1885. John Fenwick, 1862. Philip Fenwick, 1863, at the age of 74. Norah, wife of Wm. W. Diggs, 1863, at the age of 72. Robert Brown, 1870, at the age of 86.

On a farm in the Laytonsville district are these two graves:

N. Griffith, died Aug 5th 1803, in the 32nd year of his age.

Charles G. Ridgely, Departed this life 1st of April 1825, in the 63rd year of his age.

Near Brookeville, Olney district, on a farm owned by Joseph Janney, are the graves of Richard Green and wife, inscribed:

Richard Green (Major) died July 30th 1818, Aged 76 years, 8 mo.

Sarah, his wife, died March 21st 1815, Aged 77 years.

The above is said to be the second wife of Richard Green, and the sister of Mr. Joshua Howard.

General Anderson who fought in the year of 1812 is also supposed to be buried on this farm. Capt. Richard Anderson of the 4th Maryland regiment, who rendered distinguished service at the battle of Cowpens in the Revolutionary war, may probably be the same.

On Walter Mobley's farm, about one mile from Rockville:

General Jeremiah Crabb Died 19th February 1800, in the 40th year of his age. Also in Memory of Elizabeth Ridgely Griffith, His Wife, Born August 10th 1764; died in 1828, aged 64 years.

Thomas Worthington Howard died July 29th 1818. His Wife Elizabeth Ridgely, Daughter of Gen. Jeremiah Crabb, died Nov. 8th 1821.

The old graveyard which is very near the house, is almost filled with the graves of Jeremiah Crabbs' family, the place having been owned by his descendants until a few years ago. His daughter, Sarah Griffith, is buried there.

On a farm owned by the late Washington Chicester (Olney district), are several inscriptions:

Richard Johns, son of Thomas and Sarah Johns, born Oct. 15, 1775; died April 5, 1836.

Washington Bowie, son of Allen and Ruth Bowie, born 12 August 1776; died 12 April 1826, Aged 49 years and 8 months.

Margaret Crab Bowie, wife of Washington Bowie, daughter of Thomas and Sarah Johns, born 19 May 1773, died 22 July 1840.

Sarah Holliday Bowie, daughter of Washington and Margaret Bowie, born 28th Feb. 1811; died Augt. 1824.

Washington Bowie, son of Washington and Margaret Bowie, born April 20, 1805; died June 14 1844, Aged 39 years 1 month and 16 days.

Margaret Dallas Bowie, daughter of Washington and Margaret Bowie, born 9th Decr. 1803; died 1st Jany 1851.

Mary Bowie Chichester, born July 2 1802; died July 31st 1872.

Thomas Johns Bowie, Son of Washington and Margaret Crab Bowie, born Oct 21st, 1800; died July 26th, 1850, Age 49 years, 9 months and 5 days.

Catherine Worthington, wife of Thomas J. Bowie, dau. of Thomas and Elizabeth Bowie Davis, born June 26, 1803; died June 21, 1898.

Ellen Ruth Bowie, daughter of Thomas and Catherine Bowie, born Jan 11th 1838; died March 31st 1848, Aged 10 years, 2 months and 20 days.

Sarah Holliday Bowie, Daughter of Thomas and C. W. Bowie, born 22 Dec 1835; died 10th Augt. 1838, Aged 2 years, 9 months and 18 days.

On the Dorsey farm are the following stones erected by Mr. J. M. Dermott of Frederick City, Md.:

Joshua Dorsey, Born March 15th 1768; Died July 12th 1843.

Henrietta Dorsey, Born March 28th 1770; Died Sept 5th 1848.

At the Ridge farm, Zadoc Magruder's old place, are the graves of two Magruders:

Robert Pottinger Magruder was born March 23rd 1769 and died Aug 10th 1822, Aged 53 years.
Useful in life, lamented in death, an affectionate husband, a kind friend, a pious christian, who delighted in doing good.

Elizabeth Perry Magruder, Consort of Robert Pottinger Magruder, was born Oct. 13th 1770, and died April 17th 1835 [1833 ?].
She was useful in life and happy in death, through faith in Jesus Christ.

At Mt. Airy farm of the Ashton tract, Samuel Richardson and his wife are buried:

Here lies the Body of Mr. Samuel Richardson, who departed this life 19th Feb. 1764, Aged 68 years.

Here lies the Body of Mariam Richardson, who departed this life on the 21st day of November 1767, In the 57 year of her Age.
Remember man as thou Passeth by,
As thou art now, so once was I.
As I am now, so thou shalt be
So prepare to follow me.

"Greenwood," the Davis place, is about thirty-four miles from Laurel. The family cemetery on one corner of the lawn is inclosed by a stone wall. The monument was erected by Allen Bowie Davis and inscribed with the names of those who have passed away. On one side are five names:

Ephraim Davis, Died Aug 13th, 1769; Aged 33 years.

Elizabeth Howard (his wife) Died Jan 4, 1793; Aged 48 years.

Thomas Davis, son of Ephraim and Elizabeth, Died Feb. 8, 1833; Aged 65 years.

Elizabeth, his wife (dau. of Allen and Ruth Bowie), Died Nov 23 1840; Aged 69 years.

Dr. Thos. Johns Davis, son of Thos. and Elizabeth Davis, Died July 11, 1828; Aged 23 years.

On the second side are:

Rebecca Comfort, wife of Allen Bowie Davis and daughter of Thos. B. and Milcah (Goodwin) Dorsey, Died July 8, 1836; Aged 27 years.

Thomas, the beloved son of Allen Bowie and Hester Ann Wilkins Davis, Died Feb 3, 1849; Aged 8 years.

Allen Bowie, a lovely infant, son of Allen Bowie and Hester Ann Davis, Died Sept 20, 1859; Aged 9 months.

On the third side, are commemorated those who have died since 1875:

Allen Bowie Davis, Hester Ann Davis, William Wilkins Davis, Esther Wilkins Davis.

The late Mr. and Mrs. Allen Bowie Davis died, respectively, on April 17, 1889, and October 9, 1888. All the early inscriptions, if there ever were any, have disappeared. Stones bearing the following were erected by the late Allen Bowie Davis to his grandparents:

In Memory of Thomas Davis, born December the 10th 1768, and died February 8th 1833, Aged 64 years.

In Memory of Elizabeth Davis, Relict of Thomas Davis, born September the 11th 1772, and died November 23rd 1840, Aged 68 years.

Besides the inscriptions on the family monument, the memory of Thos. Johns Davis, M. D., is perpetuated on a stone covering his grave and bearing the following verse:

> Thus fade the fragile buds of earth;
> Thus fade the lovely and the brave,
> Come here ye thoughtless sons of mirth,
> And pause a while o'er virtues grave.

Two other graves are:

In memory of Mrs Achsah Goldsborough, relict of Dr. Richard Goldsborough of Cambridge, Maryland, who departed this life on the 7th day of Sept 1835, aged 67 years.

Sacred to the memory of John Bowie, M. D., Who died the 17th of February 1825, Aged 55.years.

In the Laytonsville district, the following inscriptions are found:

Zadoc M. Cooke, Born March 30th 1831; Died Sept 20th 1849, Aged 18 years.

To the Memory of Rachel Dorsey, Wife of Harry W. Dorsey, who was born March 25th 1767; Died January 24th 1844.

"Blessed are the dead which die in the Lord."

In Memory of Zadoc M. Cooke, born July 1st 1801; Died August 29th [22nd ?], 1830, Aged 29 years.

Nathan Cooke died the 7th of October 1805, in the 37th year of his age.

John Cooke, son of Nathan, Died 15th Aug 1807, in the 7th year of his age.

To the Memory of Mrs Elizabeth Magruder, wife of Otho Magruder, who died Feb 15th 1840, Aged 34 years.

Sacred to the Memory of Otho Magruder, who departed this life April 11th 1856, Aged 62 years. "For 36 years he was a ruling elder in the Presbyterian church at Rockville and Bethesda. His life was that of a Christian, his death was one of Peace and Hope and his remains were laid in the grave embalmed by the tears of a whole community."

Psalm xxxix, 37 and Psalm xii, 1, follow, making a very long inscription.

At Laytonsville, in Montgomery county, a beautiful monument of Carrara marble has been erected by Mr. Romulus R. Griffith, at his own cost, commemorative of services rendered during the Revolutionary struggle by three of his ancestors. The monument is a shaft ten feet, six inches in height, of symmetrical proportions. The only ornamentation is a beautifully chiseled sword, thirty inches in length, in relief, on two sides of the obelisk. The monument is the design and work of Henry L. Moltz of Baltimore. The inscriptions on the monument are to

Henry Griffith of Orlando, Born February 14, 1720; Died September 28, 1794. Member of the Lower House of the Colonial Assembly for Anne Arundel county, 1768–70, and for Frederick county, 1772–75.

Member of The Convention of Maryland that assembled July 26, 1775, at Annapolis, Md., and formed The Association of the Freemen of Maryland.

Major Philemon Griffith of H., Born August 29, 1756; Died April 29, 1838. Captain of Rifles at Fort Washington, Taken prisoner November 16, 1776. Commissioned Major, December 10, 1776.

Capt. Samuel Griffith of H., Born May 7, 1752; Died May 12, 1833. Commissioned Captain Third Maryland Regulars, Continental Army December 10, 1776.

H. Griffith, Died Sept 28th 1794, Aged 73 years.

E. Griffith, Died Oct 1797, Aged 33 years.

Ruth Griffith, Died in the 49th year of her Age.

H. Griffith, John Griffith, D. Griffith, Ann Wayman, H. Todd,

Other inscriptions here are:

Sacred to the memory of Henry Howard of Jno., who departed this life Feb 12th 1834, Aged 60 years.

To the Memory of Mrs Marion Nourse, wife of Rev. C. H. Nourse, and second daughter of Wm Robertson Esq., who died Nov. 11, 1847, Aged 24 years and 8 months.

Sacred to the Memory of Wm Robertson, who departed this life 20th day of Feb. 1852, Aged 67 years.

Sacred to the Memory of Nathan Dickerson, Died April 20th 1860, Aged 79 years, 7 months, 10 d.

In Memory of Margaret Dickerson, consort of Nathan Dickerson, born May 9th 1778; died December 22nd 1854.

A devoted Wife, Mother and Friend.

On a farm, belonging of late years to Wm. Griffith and before the Revolution to the Hempstone family, is the old graveyard. William Hempstone, a soldier of the Revolution, known as Major Hempstone, is buried here, but there is no stone to mark the spot. Two stones are:

In Memory of William Hempstone, Born March 30th 1793; Died July 29th 1825, Aged 32 years, 3 months, 29 days.

In Memory of Mary, a daughter of William and Ann V. Hempstone, Born March 13th 1823; Died June 24th 1827, aged 4 years, 3 m. 11 da.

At David Trundle's, near Barnesville district, Dickerson Station, is an old family burying ground. Among the stones are the following:

John Trundle, born March 6th 1753; died March 25, 1810.

Also Ruth, wife of John Trundle.

John L. Trundle, born Jan 4th 1776; died Aug 24th 1836.

In Memory of Mary, wife of John L. Trundle, who was born July 15th 1776; died Sept 7th 1831.

In Memory of David Trundle, who was born June 21st 1773; died March 1846, aged 72 years, 8 months and 15 days.

In Memory of Drusilla, wife of David Trundle, Born Nov 22nd 1775; Died Sept 23rd 1855, Aged 79 years, 10 mo. and 1 day.

Charlotte Trundle, Consort of Alfred Belt, was born Feb 6th 1787, died April 13th 1824.

In Memory of Alfred Belt, born Feb 14th 1788, died July 1st 1872, Aged 84 years, 4 mo. 17 days.

In Memory of Otho Trundle, who was born Feb 14th 1780, died Jan 27th 1823.

Elizabeth Burnes, wife of Otho Trundle, was born Dec 27th 1784; died Aug 17th 1824.

William Trundle was born Dec 1st 1804; died April 3rd 1838.

Frances N. Hempstone was born Feb 17th 1805, died Aug 25th 1840.

Lieutenant William Hempstone Trundle was born Oct 9th 1827; was killed during the Civil War, March 28th 1864.

In Memory of Benjamin Shreve, born March 15th, 1804; died Sept 25th, 1861.

In Memory of Mary Elizabeth, wife of Benjamin Shreve, born March 26th 1811; died Oct 23rd 1855.

The Shreves or Shrieves, descendants of the Trundles, still live on this farm.

At the home of Beall Gaither is a cemetery in which repose many of the Gaither family. Some inscriptions here are:

In Memory of Daniel Gaither, Departed this life Sept 16th 1818, In the 53rd year of his age.

In Memory of Henrietta, wife of Daniel Gaither, Departed this life April 1854, Aged 85 years.

Jane Gaither Departed this life Sept 19th 1844, Aged 64 years.

In Memory of Juliet (Gaither), wife of Rushrod Gartrell, who departed this life April 10th 1863, in the 56th year of her age.

Deborah (Gaither), Wife of John F. E. Magruder, Died 1864, born Aug 1st 1815.

"Blessed are they that die in the Lord."

In Memory of Greenberry Gaither, Born April 16th 1820; Died Sept 24th 1848.

Perry Gaither, Died 1854. Henrietta, wife of Perry, Died 1859. Samuel Gaither, Died 1860.

At the home of Henry Chew Gaither, deceased, three miles from "Greenwood," said to be over 125 years old, are the following:

Sacred to the memory of Henry Chew Gaither, son of Wm. and Elizabeth Howard Gaither, was born Jan 25th A. D. 1778, Departed this life Feb 12, A. D. 1845.

Sacred to the memory of Eliza, Wife of Henry Chew Gaither, and daughter of William Worthington, was born March 20th A. D. 1793. Died suddenly at West Point, June 19th A. D. 1850, Aged 58 years.

Sacred to the memory of Gen. William Lingan Gaither, only child of Henry Crew and Eliza Gaither, was born Feb 21, A. D. 1813; Died at Berkeley Springs, on the 2nd of Aug, A. D. 1858, Aged 45 years, 5 months and 11 days.

In memory of Ephraim Gaither, Born April 24th, 1780; Died May 2nd, 1857.

In memory of Sarah Elizabeth Gaither, Born April 19th 1799; Died March 27th 1872.

She was the daughter of Dr. R. and A. Goldsborough, and relict of Ephraim Gaither, half-brother of Thomas Davis.

"Clean Drinking" was granted to John Coats or Courts in 1699, for 700 acres. Later it was bought by Walter C. Jones, who established there a mill, and left his epitaph cut in the stone as follows:

> Here lies the body and bones
> Of old Walter C. Jones.
> By his not thinking,
> He lost "Clean Drinking";
> And by his shallow pate,
> He lost his vast estate.

Off this tract was taken "Hayes," where a fine old house built by the Rev. Alexander Williamson, known as the "Hunting Parson," is still standing. Parson Williamson was rector of Rock Creek church, D. C., and is said to be buried under the chancel.

CHAPTER IX

BETWEEN the years 1629 and 1630, an Anglo-Saxon settlement was planted at Kent Island on the Eastern shore of the Chesapeake. Here it took root and flourished, and so when Lord Baltimore's colonists arrived a few years later to substantiate his claims, they found others ready to dispute his title. Colonel William Claiborne stands out in local history as the head of the rebels, and as he was defeated, but still declined to acknowledge the supremacy of the new over-lord, he was banished and his lands forfeited. Some of his followers returned to England, but many settlers remained. By Gov. Leonard Calvert the island was deemed of sufficient importance to have its affairs regulated by a Commissioner, whom he duly appointed. As early as 1638, we find burgesses from the Isle of Kent attending the General Assembly, held that year at Fort St. Mary's. This island, therefore, wrangled over as it was, even to the shedding of blood, stands to us as a landmark on the plat of time, to be consulted in the laying out of the new lines of our present interests. Here there is still a farm going by Claiborne's name, and here are the site and foundations of a church, built in 1650, which serve as a connecting link in the ecclesiastical traditions, originating with the ministrations of the Rev. Richard James, the clergyman of the first Anglo-Saxon settlement. Broad Creek church, erected in 1650, and Christ church at Stevensville, its successor, erected in 1880, represent a long lapse of time in the history of a people, only the old place of worship is now but a memory; bushes and briars have been allowed to take possession of the God's acre, where the living once paid honor to their dead, and the venerable monuments have crumbled away. The only ancient tombstones reported to us in this locality, are those on the farm of James Bright, near the site of the old church, and those on Walter F. White's place, at Crab-Alley Neck.

Co-eval with the building of the church on Broad creek, in 1650, the boundaries of Kent county were defined. They embraced all the territory on the mainland lying between the Sassafras river on the north, and the Choptank on the south, a very large slice of the Eastern shore, and now divided into Kent, Queen Anne's, Talbot and a part of Caroline counties. The island that gave it its name has meanwhile fallen to the portion of Queen Anne's.

The mainland, which can be reached from the island at low tide by a causeway crossing the Narrows, is rich in old places of burial and here tombstones are still to be found, bearing the well-known names of Bennett, Blake, Carroll, Chamberlaine, Decourcy, Earle, Goldsborough, Hall, Lloyd, Neale, Rousby, Rozer and Tilghman.

Four stones are all that remain of the graveyard at Bennett's Point. There are bits of what may have been the facing of a vault, or the upright frame of Captain Greene's stone, and broken bricks scattered around. Here is found the tomb of Dorothy Carroll. The top of the slab, a perfectly preserved specimen of white marble, is ornamented with the Carroll coat of arms impaled with another, probably that of Blake—chevron between three shocks of wheat—the whole being surmounted by helmet and crest—the Carroll bird—and deeply carved in a lozenge. The stone lies apart from the rest of the group and bears this inscription:

> Here lyeth Interr'd the Remains
> of Dorothy Carroll Daughter
> of Mr. Charles Blake of
> Wye River in the Province of

Maryland, & Wife of Charles Carroll
son of Charles Carroll Esqr. of
Clounlisk, in the King's County and
Kingdom of Ireland.

She was Meek, Prudent and Virtuous
wanting no good quality that
Compose a good Christian and Wise
tender and loveing Mother and Friend.
tho' Young in years a Matron
in Behavior and Conduct.
She left Issue two sons and
one Daughter who inherit
her Beauty, and to be hoped,
they will her Virtues.
She departed this life the
8 day of July Anno Domini 1734,
Aged Thirty-one Years, Seven Months
and Twelve Days.

An almost illegible, broken gray slab, has the following inscription (the brackets indicate portions illegible):

Here lies Interred ye body [of]
Thomas Greene Mast[er and Mari]
ner of ye Towne of Ne[wcastle]
on Lyne Comma[nder of the ship]
Loveing Friendship [departed]
this life at Sea 17 August
1674 and brought here and [buried]
February 27 after[wards] ? ? ? ?

Other inscriptions on the stones of Richard Bennett and his wife are:

Here lieth the body of Richard Bennett Esq., who was born the 16th of September 1667, and died ye 11th of October 1749. His Father Died Young His Grandfather, who was also named Richard Bennett, was Governor of Virignia. No man was more Esteemed in Life In all Ranks of People than He, And this Esteem proceeded from his Benevolent & Charitable Disposition, Added to a Vast Depth of Understanding. To His Memory this Tombstone is dedicated by his Nephew, The Honourable Edward Lloyd Esq.

Here Lyes Interr'd the Body of Elizabeth, Wife of Richard Bennett Esq. She was the Daughter of John Rousby Esq. by Barbara his Wife and Dyed the third day of April Anno Domini 1740 in the 58th Year of her Age very much lamented. Requiescat in pace.

On the farm is a stone bearing the name

Queen Anne County

Mrs. C. Augusta Pratt, Born August 28, 1804; Died August 4, 1854.

At "Bolingly," Queenstown, now occupied by a hotel, are found several graves. Some of the inscriptions are:

Here lyeth the Body of Edward Neale Esq., who departed this life the 28th day of December 1760, Aged Sixty years.

Here lies the Body of Mrs. Martha Hall, who departed this Life the 31st Day of May 1789, Aged fifty-one years and five months. May she rest in Peace.

Here lies Thomas Whetenhall Rozer Esqr. who died Octr. 22nd, 1785, Aged 27. May he rest in Peace.

Sacred to the memory of Clarina Underhill, wife of Anthony Underhill Esq., of the City of New York, who departed this life on the 6th of June 1835, at Queens Town E. Shore Maryland, aged 66 years. This tomb is erected by those who most valued her while living and lamented her when lost forever.

At the "Hermitage," Queen Anne county, lie the remains of Dr. Richard Tilghman, the progenitor of the Tilghman family, also those of his wife Mary Foxley. He died in 1675; she survived him twenty years. The graveyard is kept in good order and the names of those buried there furnish an interesting list of Tilghmans who distinguished themselves in their day and generation.

"Always remember
the 5th·of November
But Doe not forgett
Death will have no lett
Consider thy end
and thy time well spend
and soe shalt thou have
a crown in thy grave."
Vale.
Ita dixit Richardus tilghmanus
B. M.

In artique chirugi
Magister
qui sub hoc tumulo
Sepultus est
Obiit Janu 7mo Anno
1675.

Other Tilghman inscriptions are:

Here Lyes Interr'd the Honourable Richard Tilghman Esqr, who departed this life the 23rd day of Janu, Anno Domini 1738, in the Sixty-Sixth Year of his Age. He Married Anna Maria, the Daughter of Coll. Philemon Lloyd, by whome he had nine Children, seven of them living at the time of his Death.

In Memory of Anna Maria Tilghman, Widow of ye Honble Coll. Richard Tilghman, who Departed this life December the 15th, 1748, in the 72d Year of her Age, at ye Joynt Expense of her Seven Children, not more out of filial Regard then Gratitude for Her pious Endeavour to lead them in the Paths of Virtue, In which She herself persevered With Constancy not frequently to be met with; thereby acquiring Self approbation And The Love and Esteem of others.

Here lyeth Elizabeth, the Daughter of Edward and wife of Richard Tilghman, who died June the 7th Anno 1767, in the 19th year of her Age. She had every qualification necessary to render her, And was, Universally Esteemed A Particular Favorite of god and Man.

Reader, Ponder well the End of Providence In Snatching from the World So useful a Member of Society; in tearing from a fond Parent and Husband So great a Part of Themselves, and by Pious Meditation Turn what seems to be Misfortune to them into Advantage to thyself.

> From Earliest Infancy 'til Life was Ended
> She Scarcely Ever in the Least offended
> Her Manner so Engaging Thought so just
> All who beheld her Lov'd Without Disgust.

Sacred to the Memory of Eleanor Martha Tilghman, an Amiable & accomplished woman, Consort of Matthew Tilghman, Daughter of Thos. Whettenhall Rozer of Notley Hall P. George's County.

Through the short Space of her Earthly Probation, She discharged with Exemplary Propriety the duties of a Good Christian, of an affectionate Daughter and of a tender & dutiful Wife.

She was born Jan'y. 10th, 1785, was Married Jan'y. 10th, 1802, and Died Feb'y 2nd, 1803, Aged 18 yrs., 25 days.

"Piety alas retards not the approach of Death."

The widower consoled himself with a second spouse, Harriet Hynson. They left descendants. He was born September 20, 1777; died October 21, 1828.

Sacred to the Memory of Anna Maria the only child of William & Eleanor Tilghman, and The sincerely beloved friend and wife of Edward Tilghman 3rd. She was born the 20th of August 1797 and died the 2d of May 1820. Possessing, and most earnestly displaying, Throughout her transient State of being here All those social and moral Virtues Which can adorn the female character, She left this world as she had uniformly lived in it A truly meek, pious and resigned Christian. Positum marito suo.

Sacred to the Memory of Edward Tilghman, son of Matthew and Sarah Tilghman, Born June 20th 1786; Died Dec. 6th 1860.

To the memory of Mrs Eleanor Tilghman, who died the 12th day of Feb. 1821, Aged 56 years.

To the memory of William Tilghman Esq., who died the 17th day of December 1800, Aged 52 years.

"He was a man to all the Country dear."

In memory of James Tilghman, Who died the 19th day of April 1809, In the 66th year of his age. For more than 19 years he was Chief Judge of the second Judicial District of Maryland.

Erected to the memory of Elizabeth Tilghman, Wife of Judge Tilghman, by her affectionate children. She died the 22 day of January 1809, In the 59th Year of her age.

In Memory of George Tilghman, Son of Judge Tilghman, who was born on the 11th Oct. 1771 and died the 30th July 1797.

On a marble cross:

Stedman R. Tilghman, Born 1st March 1822; Died 30th July 1848.

In memory of Henry Ward Pearce Jr., who died on the 26th day of March 1803, aged forty-five years.

In memory of Mrs. Anna Maria Pearce, wife of Henry Ward Pearce. who died on the 17th day of August, 1834, in the seventy-fifth year of her age.

There are other stones and inscriptions of a later date, the Cooke-Tilghmans, the late owners, being the last.

The cemetery at Centreville was laid out about the year 1845. The oldest stones are as follows:

Michael Keating died May 7, 1847, aged 51 years.

Elizabeth J. Palmer, wife of Michael Keating, died Aug. 5, 1859, in her 51st. year.

Mary E., infant daughter of Abner and Sarah G. Hall, who died Oct. 15th, 1846.

In memory of Sarah G., wife of Abner Hall, Died Sept. 4, 1851, Aged 33 yrs., 5 mos. and 13 days.

Anderton B. Peters died June 27, 1848, aged 35 years, 2 months & 14 days.

Elizabeth Nevill Died April 27th [29th], 1850, Aged 68 years.

Mary E. Goodwin Downs, b. April 7, 1824; d July 27, 1827.

Sacred to the memory of Jacob H. Simpers, who died Feb. 5th, 1848, Aged 26 yrs. 11 mos. and 18 days.

James E. Dillon died Nov. 20, 1825.

In memory of Hopewell Ford, who died December 1st 1850, Aged 65 years.

Mary Hamilton died March 21, 1815; aged 39 years, 6 months & 4 days.

In memory of Thomas H., son of Thomas and Hopewell Ford, who died Oct. 6th, 1850, Aged 43 years 3 months and 14 days.

Oakley Haddaway died March 6, 1845, in his 39th year.

Henry Harwood died April 1848, in the 35th year.

Emily Booker, wife of T. B. Booker, died May 19th, 1850, in her 48 year.

John MaBB? Died Oct. 5th, 1849, Aged 59 Years.

Elizabeth Ann, Wife of C. R. Ferguson. Born March 18th, 1823, Died July 26th, 1851.

The Earle lot contains stones moved from "Winton," according to provisions made in the will of the late Richard T. Earle. They are inscribed:

Erected to the memory of the Honourable Richard Tilghman Earle. He died on the 22nd day of November 1843, in the 78th year of his Age.

For more than twenty-five years he discharged the duties of the office of Chief Judge of the 2nd. Judicial District of Maryland with distinction to himself and entire satisfaction to the public.

His sound judgement, quick perception, nice discrimination and uncompromising unpartiality, eminently fitted him for the office he held. He was no less esteemed in all the relations of private and domestic life, his truth and weight of character having bound to him a large family of children and secured the attachment of many friends. He departed this life in a confiding trust in God's promises and in the full hope of a blessed immortality.

The grave of Mary Earle, wife of Judge Earle, who was among the best of women and lived and died unto the Lord, Bemoaned by numerous relatives and friends. She departed this life on the 11th day of December 1836, in the 54th Year of her age.

Sacred to the memory of a true disciple of our Lord Jesus Christ, Catherine Spencer Earle, beloved wife of Richard T. Earle. In peace she departed this life Feb. 18th, 1848, in the 34th year of her age.

"Blessed are the pure in heart."

Sacred to the memory of Elizabeth A. Spencer, beloved wife of Richd T. Earle, Died Aug 28th, 1868, in the 64th year of her age.

She was a woman of very decided character, a sincere Christian, with a heart full of love to God & a hand ever ready to help the needy.

Richard T. Earle, husband of the two pious wives, Catherine and Elizabeth Spencer, leaves on his monument a record of repentance and humility. He is spoken of in his obituary as a "kind-hearted, genial gentleman and well-known for his charity and benevolence."

Richard T. Earle of Winton. Born December 22, 1816; Died January 21, 1895.

"God be merciful to me a sinner."

Sacred to the memory of Henrietta M. (Earle), beloved wife of David Stewart. She departed this life on the 5th day of April 1839, in the 27th year of her age.

Sacred to the memory of Philip Henry Feddeman, who was born the 10th October 1795, and died deeply lamented on the 1st day of Septr. 1830.

In Memory of Elizabeth Ann Feddeman, Widow of Philip Henry Feddeman. She died deeply lamented on the 29th day of November 1836, in the 35th year of her age, Leaving five infant children, two sons and three daughters, to deplore their irreparable loss.

Sacred to the Memory of Old Uncle Anthony, the faithful family servant of the Hon. Richard Tilghman Earle. He died on the 22d day of Feb. 1847, aged 77.

To the Memory of Mother Polly, wife of Uncle Anthony, the friend as well as the nurse of our Mother, Mary Earle, is this stone erected by those she loved and nursed on her knee. She died on the 21st. day of October, 1843, aged 76.

A new monument to the Earle family is inscribed on the four sides as follows:

James Earle, of Craglethrope, England, Settled in Maryland with his family Nov. 1683.

Richard T. Earle, Judge of the Highest Courts of Md. from 1809 to 1834.
"Justice and Judgment are the habitation of thy throne."

Mary Earle, Daughter of Judge Tilghman, and wife of Judge Earle of Maryland.
"Her children rise up and call her blessed."
Susanna to the memory of her father and mother.

At "Readbourne" is a stone to the memory of James Hollyday:

To the memory of James Holliday Esq., who departed this life on the eighth day of October 1747.

He was for many years one of his Lordship's Council And in public and private Life Always supported the Character of a Worthy Gentleman and good Christian.

"Readbourne" house was built by the above in or about the year 1733. His wife (widow Lloyd, *née* Sarah Covington) was buried in England, where she went to visit a daughter by her first marriage, after James Hollyday's death. Other of the Hollyday stones are:

James Hollyday obit 9th Jan'y 1807, Ætat 48.

Susanna, Relict of James Hollyday, Born July 17, 1770; Died Aug. 19, 1849.

Frisby, 4th son of Ja's and Susanna Hollyday, Born April 25th 1801; Died Feb'y 15, 1821.

Anna M. C. Jones, only daughter of Ja's and Susanna Hollyday, Born 2, 1796; Died June 1823.

To Our Dear Father, Henry Hollyday, second son of Henry Hollyday, second son of James and Susanna Hollyday, Born Jan'y 15, 1798; Departed this life Sept 15, 1865.

Anna Maria, wife of Henry Hollyday, Born Oct. 9, 1805, Died March 5, 1855. A sincere Christian.

James Henry, eldest son of Henry and Anna M. Hollyday, Born Jan'y 14, 1834; Died Feb'y 2, 1846.

Mary Robins, 6th daughter of Hy' and Anna M. Hollyday, Born Sept. 18, 1845; Died Nov. 19, 1846.

Nannie Ringgold, Eldest daughter of Hy' and Anna M. Hollyday, Born Oct. 18, 1833; Died Dec. 18, 1849.

Mother Milly, A Faithful servant, Died in 1848, Aged about 75 years.

The oldest stones in St. Luke's churchyard at Church Hill are:

In Memory of David Latemer, laid here 1st of March 1795, in the 28th Year of his Age.

In Memory of John Lenox, who departed this life May 26th 1807, In the 16th year of His age.

On the Cacy place near Church Hill is a stone inscribed:

Beneath this stone are interr'd the remains of Joshua Seney, who was born near the spot which now contains his ashes, March 4th, 1756, And died Oct. 20th 1798.

From the commencement of the American Revolution, at various Periods of his Life, he filled with ability some of the highest stations and discharged with Integrity some of the most important duties to which his native State could appoint him, Preserving through the whole a Character both private and public unstained by a single vice; in 1776 a whig, a Democrat in 1798, he jealously and unceasingly maintained the liberties of his Country and died as he had lived, an honest man and a Christian.

This stone lies in an inclosure, used as a pasture, though other stones, to members of the Seney family, show that it was used as a family graveyard as late as the year 1882.

In the old cemetery at "Meadow and Vale" are many stones. Some of the inscriptions here are:

Dowdail Thompson, son of Augustine Thompson Esq., born Sept. the 23rd, 1718; Died April ye 28th 1756, Aged 37 years.

Here Lyeth ye body of Augustine Thompson Esqr., who departed this Life ye 26 Day of February 1738, Aged 48 years.

Underneath this stone Lies Interred the Body of Mrs. Augustine Thompson, Wife of Ezehiel Forman Esquire and Daughter of Captain Thomas Marsh and Mary his wife. She was born the 14th day of April 1740 and Departed this Life the 21st of February 17, ——[?].

This stone is consecrated to the memory of the best of Mothers by her affectionate son Thomas Marsh Forman.

Here lies the Body of Mary, wife of Capt. Thomas Marsh and Daughter of Augustine Thompson Esq., who Departed this Life the 14th of June 1740, Aged 25 years.

On footstone: "Prepare to follow."

Here Lieth the Body of M. Ann Marsh, wife of Capt. Thomas Marsh and Daughter of Willm. Frisby Esq:, who Departed this life the 21st of April 1756, Aged 34 years.

To the Memory of Coln. John Thompson, who departed this life Sept. 7th, 1803, Æ. 63 years.

Sacred to the memory of Elizabeth Thompson, daughter of Dr. Wm. Murray and relict of Col. John Thompson, who died March 29th 1840, aged 27 years and 7 months.

"Let me die the death of the righteous: let my last end be like his."

John Keene of M., Born Nov. 28th, 1777; Died Jan'y 28th 1815.

Beneath this stone are interred the Remains of Doctor Samuel Thompson, who died on the 17th day of November 1799, Aged 51 years and 7 months.

Col. Samuel T. Harrison Died June 3rd, 1863, Aged 59 years.

"Blessed are the pure in heart for they shall see God."

In memory of George Anna H., Wife of W. H. Newnam and Daughter of W. L. B. Deford, Born March 5th 1845, Died April 16th, 1874.

In Memory of Margaretta, wife of W. H. Newnam and Daughter of Col. Saml. T. Harrison, Born Oct. 1, 1830, Died July 1, 1867. Aged 36 years and 9 months.

John A. Newnam Died July 4, 1860, Aged 5 months and 24 days.

Spencer Harrison Died May 27, 1865, in the 28th year of his age.
"Here the prisoner is at rest."

Susan F. Harrison Died Sept. 2, 1862, Aged 57 years.
"Return unto thy rest O my soul, for the Lord hath dealt Bountifully with thee."

At Crossly farm are two stones:

Ann Elizabeth, wife of John McKenny, who departed this life October 27th A. D. 1825, aged 21 years.
"All that are in the graves shall hear his voice and come forth."

Mary Ambrose, wife of John McKenny, who departed this life Oct. 31st A. D. 1836, In the 30th year of her age.
"There shall be a resurrection of the dead, both of the just and the unjust."

The present Wm. McKenny heirs, who own fifty-six farms, on several of which are graveyards, descend from one of the above. Wm. McKenny is buried on the old Goldsborough farm near Centreville, which came into his family through his wife.

At "Ripley," owned by Mr. James Brown, the oldest stones are inscribed as follows:

James Brown died Feb. 9, 1822, aged about 57 years.

Mary Ann, wife of James Brown, died suddenly in the garden June 5th 1827, Aged about 43 years.

Here calmly lie and sweetly sleep the cherished remains of Mary E. Tilden, who departed this life on the 7th Feb. 1837, aged 55 years. Leaving behind her a disconsolate husband, who pays this tribute to her memory to deplore her loss.

James Brown was a colonel in the war of 1812. Mrs. Mary E. Tilden was the sister of Col. James Brown, and mother of Mrs. Mary E. Leason and John Brown Tilden, who are also buried here. In the corner of the graveyard some of the Carmichaels are buried, but without stones.

"Round Top," the old Carmichael place, now owned by the Ford heirs, gives us this inscription:

Here lieth the Body of Mrs. Margaret Holt, wife of Mr. Arthur Holt and Daughter of William Carmichael Esq., who departed this life the 20th day of May 1767, Aged 26 years.

The following inscriptions are taken from the tombstones at Cloverfields Farm:

Anna Maria Hemsley, died 1790, aged 64 years.

Wm. Hemsley, died 1763, aged 33 years.

Anna Maria Lloyd, wife of Robert Lloyd and youngest daughter of the Hon. Richard Tilghman, in the 54 yr. of her age.

Sarah, second wife of Wm. Hemsley and 3rd daughter of Alexander Williamson, died 1794, aged 45 years.

Wm. Hemsley, died 1812, 76 yrs. old.

Anna Maria Lloyd, daughter of James Lloyd Esq. of Kent, and Elizabeth Tilghman, his wife. Born 1782; died Nov. 1808.

Maria Hemsley, wife of Wm. Hemsley, daughter of James Lloyd Esq. of Kent, and Elizabeth Tilghman his wife. Born 1784; died 1805.

Elizabeth Hemsley, wife of Philemon Hemsley, daughter of James Lloyd Esq. of Kent Co. Md. Born April 1784; died 22nd December 1808.

Wm. Hemsley, eldest son of Wm. & Henrietta Maria Hemsley. Born 1766; died 1825.

Henrietta Mariah Earle, wife of Thomas Earle and daughter of Wm. and Sarah Hemsley, born 10th December 1779; died 25 December 1821.

In Memory of Elizabeth, daughter of James and Elizabeth Tilghman. Born April 1783; died Aug. 1839.

St. Paul's is one of the original parishes, laid out by act of Assembly in 1692, and beneath the shade of its far-spreading oaks there are many ancient looking tombs. The spot is a most attractive one, but it has been impossible to get a full list of the old graves. The most ancient is David Coley's. He departed this life October 20, 1729. His epitaph is of the admonitory form, variants of which are to be found in England as early as the fourteenth century, while in France we have examples as early as the thirteenth.

> Behold & see now where I lye,
> As you are now so once was I
> As I am now, so must you be,
> Therefore prepare to follow me.

The inscription of one old tomb we are able to give in full:

Beneath this marble is the body of Jas. Tilghman Esqr., Who having faithfully performed the duties of a husband, a father & a citizen, Descended into the Grave at a mature age, In full hope of a happy Resurrection.

By the Public he was respected and by his numerous Friends and Relatives Esteemed and regretted; By his children, Honored, loved and lamented.

He died in Chester Town, August 27, 1793, In the 77 year of his Age.

St. Peter's, the first chapel of ease of St. Paul's parish, better known as the I. U. church, stands amidst graves of a later date. A monument has been erected there in recent years to Col. Philip Reed, a hero of the war of 1812, and the remains of his wife repose beside him. Emmanuel church, built about the year 1770 as a chapel of ease to I. U., after it became a separate parish, is in Chestertown, and the graves that once lay around it were removed to the public cemetery, laid out more than half a century ago.

A tablet in Emmanuel church reads.

Consecrate To the memory of a good Woman, Sarah, The truly beloved wife and highly esteemed Friend of Thomas Bedingfield Hands She was Pious without Hypocricy Virtuous without Affectation The dutiful Daughter, the endearing Wife The tender Parent And the kind innocent neighbor She lived thirty-three years, seventeen thereof in the Marriage state, and died Oct 5th 1754. Gentle Passenger Let the example of her Virtues The purity of her morals and the simplicity of her manners Stir thee up to the practice of the Same; That thy memory, like hers, may diffuse around a sweet smelling savour. Pos. 1757.

In the public cemetery, near Chestertown, are the following:

Sacred to the memory of Beddingfield Hands, who died on the 3rd of March 1821, aged 30 years.

Blessed are the dead who die in the Lord.

Sacred To The memory of Catherine Ringgold, Widow of Beddingfield Hands, And afterwards wife of Richard Ringgold. She was born on the 23rd of April 1782, And died on the 11th of Feby. 1849.

I shall be satisfied to rise in thy likeness.

In the Constable lot on the hillside is a very much broken slab to the memory of

Wm. S. Constable, who died Dec. 30, 1851, in the 45th year of his age.

Sacred to the memory of Susanna, Consort of William S. Constable and daughter of the late Thos. and C. Munemy of Baltimore, who departed this life Sept. 28th, 1834, in her 19th year.

Possessing every virtue that adorns, and endowed with every quality that endears, her memory will be affectionately cherished by all who knew her worth.

Wm. S. Constable married secondly in 1840, Catherine, the sister of his first wife. They had six children.

To the memory of John Constable, who died Feb. 1844, aged 78 years.

Christiana Constable, departed this life Jan. 13, 1849. Aged about 68 years.

In memory of Capt. Robert Constable, who departed this life Nov. 7th, 1833, Aged 47 years, 11 months, 10 days.

In memory of Mrs. E. A. Constable, Consort of Robert Constable, Departed this life Dec. 8th 1827.

It may be truly said: "For her to live was Christ, To die was gain."

Margaret Constable departed this life Oct. 7, 1821, Aged 63 years.

In the same lot is a stone to the memory of Maria Constable, who married Rev. James Hanson, and died *s. p.*

Mrs. Maria Hanson, who departed this life Sept. 18, in the year of our Lord 1845, in the 25th year of her age.

An iron railing incloses a lot containing three stones removed from the "Hall," one of the Hanson estates near Chestertown, all of later date than 1850. Mrs. Courtney Hanson, Edward Anderson Hanson and Mrs. Catherine Wroth, daughter of Geo. and Rebecca Hanson, are buried here. The lot was inclosed by Miss Lavinia Hanson.

Ann Chapman died March 13, 1838, aged 30 years.

Charles Caviller died Aug. 28th, 1815, aged 66 years.

Mary T., wife of James Beck, born Dec. 1, 1781, died August 11th 1844.

Mary T., wife of Francis Baker, born Nov. 11th, 1816; died Sept. 8, 1841.

John Bordley died Jan. 4th, 1701[?], aged 40.

Thomas Palmer Blakiston, son of John & Elizabeth Blakiston of Philadelphia, died Aug. 7th, 1825, aged 15 years.

Cary Clare Chambers, daughter of E. F. Chambers, born July 15th, 1832; died Aug. 28th, 1844.

Elizabeth C. Chambers, wife of Gen. Benjamin Chambers, born June 11th, 1762; died Dec. 27th, 1820.

Gen. Benj. Chambers, born Oct. 16th, 1749; died Jan. 10th, 1816.

"He served his Country with Fidelity in the war of 1776, in the war of 1812, and in various public offices, which he filled with honor to himself and usefulness to the Community, And at his death enjoyed the esteem and respect of all who knew him, The warmest affection of a beloved family, and the Consoling hopes of a Christian."

To the Memory of Thomas Ringgold Of Chestertown, Merchant, who died on the 1st. of April, 1772, in the 57th Year of his age, This marble is erected by His afflicted Widow.

By a steady Industry He acquired an ample fortune, With unblemished reputation; And his Death was a misfortune Not only to his Family, But to his friends, His neighbors and His Country.

Sacred to the memory of A good woman, Anna Maria Ringgold, The Widow of Thomas Ringgold Esqr. She died July 1794, In the 70th Year of her Age. Her unaffected piety was an example to all, And her virtues & the Innocency of her manners, Not only Endeared her to her Family & Friends, but secured to her The Love and esteem Of all who knew her.

Sacred to the Memory of Thomas Ringgold Junr. Esqr. of Chester Town, Mary Ringgold, his afflicted widow, has caused This Marble to be erected.

In His Public Life Independent & unbiased, He always Served his Country Faithfully. His Private Virtues were equal to His Public Character. The Affectionate Husband; The tender Parent and the Indulgent Master; a sincere Friend and the good Neighbor to all. Hence his Death became a Public as well as a Private loss. Obt. 26th October 1776, age 32.

Elizabeth, wife of Richard Ringgold, died Aug. 3rd. 1814, aged 38 years.

Richard, consort of Elizabeth Ringgold, died July 25th 1845, aged 65 years.

Mrs. Isabella Jane Richardson, died Oct. 22nd. 1800, aged 50 years.

Harriet Malvina Chapman Spencer, died Nov. 7th, 1844.

Elizabeth, wife of Isaac Spencer, died Dec. 17th, 1819, in her 44th year.

Isaac Spencer, died Oct. 21st. 1852, in his 62nd. year.

Absolom Sparks, born Oct. 12th, 1805, died Dec. 23, 1833.

Annette T., Harris W., and Polly, children of George & Mary Vickers, before 1850.

Wm. Harris born 1768, died Jan 28th, 1827.

Dr. Wm. Jones Clarke, born in Phila. Dec. 8th, 1796; died in Chestertown Sept. 1st. 1822.

Capt. James Craige died April 1795, aged 54 years.

John G. Gruber died June 2nd. 1834.

Isaac Hines born April 20, 1794; died July 16th, 1842.

Sarah R., wife of William Jacobs, died Jan. 29th, 1811, aged 22 years & 3 months.

Elizabeth Augusta Jones, wife of Rev. C. F. Jones D. D. & daughter of E. F. Chambers, born July 9th, 1820; died Nov. 1st. 1850.

Arthur M. Merritt died March 9th 1849, aged 46.

Wm. J. Maslin died Oct. 1826.

Martha J., wife of James Alfred Pearce, born April 13, 1807; died March 8th, 1845.

Thomas Worrell born Feb. 14th, 1768; died Sept 30, 1825.

Elizabeth G. Worrell, born Sept. 25th, 1794; died Feb. 17th, 1846.

Amy Amanda Ware, daughter of Rev. Thos. & Barbara Ware, died Aug. 22nd. 1823, aged 19 years and 9 months.

Anthony Banning died Dec. 27th 1787, in the 47th year of his age. This tomb was erected by his daughter Catherine Banning.

On the Whitehouse farm, owned by Mrs. Walker, this inscription is on a flat slab, fallen from its supports. The graveyard, a neglected spot inclosed by an osage orange hedge, lies about a stone's throw from the house.

Sacred to the memory of Simon Wilmer, who died Oct. 19th, 1798, in the 49th year of his age; and Ann, his wife, who died 3rd. of April 1789, Aged 43; also to Mary, his wife, who died at Alexandria D. C. March 29th, 1831, Aged 68.

"The hoary head is a crown of glory, if it be found in the way of righteousness. I know that my Redeemer liveth and that he shall stand at the latter day upon the earth And though after my skin worms destroy this body, yet in my flesh shall I see God. Prepare to meet thy God."

Shrewsbury church was already standing in 1701, when its records begin. One of its early vestrymen was Col. Edward Blay, who in 1709 gave to the parish two acres of ground, where the present edifice stands, which was added to later by the munificence of his great-grandson, Dr. William Blay Tilden. This churchyard is now beautifully laid out with walks and shrubbery. It contains many old graves. Among the inscriptions may be noted:

Mr. William Gough, who departed this life on the 1st. day of October 1795, aged 58 years.

In memory of James Briscoe, who departed this life Nov. 24th 1800, aged 53 years.

"An honest man's the noblest work of God."

Here lye the bodies of Jervis and Hannah, son and daughter of Henery Spencer, who departed this life Feb. 10th 1742-3; Jervis aged 13, Hannah aged 16.

> Farewell our friends and parents dear
> We are not dead but sleepeth here
> Our debts is paid, our graves you see
> Prepare yourselves to follow we.

Here lieth the body of Anthony Cameron, who departed this life Sept. 14th, 1751, aged 68 years; and of Joseph, his son, who departed this life Oct. the 4th, 1749, Aged 34 years.

In Memory of James Wallace, who died Jan'y ye 29th, 1740, Aged about 47 years, and John Wallace, who died Jan'y ye 7th, 1746, aged about 45 years, also Robert Wallace, who died Jan. ye 29th, 1730, aged about 23 years.

Sacred to the Memory of Mary M. Blackiston, wife of Thomas M. Blackiston, who departed this life April 10th, 1845, Aged 56 years 4 months and 9 days.

Sacred to the memory of James Blackiston, who departed this life on the 12th of September, 1816, aged 72 years, 2 months and 2 days.

> O native reason
> We own thy matchless sway
> Thou canst direct our course—
> When Virtue points the way—
> To honour and Benevolence,
> To Love and Charity.
> My friend is now no more
> He trod this thornless road.
> His mind was virtue's residence
> And Honour's pure abode.

In memory of Colin Ferguson born in 1780, died suddenly on the 11 June 1849, Aged 69 years.

> Leaves have their time to fall
> And flowers to wither at the North wind's breath,
> And stars to set; but ah!
> Thou hast all seasons for thine,
> O Death.

Ann Alethea, wife of Dr. J. E. Marsh, died Sept. 15th, 1846, aged 22 years, 8 months and 4 days.

Raymond Biddle died Nov. 13, 1843, in the 62nd. year of his age.

In memory of Almon Gunnison, a native of New Hampshire, who died in Georgetown roads, Md., on the 6th day of October 1842, in the 25th year of his age.

In Memory of Eliza Pearce, wife of William Pearce, who departed this life April 12, 1821, aged 28 years.

Sacred to the memory of McCall Medford, who departed this life on the 27th day of Nov., 1825, in the 54 year of his age.

In memory of Mr. Edward Freeman, who departed this life May 15th 1791, aged 35 years and 7 months.

The decease of this amiable man is a source of deep affliction to his family and friends.

Here lyeth interred the body of Daniel Bryan, Late of Kent County in Maryland, Merchant, who departed this life on the 29th day of September, 1754, aged 58 years.

In memory of Mr. John Corrie, who departed this life Feb'y the 19th 1798, aged 49 years.

In memory of Elizabeth Latham, who departed this life November 18th 1795, in the 63rd year of her age.

This stone designates the spot where the remains of John Latham are interred, who departed this life on the 11th Jan'y 1811, in the 19th year of his age.

This stone designates the spot where the remains of Eliza, daughter of Geo. and Elizabeth Medford, are interred. She departed this life on the 1st of Oct. 1826, in the 30th year of her age.

She was a dutiful daughter, an affectionate sister, a beneficent neighbor and a firm believer in the evidences of the Christian Religion.

This stone designates the spot . . . Elizabeth Medford, relict of George Medford, who departed this life on the 9th of July 1827, in the 61st year of her age.

She was an affectionate wife and parent, a kind Mistress to her servants, a good neighbor and a general philanthropist, And a confirmed Christian.

Sacred to the memory of Mrs. Mary Yeates, Consort of Col. Donaldson Yeates, who departed this life Dec. 25th 1809, in the 58th year of her age.

In memory of Ebenezer Reyner, who died Jan'y 24th 1748, aged 51 years, 10 months; also Margaret, his wife, who departed this life May 16th 1748, aged 30 years 11 months.

> Death thou hast conquered.
> We by thy darts are slain;
> But Christ shall conquer thee
> and we shall live again.

My friend Thomas H. Wethered, aged 22 years, 8 mos. and 2 days.

Sacred to the memory of Samuel Wethered, who departed this life Feb. 12, 1829, in the 56 year of his age.

Eliza Y. Wethered, wife of Samuel Wethered and daughter of Donaldson and Mary Yeates, died 5th Jan'y 1825, in the 41st year of her age.

In memory of James Murray Spencer, who was born Dec. 27th 1810, and died April 28th 1846, Aged 36 years.

In memory of Coll. Wm. Spencer, who died March 1821, Aged 56 years.

Sacred to the memory of Eliza Sophia, wife of the Rev. John Owen, Rector, Born April 18th 1806; Died in the Lord April 22nd 1849. Erected by the ladies of the Parish.

Sacred to the memory of Caroline Pleasants, Daughter of Nathaniel Wattles Esq., and wife of the Rev. Chas. E. Pleasants. This monument is erected by the ladies of the parish, in testimony of their regard for her great moral worth, her purity of character and unbounded benevolence of heart.

She was born in Alexandria D. C. July 26th, 1815 and died in this county Oct. 16th, 1841.

> As daughter, sister parent, friend and wife
> A noble pattern of the Christian life.

Here lyeth the body of John Daniel, son of Mr. Joseph Daniel of Warrington, in the County of Lancaster; died April 18th 1731, in the 41st year of his age.

Erected by C. Pearce to the memory of her Beloved Grandmother, Mrs. Catherine R. Forrester, and to that of the Rev. Geo. Wm. Forrester, Rector of Shrewsbury Parish, over which he presided forty years. Distinguished for their piety, their virtues and their talents, Their lives were devoted to their duties, and they now rest together in humble Hope of a blissful Eternity.

In memory of Jennet Black who departed this life April 22, 1774, aged 32 years.

Sacred to the memory of James Black M. D., who departed this life Oct. 27th 1804, aged 32 years.

Margaret Wilson Black, relict of the late Doctor James Black, who departed this life Sept. 7th, 1815, aged 33 years.

In memory of Susan Henrietta Wallis, who departed this life Dec. 15th, 1827, aged 21 years.

Col. Edward Blay and his wife, Madam Ann Blay, are buried in a private graveyard at Blay's Range, about one mile northwest of Shrewsbury church. In the vault containing their remains, is a tablet with the following inscription:

Within this enclosure are the remains of the following named persons: Col. Edward Blay & wife of England; William Blay (only son of Edward

& wife) and wife Isabella, daughter of Col. Pearce, with their issue: Rachel, Catherine, Isabella, Edward & William.

Rachel Blay & Peregrine Brown of England, her husband, and their son Peregrine; her second husband Aquilla Pearce & their daughter Martha.

Catherine & John Tilden and their children: Isabella & Richard Wethered of London, her husband, and their children William, John, Samuel & John [William excepted].

This inscription and the enclosure done by the direction of John Wethered, who died on the 21st. of February 1822, in the 77th year of his age.

There are no stones with inscriptions in the graveyard. Another worthy, associated for many years with Shrewsbury parish, was Gen. John Cadwalader, a native of Philadelphia and a soldier of the Revolution. Until the end of the last century a fine marble altar tomb stood in the churchyard to his memory, "placed there," according to the inscription, "by his affectionate children" to mark the spot where his remains were deposited. His Philadelphia descendants, however, have since had it removed to Laurel Hill cemetery on the banks of the Schuylkill, and in this monument Kent county has lost a valued legacy. Gen. John Cadwalader departed this life February 11, 1786, aged 44 years, 1 month and 1 day. The epitaph on his tomb written by his violent political enemy, Thos. Paine, speaks of his character as a soldier and statesman, of his inflexible patriotism, his heart "incapable of deceiving," his nice sense of honor, his qualities as a friend and his domestic virtues.

These inscriptions are found at "Spencer Place," on Grey's Inn creek:

Sacred to the memory of Mrs. Martha (Wickes) Spencer, consort of Richard Spencer, who departed this life, March 13, 1818, in the 69th year of her age, after living happily together 47 years.

Sacred to the memory of Richard Spencer, who departed this life April 25, 1825, in the 93rd. year of his age, after living a happy and exemplary life.

Richard Spencer, the son of Richard and Martha (Wickes) Spencer, departed this life February 19th, 1836, in the 56th year of his age.

Sophia Spencer, consort of Richard Spencer, departed this life June 11, 1826.

Martha Sophia Spencer, the daughter of the second Richard Spencer of Kent County, Maryland, died at Columbus, Geo. June 1838, in the 19th year of her age.

St. Paul's churchyard, St. John's parish, Hillsborough, in Caroline county, contains these two stones:

James H. Barton born March 15th, 1819; died April 21st 1845.

Mary E. Seth Holt, wife of Dr. John H. Holt, born March 3rd, 1811; died June 27th, 1843.

In a field back of the main business streets are some well-preserved memorials to members of the Tillotson family.

John Tillotson died 5th day of August 1853, aged 29 years. He was a kind husband, an honest man; to love him was only to know him.

William Tillotson Esq., born Nov. 14th, 1748; died Sept. 17th, 1810.

In the cemetery of Denton lies the body of a centenarian, Nathan Trifett, who died October 15, 1873, aged 104 years.

The oldest inscription in the Methodist churchyard is to the memory of Hannah M. Numbers, wife of Thomas Numbers, who died May 26, 1850, aged 36 years.

The Catholic cemetery is also of comparatively recent date, the earliest tombstones being inscribed to the memory of Elizabeth G. Collins, daughter of Gen. William Potter, who died June 15, 1850, aged 57 years; Joseph Richardson, born June 14, 1770, died January 16, 1848; Elizabeth G. Richardson died July 29, 1842, aged 52 years, 4 months and 4 days and Elizabeth Turner, daughter of John Griffith in Dorchester county, Md., born March 3, 1770, died September 29, 1841. Her first husband was James Ewing of Caroline county, Md., after whose death she married Jesse Turner of Kent county, Delaware, whom she also survived. Monument erected by her son Robert Ewing of Philadelphia, Pa.; Elizabeth Whitney, wife of Frank Whitney, born December, 1747; died October 28, 1828, ends the list.

CHAPTER X

BEFORE Talbot county was forced to cede a portion of its territory to Queen Anne's, it was divided into three flourishing parishes. These were St. Paul's or "Old Chester," St. Peter's or "Whitemarsh" and St. Michael's of which Old Christ Church is the present representative. The early church of Old Chester is now no more, and all signs of its churchyard have long since been obliterated, but in the town of Centreville, about two miles distant, stands the present St. Paul's, interesting on account of its many memorials to the Earle family. Whitemarsh church had a longer lease of life, and as it stood for about two centuries in the same locality, the tombs of many generations of parishioners remained about it, after the tide of settlement had swept in other directions, and left no one to worship within its walls. In the year 1897, however, its doom was sealed; for while efforts were being made to clean up its neglected graveyard, the old church caught fire and a portion of its brick walls tottered and fell, leaving only a mass of charred ruins. Some of the monuments near it suffered in its fall, among them that of Robert Morris, father of the Revolutionary worthy of the same name. It consisted of a fine slab mounted on marble supports and was broken in too many pieces to be restored. In 1898 its condition was reported to one of Mr. Robert Morris' descendants, Mrs. Charles C. Harrison of Philadelphia, and through the agency of the Memorial Committee, a local stonecutter was engaged to make a new slab like the first, and to copy the lettering from the broken bits, which was done. The inscription reads as follows:

In Memory of Robert Morris, a Native of Liverpool In Great Britain, Late a Merchant at Oxford in this Province.

Punctual Integrity influenced his Dealings, Principles of Honour governed his Actions. With an uncommon Degree of Sincerity, He despised Artifice and Dissimmulation. His friendship was firm, candid and valuable, His charity frequent, secret and well adapted. His Zeal for the Public Good, active and useful. His Hospitality was enhanced by his Conversation, Seasoned with cheerful Wit and a sound Judgement.

A salute from the Cannon of a Ship, The Wad fracturing his Arm, Was the Signal by which he departed, Greatly lamented as he was esteemed, In the fortieth year of his Age On the 12 day of July M. D. C. C. L.

In the old churchyard lie the remains of the Rev. Daniel Maynadier, rector of St. Peter's parish from 1717 to 1745. He was very old at the time of his death, and the generally accepted tradition that he was a Huguenot, driven to this country from France by the revocation of the Edict of Nantes (1685), is worthy of belief. A singular story is told of his family. His wife, after a brief illness, died and was buried with rather unusual haste. The worthy man, overcome by grief, retired early, but was aroused from his slumbers shortly before midnight, by a knocking at the front door. Imagine his feelings when upon opening it there stood his wife, faint and terrified, but alive and in the flesh! She had been hastily coffined, without the removal of a valuable ring, and one of the attendants, aware of the fact, had exhumed the body just after nightfall, for the purpose of robbing it. But the ring clung to the finger and an effort was made to sever the joint. Blood flowed, the corpse groaned, moved and regained consciousness, and the would-be robber of the dead fled in terror from the scene. The lady, thus happily saved from the grave, made her way through the darkness to the desolate home whence she had been carried a few hours before, and lived for many years afterwards.

The tombs remaining in Whitemarsh churchyard bear the following inscriptions:

In Memory of Thomas Goldsborough, who departed this life on the 11th day of May 1804, Aged 29 years.

He found the Savior in his early youth.
He loved his precepts and espoused the truth,
Careless of all the world calls grand and good,
A way-mark to the realms of bliss he stood.
His happy spirit, wishing all to rise
And go with him to Manshions in the skies,
From lasting heavenly bliss was bid remove
To the full fountain of redeeming love.

In Memory of Mrs. Rachel Goldsborough, who departed this life on the 16th day of Jan'y 1815, in the 60th year of her age.

Twenty-five years have rolled their suns around
Since the rich pearl of heavenly grace she found.
Firm as a rock against the waves she stood,
A steadfast witness of redeeming blood.
When death appeared he found her on the wing;
Death had disarmed the monster of his sting.
In holy rapture closed her mortal days
While every breath was love or joy or praise.

Sacred to the memory of Elizabeth, Consort of Thomas Parrott, who departed this life May the 23rd A. D. 1816, in the 42nd year of her age.

William Harrison Jr. Born July 8th 1780 and Died Nov. 29th, 1827.

In memory of Richard W. Thompson, a native of Dublin, Ireland, who departed this life Oct. 12th, 1826, in the 51st year of his age.

In memory of John Sawyer, son of Wm. and Rebecca, and consort of Alice Sawyer, who departed this life May 21st 1825, Aged 58 years.

In Memory of Mr. James Kennedy, who departed this life Septr 27th 1787, aged 39 years.

"In sure and stedfast hope to die
And claim his mansion in the sky.
Hear, here his faith laid down
The cross exchanging for a crown.
He knew and felt his sins forgiven
And found the calm[?] of his heaven."

The above verse is so nearly obliterated, that all lapses of continuity must be excused.

Thomas Bullitt Departed this life Octr. 11th 1821, In the 23rd year of His Age.

To the Memory of Thomas James Bullitt, who departed this life 25th November 1840, Aged 77 years. By his daughter E. H. Hayward.

Mary Bullitt, the wife of Thomas J. Bullitt, departed this life on the 24th Feb'y 1812, Aged 55 years.

To the memory of Jeremiah Nichols, Son of The Rev. Mr. Henry Nichols, who departed this life Oct. 8th 1753, Aged Forty years, Six months and sixteen Days. This tomb is Dedicated by His Sorrowful Relict Deborah Nichols.

Here lieth Elizabeth Nichols, Daughter of Jeremiah Nichols and Deborah his wife, who departed this life Sept. 1747.

In memory of Mary MacCallow [MacCallum?], who died 11th day of August 1773, Aged about 30 years.

Sarah Galt, obit Sept 26, 1808.

Here lieth the body of Elizabeth, wife of Philip Walker, who departed this life March 19, 1755, in the 36th year of her age.

Thos. Richardson Merch't, 1728? [Inscription effaced.]

John Thompson, Merchant, Died March 14, 1742. [Inscription illegible.]

Here lieth the body of John H——? Taylor of Talbot Co., who departed this life Mar. 23rd, 1797, Aged 47.

Rachel James, D.A.U.G.H.T.E.R of L. Booker, Died 17 day of June 770, age 31 years, The wife of Alex. James.

The late Mr. Mulliken is quoted as saying that Lambert Booker, the father of Rachel, as above, died in 1763 and requested to be buried at Whitemarsh, between the two doors, but Mr. Mulliken added that he did not know whether this was done.

On the Talbot shore of Wye, about a mile above where it pours its waters into Miles river, may be found, amid tangled vines, weeds and marsh grass, a gravestone, now nearly submerged in the oozy soil, bearing this inscription:

Here lyeth immured ye bodye of Francis Butler, Gent., son of Rhoderick Butler, Gent., who was unfortunately drowned in St. Michael's River the 3rd. Mar. 1689, aged 42 years or thereabout. Momento Mori.

Francis Butler, who is buried here, was elevated to the post of high sheriff of Talbot county, shortly after his arrival in Maryland, but lived but a few months to enjoy the honors of his position.

Robert Morris, senior, is designated on his tombstone as a "merchant at Oxford." This center still keeps its name, and at "Plinhimmon," an old estate whose beautiful family burying ground has been given to the people of Oxford as a public cemetery, is a monument erected to the memory of Mrs. Tench Tilghman. The same serves as a cenotaph to her husband. The inscriptions are:

To Mrs. Anna Maria Tilghman. The affection and veneration of a daughter and grandson have caused them to erect this monument to Anna Maria Tilghman, daughter of the Hon. Matthew Tilghman and widow of Lt. Col. Tilghman.

Her pure character, combining every christian grace and virtue, attracted the devoted love of her family connections and the admiration and esteem of all who knew her. Born July 17th 1755, Died Jan. 13th, 1845.

Tench Tilghman Lt. Col. in the Continental Army, and aid-de-camp of Washington, who spoke of him thus: "He was in every action in which the main army was concerned. A great part of the time he refused to receive pay. While living, no man could be more esteemed, and since dead, none more lamented. No one had imbibed sentiments of greater friendship for him than I had done. He left as fair a reputation as ever belonged to a human character." Died April 18th, 1786, aged 42 years.

Colonel Tilghman died in Baltimore and is not buried near his wife. He was interred at Old St. Paul's cemetery on Lombard street, but his epitaph may as well be given here:

In memory of Col. Tench Tilghman, who Died April 18th 1786, In the 42nd. year of his age, very much lamented. He took an early and active part In the great contest that secured The Independence of The United States of America. He was an Aid-de-camp to His Excellency, General Washington, Commander-in-chief of the American armies; And was honored with his friendship and confidence. And He was one of those whose merits were distinguished, And Honorably rewarded by the Congress. But still more to his Praise, He was a good man.

The inscriptions at "Peach Blossom" are:

In Memory of Elizabeth Goldsborough who died the 2nd Day of Octr. 1746, Aged 36 years, and of Greenbery, Henrietta Maria, William and Elizabeth Her children, this Erected by their most Affectionate and Sorrowful Husband and Father William Goldsborough.

Here is deposited the Body of the Hon. Wm. Goldsborough Esqr., who died the 21st of Sep. 1760. Aged 51 years.

He was sometimes a Member of the Lord Proprietary's Council and one of the Judges of the Provincial Court and was Justly Esteemed a Faithful

Councillor, an upright Judge, an Honest man and a good Christian. To his Memory This Stone is Inscribed by Henrietta Maria, his Widow.

To the memory of George Robins, Gent., who died December 5th 1742, aged 44 years. Henrietta Maria, His widow Dedicated this stone.

Robins Chamberlaine, Son of James Lloyd and Henrietta Maria Chamberlaine, died the 22nd day of April 1773, aged 4 years, 7 months and 8 days.

At "Plaindealing" we find the following inscriptions:

In Memory of Col. Thomas Chamberlaine Of Talbot County, Eldest son of Samuel and Henrietta Maria Chamberlaine, who died May 13, 1764, Aged 33 years. This stone is erected by his Sorrowful Widow, Susanna Chamberlaine.

Underneath lieth intered the Body of Mrs. Henrietta Maria Chamberlaine, late wife of Mr. Samuel Chamberlaine and eldest daughter of Col. James Lloyd of Talbot County. She Departed this life on the 29th Day of March 1748, Aged thirty Seven Years, Two Months and three Days.

Several stones mark the graves of members of the Hayward family at "Locust Grove," and the following inscriptions are found:

In memory of Elizabeth R., wife of Barclay Haskins and daughter of Thomas and Mary Hayward, who died March 17th 1845, Aged 36 years.
"These are they which came out of great tribulations, and have washed their robes and made them white in the blood of the Lamb." Rev. 7, 14.
"Blessed are the dead who die in the Lord."

Thomas Hayward Esq. departed this life July 3rd. 1833, Aged 66 years, 8 months and 26 days. This tribute of love is dedicated to his memory by his wife Mary Hayward.

If we believe that Jesus died and rose again, even so, them also which sleep in Jesus, will God bring with him.

Geo. Robins Hayward Esquire, departed this Life Dec. 19th, 1811, Aged 44 years and 3 months. This tribute of love is dedicated to his memory by his wife Margaret Hayward.

>Gentell Readers
>Be not Slothful but Followers
>of those who through faith and
>patience inherit the promises.
>"Life is short, Eternity how long."

At "Orem's Delight" is an inscription:

In memory of Elizabeth, wife of Jas. Wrightson, Who died Dec. 24th 1842, In the 54th year of her age.

At "Belleville," Oxford Neck, on land held for many

years by the Bozmans and Kerrs, is an old graveyard where the only monument reported, is to the memory of Hon. John Leeds Kerr, senator from 1841 to 1845. He was the son of David and Rachel Leeds Bozman Kerr, who together with John Leeds Bozman, the Maryland historian, are also buried there.

"Mt. Pleasant" was the Nichols' homestead, but here there is only one stone left to mark where there was once a graveyard.

"Hope," another old estate belonging first to the Lloyds and then to the Tilghmans, had its ancient graveyard also; but I have to trust to memory here, being under the impression that like so many other private cemeteries, which have passed to strangers, the ashes of the dead have been removed to some public cemetery for protection.

Opposite Oxford is the "Isthmus," for many years the home of the Banning family. Jeremiah, Anthony and Henry Banning were born there, and it became Jeremiah's home in later years. Their father was James Banning and at his death their mother married Nicholas Goldsborough, who proved to be a good stepfather. At the time of Robert Morris' tragic death in 1750, Jeremiah was a boy of seventeen. The event made an indelible impression on his mind and in the journal he left behind him, all his early recollections and those of later years are graphically depicted, giving interesting information about the locality in which he lived.

At the "Isthmus" is one solitary grave to the memory of Susanna Banning, probably a descendant of Capt. Jeremiah Banning. She died July 4, 1851.

At "Pleasant Valley" is the following inscription:

Here lyes Interr'd the Body of Richard Carter, son of Thomas Carter of Kirkly Wisk, in the County of York In Great Britain, Yeoman, who departed this Life the 4th day of March 1708, in the Seaventy First Year of his age.

"Grosses" was so named after one of its owners, Jacob Grosses. It belonged to the Lloyds before 1735, afterwards becoming the property of the late Dr. Charles Tilghman. Two inscriptions are found there:

Here lyeth the body of Anna Maria Goldsborough, daughter of William M. and Margaret Tilghman, born the third of November 1737, and departed this life February the 4, 1768.

Henrietta Maria Tilghman, Daughter of William and Margaret Tilghman, Who departed this life on the 21st Day of October 1787, Aged 38 years and three days. As a small tribute to her memory this stone is inscribed by her affectionate sister Mary Tilghman.

Several well-grown holly trees, in a cultivated field, at the Adkins place, direct one to the spot where lie the following:

Here lies the Body of John Edmonson, who died June 1st, 1841, Aged 68 years. He had the esteem of all who knew him and he deserved it.

Here also is buried his only child, Anne Harvey Edmonson, Born June 27th 1802; Died Sept. 1st, 1824.

The above inscriptions are on one stone, which is broken in five pieces.

Here lies the body of Lucretia Teackle, who was born October 28th 1766, and died June 5th, 1826.

She lived respected and died lamented. This stone is erected to her memory by her affectionate children.

Here lies also the body of Rachel Teackle, daughter of Severn & Lucretia Teackle, Born July 26th, 1788; Died Aug. 3rd 1828.

On a farm in the Bay Hundred district, owned of late years by the heirs of Mr. James Hazlett and once known as "Cromwell," but now as "Delmore-end," is the tomb of Thomas Impey. "He was born at Delmore-end in Hartfordshire. He Died 9th October 1686."

On account of its age and of the prominent people buried there and also because of the beauty of its tombs and their quaint inscriptions, the old Lloyd burying ground at "Wye," the home of the Lloyds since 1660, is the most interesting in Maryland. The family badge of a lion rampant, appears on variously carved shields. The crest, also a lion, sometimes

THE GRAVE-YARD AT WYE HOUSE, TALBOT COUNTY

surmounts a helmet with elaborate mantling, and at others is wanting.

Col. Philemon Lloyd, one of our well-known dignitaries, was buried here in 1685, his wife, a namesake of the unfortunate Queen Henrietta Maria, following him in 1697. Three daughters, all of whom died before 1695, are buried here also. The oldest stone in this graveyard is that of Capt. James Strong, of Stepney, in the county of Middlesex. Above the inscription is a coat of arms where palmer shells and crosslets fitchee are conspicuous. This stone is cracked in six places and restored. The inscription reads:

Here lyeth Interred the Body of Capt. James Strong of Stepney in the County of Midd: Marrine, second son of Capt. Petter Strong. Departed this life y 8 day of Jan. 1684, A . . . yeare 2 months XI dayes. Le . . . one Son . . . on . . . Daught . . .
"The memory of ye . . . st is Blessed"

The tomb of Madam Henrietta Maria Lloyd shows the Neale coat of arms impaled with that of Lloyd on one lozenge, and impaled with that of Bennett on another. It consists of a fesse with two crescents above and one or two hunting horns below. On the Bennett half of the shield are three half lions heraldically placed. The same appears on the broken tombstone of Roger Newman, mentioned elsewhere, where it is impaled with the Lloyd lion. Zieber, in his book on *Heraldry in America*, erroneously gives the name as Newberry. The connection between Roger Newman and these two families, if it ever existed, is now lost to posterity.

The Lloyd inscriptions are as follows; brackets indicating the portions that are illegible:

Here li's inter'd the Body of Coll Philemon Lloyd, the son of E. Lloyd & Alice his wife, who died the 22d of June 1685 in the 39th year of his age leaving 3 sons and 7 daughters All by his beloved wife Henrietta Maria.
"[No] more than this the Author says
[B]ut leaves his life to speak his praise."
Memento Mori.

This stone is in three pieces restored.

> Shee that now takes her Rest within this tomb
> Had Rachell's face and Lea's fruitful womb
> Abigall's wisdom Lydea's faithful heart
> With Martha's care and Mary's better part.

Who Died The 21st Day of M . . . Dom. 1697, Aged 50 years . . . Months 23 Dayes. To whose Memory Richard (Bennett) Dedicates this Tomb.

Most of the lines are incomplete at the end, but have been filled in here to give the sense.

Jane, Mary and Elizabeth, daughters of the above, died respectively in 1690, 1690 and 1694.

Philemon Lloyd, son of Colonel Lloyd, was one of the council, and was secretary of this province. The inscription on his stone is:

Here lieth Interr'd the Body of Philemon Loyd Esq: son of Coll: Philemon Loyd and Henrietta Maria his wife, who departed this life the 19th of March 1732 in the 60th Year of his Age.

The stone of Col. Edward Lloyd has been broken in eight pieces. It has been restored, three bits being lost. The inscription reads:

Here Lieth ye Body of the Honourable Collnl Edward Lloyd, Eldest son of C[o]lnl Philemon Lloyd and [H]enrietta Maria his wife, [who] was born ye 7 of Febry 1670 and [di]ed March ye 20, 1718. He had by [h]is wife Sarah, 5 Sons and one Daughter, all living Except one Son. He served his Country in severall Honourable Stations, both Civil and Military, and was of ye Council many years.

Here lieth Interr'd the Body of Edward Lloyd Eldest son of . . . Edward Lloyd and S . . . his Wife, who died the 14th day of Feb . . . ua . . . Aged two years five Mon . . . And three days.

Here lieth interr'd the Body of Philemon Lloyd, second son of Coll Edward Lloyd and Sarah his wife, who died March the 5th 1729, Aged 20 years 11 months and 5 days.

> When Parents by their tender care and pains
> Have rais'd their Offspring to maturity,
> And then expect to reap the Joyfull Gains
> Of their Assistance and Posterity,
> Grim death Appears and crops ye blooming flowers
> And turns their Joyfull hopes to Sudden Grief.
> Against this frail uncertain State of ours,
> What thoughts can Shield or give us some relief?

> Why, only this that God's entirely good
> And governs all things by his providence;
> Then all that happens must be understood
> His goodness and his wisdom did dispens.
> Tho' we frail Creatures cannot comprehend
> The great designs of his Eternal Will,
> Yet we may Certainly on this depend,
> That all is for our good and nothing ill.

Here Lyes Interr'd the Body of Mr. Iames Lloyd, who was born August the 14th 1715; Died September the 14th 1738.

> If Youth and Beauty, Virtue and good sense
> Could guard against the fatal stroke of Death,
> He'd longer liv'd and not Departed hence
> Till far in Age, and Nature wanted Breath;
> But so it is, that human Life was giv'n
> To make a short Probation here on Earth,
> That we might qualifie ourselves for heaven
> And there Enjoy a new Eternal Birth;
> Then he who soonest near Perfection Draws
> And fitts himself for Vast Eternity,
> Is soonest eas'd from human Nature's Laws
> And in Eternall Bliss is Ever Free.

Here lieth intered the remains of Captain Richard Lloyd, who was born the 13th of August 1750, and departed this life Septr. 22d, 1787.

Here lie interred The remains of Mrs Ann Lloyd, wife of the Honble Col: Edward Lloyd, who Departed this life the 1st of May 1769, Aged 48 years.

Here lie interred The remains of Hon Col. Edward Lloyd, who departed this life The 27th of January 1770, Aged 59 years.

Here lieth intered the remains of Colonel Edward Lloyd, who was born the 15th of November 1744, and departed this life the 8th of July 1796.

Here lieth intered the remains of Elizabeth Lloyd, who was born the 17th of March 1750, and departed this life the 17th of Feb'y 1825.

Here lieth intered the remains of Col. Edward Lloyd, who was born the 22d of July 1779, and departed this life the 2d of June 1834.

St. Luke's, Wye, has its history and its traditions also; among the latter is one to the effect that a colonial rector is buried beneath the chancel, his name having been forgotten. A few years ago, the Rev. Mr. Batte, then in charge of the parish, found pinned to the altar cloth a scrap of paper with the following words:

May 12th, 1897.
The remains buried under this altar are those of the Rev. Christopher Wilkinson—I am a descendant of the above—

Mrs. A. C. Taylor,
Ellicott City, Md.

Another rector, buried at St. Luke's, was the Rev. Elisha Riggs, whose epitaph reads as follows:

Beneath this stone lie the remains of that eminent & faithful servant of God, the Rev. Elisha Riggs, Rector of this parish from A. D. 1797 until his death, Feb. 6th, 1804. "The Memory of the just is blessed."

A large vacant area, under the trees beside the church, is pointed out as the oldest part of the burying ground, but there is not a stone or mound visible. In the newer portion are lots inclosed with iron railings, containing memorials of a comparatively recent date, on which are inscribed the names of Davis, Rose and Davison. The oldest inscription discovered is:

To the memory of Mary, wife of Greenberry Griffin, who departed this life February 20th 1821, In the 48th year of her age.

The church, a venerable structure built as a chapel of ease to St. Peter's parish, is near Wye Mills. In the same neighborhood is the Coppage place where the remains of an old graveyard have been reported. Just over the border in Queen Anne's are two old Paca places and a Carmichael place, all of which have family burying grounds. In one of these, William Paca, the "Signer," and his wife are said to be buried, but the stones, if there be any, are covered with periwinkle and wild honeysuckle, and the inscriptions are inaccessible.

Underneath Christ church, St. Michael's, lie the remains of a former rector of the parish, the Rev. Henry Nicols. The stone marking his grave shows a Latin inscription, as follows:

Jacent Exuviæ H. Nicols, A. M., Collegii Jesu Ox: Olim Socii; Hujus Ecclesiæ Pastoris, Indignissimi per annos 41. Nati Aprilis 3, 1678. salvam fac Animam Christe, Pro meritis tuis. Vixit Annos 70. Sal fatuum Conculcate. Hæc ipse jussit insculpenda.

There is a very old marble tablet on the wall of the church, inscribed with the name of John Chamberlaine, who departed this life, June 1, 1721, in the 31st year of his life. It also bears his coat of arms; a shield on a lion skin surrounded by eight stars.

There are, or were, in 1871, three old tombstones at the rear of the church. Two of them are broad, flat slabs, one being to the memory of Tamberlain Davis, who died February 20, 1731, in the 33d year of his age, and about whom not even a tradition is left; the other to Mr. James Edge of Talbot county, Gent., who departed this life the sixth day of January, 1759, aged 47 years. On the third stone appears simply the name Thomas Edge, Obt. 15 Sept. 1742, Æt 28 years.

Capt. James Murphy, who perpetuated the title of one of the first tracts of land laid out in the county, died in 1698 and was buried on Rich Neck, a few miles from St. Michael's. The exact wording of the inscription on his tomb has not been obtained.

Other inscriptions at "Rich Neck" are:

In Memory of Mrs. Margaret Ward, Daughter of Coll. Phill. Lloyd, who died September the 12th A. Dom. 1747.

Hon. Matthew Tilghman Ward Esqr., who not long before his Death Composed the following Epitaph:

> This was the Second Partner of my Bed
> With whom a long and happy Life I've lead.
> Tho' without Children to Assist in years,
> Yet free from Parents' cares and Parents' fears.
> In love and Friendship all our Years were spent,
> In moderate Wealth and free from want, content,
> Our pious Souls, with pious thoughts inspired
> To worship God and profit man; desired
> Religious laws and customs to pursue,
> Not slighting old ones nor too fond of new,
> But chusing such as since they first began,
> Best serv'd ye Praising God & common Good of man.

To the Memory of Matthew Tilghman Esqr, Who Departed this life on the 4th Day of May 1790, In the 73d year of His Age. Also of Ann Tilghman His Wife, Who followed Him on the 15th Day of March

1794, in the 72d year of Her Age. This Monument is Inscribed By their Surviving Children As the last tribute of their Affection And Respect.

In Memory of Matthew Ward Tilghman, Eldest Son of Matthew Tilghman and Ann his Wife, Died March the 17th 1753, in the 9th year of his age.

Alas! how uncertain is Life. In youth and full Health, A fated stroke on his Leg fractured the Bone, and within three days Put an end to his Life, and to his Parents' early Hope.

Inscriptions on the altar tombs at "Spencer Hall," Talbot county, copied by Richard Henry Spencer, in September, 1871, are as follows:

Mary Spencer, Departed this life the 2nd day of June 1807, aged 45 years.

In memory of Dorothy Spencer, who departed this life on the 25th of Aug. A. D. 1812, aged 21 years.

In memory of Col. Perry Spencer, who departed this life on the 15th November 1822, in the 67th year of his age.

"A man's good deeds are his best monument."

In memory of Capt. Richard Spencer, who departed this life on the 26th Jan'y A. D. 1819, in the 59th year of his age.

In memory of Mrs. Eleanor Spencer, wife of Capt. Richard Spencer, who departed this life on the 5th day of August A. D. 1829, in the 64th year of her age.

In memory of Ellen Spencer, daughter of Joseph and Frances Spencer, who was born June 24th A. D. 1815, and died August 9th, A. D. 1829.

In memory of Lambert Wickes Spencer, who departed this life Oct. 5th 1836, in the 60th year of his age.

Inscriptions on tombs at "Hampden," Talbot county, Md., copied in 1873, before they were removed to Spring Hill cemetery, Easton, Md.

Here lyeth ye body of Elizabeth Martin borne in Hertfordshire, late wife of Thomas Martin, who departed this life in the year 1676, aged 40 years.

> A dame of virtue, and esteemed to be,
> Who seldom was from home or family.
> O Lord of Mercy, since it is our fate,
> Prepare us for the immortal state.

She was Elizabeth Day, born in Hertfordshire, Eng., in 1636. Her husband, Thomas Martin, of "Hampden," born, it is claimed, in Dorsetshire, Eng., in 1629, died in Talbot county, Md., in 1701, aged 72 years.

Here lyeth the body of John Day borne in Maryland, who departed this life in the yeare Anno Dom. 1676.

He was the nephew of Elizabeth Day, wife of Thomas Martin.

Here lyeth the body of Elizabeth Martin, borne in Maryland, ye daughter of Thomas Martin. She departed this life in the yeare Anno Dom. 1676.

Here lies the body of Thomas Martin, who departed this life April 29th, 1782, Aged sixty-two years, ten months & thirteen days.

Honesty, sobriety and industry constituted him a useful and good citizen; affection and tenderness endeared him to his family, while a sincere benevolence secured him the esteem and respect of his neighbors.

Here lies the body of Mary Ennalls Martin, wife of Thomas Martin, who departed this life December 4th, 1771, Aged forty-seven years, three months and thirteen days.

The mother who instils useful instruction into the tender minds sows the seed of Virtue, and Her children arise up and call her blessed.

Here lies the body of Mary Martin, the second wife of Thomas Martin, who departed this life Dcember 1st. 1796, Aged 65 years, 4 months and 15 days.

As a tribute of affection and grateful remembrance, this stone is erected by one of her affectionate stepsons, Joseph Martin.

Mrs. Martin was the eldest daughter of the Rev. Thomas Airey, rector of Christ Church, Cambridge, Md., and his first wife, Elizabeth Pitt. Her youngest sister, Louisa Airey, married Robert Gilmor of Baltimore. Rev. Thos. Airey was born at Kendal, Yorkshire, Eng., in 1701. He came to this province in 1726, and was inducted into the office of priest of Great Choptank parish, Dorchester county, in 1728, by letter received from the Lord Proprietary, Charles Calvert, Governor of Maryland.

A large white monument of imposing design marks the grave of Hon. Daniel Martin, at Spring Hill cemetery, Easton. It is inscribed:

To the memory of Daniel Martin, who departed this life on the 11th day of July 1831, aged 50 years and 7 months, this stone is dedicated. He was distinguished by the confidence of his fellow-citizens, having been often called to fill various posts of honor and of trust. In the last of these as Governor of his native State, to which he had been twice elected, he descended to the tomb. Thus closed his bright career of honor and usefulness. In the death lamented as in life he had been honored.

To the Spring Hill cemetery have been removed many of the bodies that once reposed in the old Whitemarsh churchyard, as well as others from private burying grounds, on estates that have passed to strangers. The oldest gravestones here, taken from Mr. A. L. Richardson's list, made in 1906, are as follows:

Margaret Allen, wife of Bennett Allen, born Aug. 10, 1810; died Sept. 24, 1842.

Marion E. Bullen, daughter of Wm & E. E. Bullen, d. Aug. 15, 1843, aged 7 years, 10 months & 23 days.

Harriet Bennett, wife of the late Thomas Bennett, d. Jan. 8th 1832.

Thomas Bennett, d. at Annapolis Feb. 23, 1827, in his 34th year.

Rachel Bennett, d. April 25, 1845, in her 72d year.

John Bennett, d. Jan 27, 1838, in his 69th year.

Thomas Carter, d. June 14, 1850, aged 63 years.

Thomas Edmund & James White Cox, children of Whittington & Susan A. Cox, 1833 & 1845.

Elizabeth Dawson, d. Oct. 1, 1842, in her 92d. year.

T. H. Dawson, d. Nov. 14, 1841, in his 60th year.

Thomas Scott Dawson, d. Aug. 11, 1842, aged 30 years, 10 months & 4 days.

John M. G. Emory, d. Dec. 17, 1836, in his 52nd year.

P. H. Feddeman, d. Sept. 3, 1845, aged 29 years and 1 month.

Anna M. Feddeman, d. July 27, 1845, aged 28 years, 6 months & 27 days.

Mary Feddeman, daughter of Daniel & Rebecca Feddeman, d. Oct. 14, 1846, in her 39th year.

Eli H. Furniss, d. May 12, 1846, in his 45th year.

Mary E. Faulkner, wife of Thomas M. Faulkner, died March 2, 1846, aged 29 years.

Ann M. Faulkner, wife of Wm. H. Faulkner, d. Oct. 9, 1845, aged 21 years.

Caroline F. Faulkner, wife of W. H. Faulkner, d. Aug. 14, 1848, in the 21st. year.

Benjamin Faulkner, d. Sept. 28, 1844, aged 27 years, 4 months & 12 days.

Samuel Groome, died March 14, 1828, aged 50 years, 10 months & 5 days.

Talbot County

Eliza Groome, wife of Peregrine Groome, d. March 5, 1845, in her 67th year.

Alex. Graham, d. Dec. 1, 1845, aged 56 years.

Eliza Clementson Graham, d. Sept. 3, 1833, aged 33 years.

Henrietta Maria, Samuel C. & Francis Goldsborough, children of John C. & Mary E. Goldsborough, all died before 1847.

Henry Goldsborough, d. Aug. 7, 1832, aged 40 years.

Margaret Goldsborough, wife of Henry Goldsborough, d. Apr. 8, 1863, aged 72 years.

John Goldsborough, d. Aug. 12, 1840, aged 73 years.

Mrs. A. M. Goldsborough, d. Jan 26, 1836.

John C. Goldsborough, b. Sept. 22, 1801, d. July, 1844.

Mary Goldsborough, widow of Dr. Howes Goldsborough, d. March 14, 1821, aged 47 years.

Dr. Nicholas Hammond, d. Nov. 10, 1831, aged 56 years.

Col. Wm. Hughlett, b. April 16th 1769 near Greensborough, Caroline Co., d. Dec. 7, 1845, aged 76 years, 7 months & 21 days.

Mary Hughlett, widow of Col. Wm. Hughlett, b. Sept. 19, 1793; d. Dec. 19, 1863.

John A., Susan & Henrietta Hambleton, children of Samuel & Elizabeth Hambleton, died between the years 1847 & 1849.

Rev. Charles W. Jacobs, minister of the Methodist Protestant Church, b. in Alexandria, D. C., Oct. 30, 1812; d. in Easton, Md., Jan. 20, 1833.

Wm. Owen Kennard, infant son of Samuel T. & Elizabeth Kennard, d. Nov. 5, 1830.

Samuel T. Kennard, b. March 16, 1793; d. Sept. 17, 1845.

Amelia H. Kennard, d. March 1, 1827, aged 22 years, 7 months & 15 days.

Frisby Kirby, d. May 6, 1828, in his 41st. year.

Martha J. Kirby, wife of Frisby Kirby, d. June 25, 1851, in her 31st year.

Jacob Loockerman, b. Jan. 22, 1759, d. June 17, 1839.

Mary Loockerman, wife of Jacob Loockerman, b. May 23, 1774; d. Sept 14, 1840.

John Loockerman, son of Jacob Loockerman, b. Dec. 9, 1789; d. Dec. 24, 1846.

Ennalls Martin, M. D., b. Aug. 23, 1758; d. Dec. 16, 1834.

Sarah H. Martin, wife of Ennalls Martin, M. D., b. in Worcester Co., Md., Nov. 22, 1768; d. in Easton, June 3, 1835.

Mary A. Marshall, daughter of Richard & Henrietta Marshall, b. Feb. 9, 1809; d. Nov. 13, 1835.

Martha A. Mackey, wife of Alex. H. Mackey, b. Dec. 23, 1815; d. Sept. 27, 1843.

Miss Matilda McCallamont, d. Feb. 4, 1832, aged 24 years.

Susannah Murray, wife of John A. Murray, d. Sept. 2, 1846, in her 41st. year.

William Newman, d. March 5, 1847, aged 69.

Margaret Newman, d. Nov. 11, 1826.

John Ozman, died March 21, 1848, aged 28 years.

Lucy Ozment, wife of John Ozment, d. Dec. 21, 1845, in her 58th year.

Maria Josephine Pascault, daughter of Alexis A. & Maria E. Pascault, b. July 3, 1849; d. Oct. 12, 1850.

Mary Eliza Plummer, d. Sept. 19, 1843, in her 17th year.

Mrs. Caroline Rowlenson, wife of Wm. T. Rowlenson, d. March 19, 1849, in her 24th year.

Elizabeth Spedden, d. Jan. 30th, 1831, aged 32 years, 9 months & 26 days.

Sarah S. Singleton, b. June 22, 1793; d. Nov. 27th. 1847.

Ann M. D. Singleton, wife of Thomas B. Singleton, d. Oct. 6, 1843, in her 40th year.

Mrs. Sarah Sherwood, d. March 5, 1846, aged 65 years, wife of the late Capt. Philemon Sherwood.

Mary Satterfield, wife of John Satterfield, d. Oct. 1, 1841, in her 26th year.

Quakers appeared in America in 1656, and in Maryland the year after. Though a proclamation was issued against them in 1658, we find them holding minor offices here in 1665, and relieved, three years later, from taking the oath in testamentary cases. In 1692, they were allowed to "affirm" where an oath was required from others. Thus we see how the industrious and peaceable Friend was welcomed in Maryland, and in less than thirty-six years had established for himself a reputation as a person of firm convictions and religious scruples, and as a law-abiding citizen, whose word could be accepted without challenge.

A local writer, probably the late Samuel Harrison of Talbot county, speaks of the simple burial customs of the Quakers in these words:

"They, who look forward with such confidence to our

The Old "Tred-Avon" Friends' Meeting-house
Built in 1684 and over two hundred years old when destroyed by fire a few years ago

immortality beyond the grave, are not apt to be solicitous for their transitory fame, that most glowing epitaphs upon perishable marble bestow; and they build no shrines to which pious pilgrimages may be made, over the relics of their saints."

Back of the old meetinghouse, built near the Tred-Avon, in 1684, as a successor to the earlier one at Betty's Cove, there are neat rows of little tombstones, showing how the Friends of yore cared for their dead. To be sure there is nothing here to reward persons in search of scraps of family history, or of curious epitaphs that mostly provoke a smile; only, in the carefully preserved "Minuits" of the great Tred-Avon Meeting may be found an unbroken record of a Christian sect, planted in a new country and holding its own for two centuries and a half.

Quite a remarkable man, who stands out prominently in the early history of the Friends in this country, was Wenlock Christison. Persecuted in Massachusetts, where he was thrown into prison and condemned to death, he found refuge in Maryland upon his escape. In 1670, Peter Sharpe, a member of the same faith, gave him 150 acres of land in Talbot county, and remembered him in his will besides. Other gifts of servants and lands followed, and honors also were heaped upon him. At his house was held in 1677, the first man's or business meeting of which there is any record, and as late as 1678, he was a member of the House of Burgesses; but, as early as 1679, his wife appears on the Minutes as *about to marry again!* Such was the demand for wives in the first fifty years of settlement, and even later on, that the only way for a widow to rid herself of the importunity of many suitors was quickly to take to herself a second spouse.

In 1681, John Edmonson was elected to fill the place in the Meeting left vacant by Christison's death, and shortly after the old meetinghouse at Betty's Cove was abandoned for the wooden building on the Tred-Avon, erected in 1684, and still standing up to within ten years ago. Not a fragment is left of the earlier building, or a scrap of stone, to show where the first body of Quakers met, worshiped and were buried.

CHAPTER XI

CECIL county, at the head of the Chesapeake Bay, is watered by the Susquehanna, the Sassafras, the Elk and the South Elk rivers. From the first, this section offered natural advantages as a place of settlement and had become an active business center while it still formed a part of Baltimore county. In fact, the first Baltimore town was located, it is said, on the banks of the Elk river below where Elkton now stands. On June 9, 1692, however, when the laying out of parishes had been decreed by Act of Assembly, Cecil enjoyed a separate existence, and on the twenty-second of November of the same year, the county commissioners divided it into two parishes called respectively North and South Sassafras. A few years later in adjusting the border lines between Cecil and Kent counties, South Sassafras was evidently juggled out of existence, for we hear of it no more; but the growth of Shrewsbury parish, Kent county, south of the Sassafras river, can be traced from this time.

The loss to Cecil was made up for, in 1706, by the creation of St. Mary Anne's or North Elk parish, and at the present day most of the ecclesiastical traditions of the county cluster about the two churches, St. Mary's, North Elk, and St. Stephens, North Sassafras. The former was built in 1742, and the latter, though it has seen a succession of church edifices—not always on the same site—celebrated its two hundredth anniversary in May, 1893. This church stands at the head of the Bohemia river. Three of the commissioners, Casparus Herman, William Ward and Henry Riggs, were among its first vestrymen; John Thompson, Edward

Jones and Matthias Vanderhuyden being the others. Three hundred and twenty-one persons represented the taxables, who contributed to the support of the parish, and tobacco was the staple with which their obligations were discharged.

There were many delays about the building of St. Stephens, but in 1703 it was sufficiently advanced for the vestry meeting to be held within its walls. In 1706 it was dedicated by the rector, Rev. Richard Sewell. Another rector, the Rev. Hugh Jones, officiated here for thirty years, being held in high esteem by the whole community. He died in 1760, at the age of 90 years and was buried near the church.

It is a pity that we have been unable to explore either this ancient churchyard or that of St. Mary Anne's, North Elk. The vestry records of these two parishes are rich in names of men, prominent in the affairs of the Province in early times. In St. Mary's church is the tomb of Rev. Joseph Coudon, one of its rectors, whose ashes repose beneath the altar. His epitaph reads thus:

In Memory of Reverend Joseph Coudon, Rector of St. Mary Anne's Parish, A Zealous and Indefatigable Preacher of the Gospel, Who Departed this Life the 13th, April, 1792, And in the 51st year of his age.

With Augustine Herman is associated the laying out of Cecil county, and his Manor of Bohemia forms one of the centers of local history and tradition. His "monument" stone, as he calls it in his will, has of late years been inserted in the walls of the present dwelling, and it was probably prepared in his lifetime, for it does not record his death, which occurred about the year 1686. We do not know whether it ever marked his grave, and although it was used by a later generation as a door to a vault, it can hardly be considered a memorial of anything but what is represented on its surface. It reads:

Avgvtine Herman, Bohemian, The First Founder, seater of Bohemea Manner, Anno, 1661.

Six generations are supposed to be buried in the Baldwin-Milligan-McLane graveyard, on a farm known as "Bohemia."

Of the first the graves have been disturbed, the stones broken and defaced. The second is represented by Col. John Baldwin, his wife and Mrs. Van Bibber. The others can be listed with the dates.

Third generation: George Milligan, died at Bohemia, 1783. Catherine, his wife, daughter of John Baldwin, 1759. Mrs. Thompson, daughter of John Baldwin, 1766.

Fourth generation. The last three have been removed: George Milligan, son of George, died about 1758. Mary, daughter of George Milligan, and wife of James Christie of Durie, Fife, N. Britain, died at Baltimore, December, 1774. Margaret, daughter of George Milligan, died at Philadelphia, 1792. Robert, son of George Milligan, died in Philadelphia, 1805. Sarah Jones, wife of Robert, died at Bohemia, 1795.

Fifth generation: Mary, infant daughter of James Christie, died in Baltimore, 1774. Catherine, wife of Louis McLane, and daughter of Robert Milligan, died in Baltimore, was buried here in 18 . . . (?), being afterwards removed.

Sixth generation, the last two of which have been removed: Catherine, infant daughter of Louis McLane, died at Washington, 1818. Kitty McLane, daughter of Louis McLane, died at Baltimore, aged 20. Catherine Christie, daughter of Thos. Christie and granddaughter of James Christie, Scotland, died at Wilmington, Del., aged 13 years, 1826.

The "Cromwell" burying ground, on "Success farm," brings us in touch with the descendants of the Protector's Uncle Oliver, after whom he was named, and who represented the elder branch of the Cromwell family, seated at Hinchingbrook, near Huntington, England. That is to say, William and John Cromwell, who came to Maryland on board the

Benona Eaton, March 11, 1671, and took up land here, are supposed to have been the grandsons of the elder Oliver. William became a member of his Lordship's Council, married twice, returned to England and died there in 1684. His descendants in Maryland intermarried with the Dorseys and Hammonds of Howard and Anne Arundel counties, and after the Revolution, " Success " farm was inherited by John Hammond Cromwell, who is buried there. On a monument is preserved his name, with those of his descendants interred near by:

John Hammond Cromwell, 1745–1819; Mary Hammond Dorsey Cromwell, wife of John H. Cromwell, died 1795; Oliver Cromwell, 1775–1792; Eliza Cromwell, 1789–1796; Elizabeth, 1786–1787; Mary, 1792–1793; Rebecca C. Wilson, 1780–1806; Louis Harlen, 1774–1825; Frances Dorsey, sister of John W. Cromwell, died in 1820; John C. Reynolds, M. D., late a surgeon in the army of the U. S., b. Feb 6, 1810; d. Feb 20, 1849.

On " Success " farm still stands the old homestead with its quaint curb-gabled roof, built more than two hundred years ago. It is now owned by members of the Nickle family, descendants of John Hammond Cromwell.

Ten years ago, in response to the writer's request for information about the graves or burial places of Cecil county, the following report from the late A. W. Evans was received:

"The work contemplated by the Colonial Dames of America, Maryland Society, is a very worthy one, deserving assistance—if such can be given. It is, however,—as laid out in the circular of the committee—one of great extent, involving considerable expense. To state who were the 'men of mark' in Cecil county would be, with a few exceptions, rather difficult. I am aware of but one Governor given by this county to the State,—viz., Governor Thomas W. Veazey—and that was in the fourth decade of this century. He was probably buried either at St. Steven's church, or at his home plantation in Sassafras Neck, now in the possession of his daughter. In the seventeenth and eighteenth centuries we have the founders of families—all very respectable people, gentlemen and yeomen—not, perhaps, very distinguished, but very numerous; and the justices of the county, and other officials—also very numerous. A list of these would have to be prepared, as far as possible, as preliminary to the work. Augustine Herman and George Talbot, in the seventeenth century, did much in the formation of the county; but the latter died in Europe.

"When we come to the Revolution, in which Cecil, though settled by such diverse nationalities, was, with singular unanimity, very patriotic, or rebel, a number of her sons who were officers in the war can be named. The following is an imperfect list of these 'men of mark':

"Walter Alexander, Captain of Militia of the Flying Camp, in 1776; buried at Hd. of Christian Church, with a stone which is correct as to his age, but in error as to the year of his death, which is given as 1780. He died in April, 1778.

"Herman Arrants, Lieutenant Flying Camp Militia; removed to Kentucky after the war.

"Jacob Arrants (I am not quite certain of the given name), Lieutenant of the Flying Camp Militia; burial place not known—probably in Elk Neck.

"Henry Dobson, Captain 3d Maryland, Continental Line, killed at Eutaw Springs, S. C., 1781, and probably buried there. There is a family graveyard of the Dobsons near Elkton, but no stone over anyone.

"Hezekiah Foard, Lieutenant 1st Maryland, Continental Line; survived till 1833; burial place not known.

"Elihu Hall, Major of Militia; died 1791; burial place not known.

"Elihu Hall (son of last?), Ensign or Lieutenant, 1st Maryland, Continental Line; burial place not known. This family was of the northwestern part of the county.

"Henry Hollingsworth, Colonel of Militia; died 1803; buried at Elkton, with a stone.

"Thomas Hughes, Major or Lieutenant Colonel of Militia; burial place not known—perhaps in Harford county.

"Stephen Hyland, Colonel of Militia; died 1806; probably buried at his place, Harmony Hall, in Elk Neck.

"Edward Oldham, Captain 5th Maryland, Continental Line; burial place not known—perhaps at St. Augustine church.

"Nathaniel Ramsay, Lieutenant Colonel, 3d Maryland, Continental Line; died 1817; buried at Baltimore.

"John Rudolph, Major in Lee's Legion; died December, 1782, in South Carolina, and probably buried there.

"Michael Rudolph (cousin of the last), Captain in Lee's Legion, and afterwards Major in the Establishment of the U. S. Lost at sea in 1793.

"Edward Veazey, Captain in Smallwood's Regiment; killed at Long Island, August 27, 1776, and probably buried there. The ground remained seven years afterwards in the possession of the enemy.

"William Veazey, 1st Lieutenant Flying Camp Militia; burial place not known—probably in Sassafras Neck.

"George Wallace (of Cecil county), Lieutenant in a Delaware Regiment; died about 1795 and buried at Hd. of Christian meetinghouse, with a stone.

"Michael Wallace, Surgeon in Smallwood's Regiment; died about 1798; probably buried in Sharp's graveyard, but no stone.

"And there were probably many other officers of the Militia, who saw service, and whose names further research might discover.

"Natives of the county who grew to manhood in it, but migrated, were John McKnit Alexander (uncle of Captain Alexander, above), of the Mecklenburg Declaration of Independence; died 1817, and buried in North Carolina; and Abraham Kirkpatrick, Captain 4th Virginia, Continental Line, who has a monument at Pittsburg, Pa.

"If to all these we add the names of the many men who founded families in the county in the seventeenth and eighteenth centuries, or who were otherwise conspicuous, it will be seen that the task outlined by the circular of the Colonial Dames, is sufficiently extensive. If a suggestion might be offered as to a beginning, it is that monuments be erected, first only, to the following, viz.:

"To Augustine Herman, founder of 'Bohemia Manor,' who died in 1686, and was buried on the bank of the Bohemia river, at a spot which can be closely identified. It is much more suitable that this should be done by Americans than by the Bohemians or foreigners of Baltimore city.

"To that gallant and able soldier of the Revolution, Captain Michael Rudulph, of Lee's Legion. As he died at sea his monument might be appropriately placed at Elkton, at or near which he was born.

"If Cecil county would erect a monument inscribed with the names of her sons who served in the Revolutionary war, it would be a worthy memorial.

"Perhaps the above does not exactly meet the idea of the circular, for the carrying out of which a local, or Cecil county branch of the Colonial Dames seems indispensible. Such a branch might do something to further the views of the committee. Others are not likely to take any steps in the matter. 'The men of mark' of old times have not all left posterity in the county or elsewhere; in many instances their places of burial cannot be determined; and to a great extent, the present inhabitants are not descendants of those who dwelt here in the eighteenth century.

"A. W. EVANS.

"Elkton, February, 1898."

Of the Episcopal churches originally established in Somerset county there is now not a trace. St. Andrews in Princess Anne, built as a chapel of ease to Somerset parish, between 1769 and 1771, is perhaps the best preserved of those that come later. In the old churchyard are to be found the following names and inscriptions, for most of which we are indebted to the lists of Mr. Albert Richardson, in the first issue of the *Bulletin of Original Research:*

Lydia Brittingham, wife of James Brittingham, born Oct 28, 1803; died Aug. 27, 1831.

Mary E. Crosdale, daughter of Col. William Walter and Anne Holland, and Relict of Rev. Henry Crosdale, born March 24, 1820; died April 23, 1885.

Hic Jacet Henricus Crosdale, Presbyter Ecclesiæ Catholica et olim Rector Hujus Parochiæ. Obit XII Die Aug., Anno Salutus MDCCCXIV. "Credo quod Redempter meus vivit."

Wm. H. Collier, d. Dec 7, 1844, in his 59th year.

Sarah Bishop Dashiell, daughter of Wm. & Esther Cottman, and Relict of George Dashiell, b. Feb 9, 1811; d. Sept 17, 1849.

Geo A. Dashiell, b. June 9, 1737 [1787 ?]; d. Sept. 3, 1835.

Geo. Wm. Dashiell, son of Geo. and Sarah Bishop Dashiell, b. April 29, 1829; d. Jan 20, 1849.

Mary B. Harris, d. Sept. 27, 1850.

Col. Arnold E. Jones, b. Aug 21, 1785; d. July 13, 1839.

Matthias Jones, M. D., d. May 8, 1826.

Milcah Gale Jones, relict of Dr. Matthias Jones, d. Oct 17, 1836, in her 64th year.

Mary H. Jones, wife of Samuel W. Jones, d. Feb 28, 1831, in her 23rd year.

Samuel W. Jones, b. July 13, 1804; d. Aug 7, 1869.

Elizabeth Johnston, consort of Wm W. Johnston, d. March 2, 1831, aged 18 years & 9 months.

Three infant children of William W. & Rosina Johnston, between the years 1831 & 1842.

George Johnston, b. Dec 3, 1764; d. Oct. 5, 1846.

Rider Henry Rackliffe, d. Aug 20, 1818.

Wm. R. Stevenson, son of George D. & Henryetta Stevenson, b. Nov 6, 1824; d. Sept 28, 1850.

St. Mary Anne's, or North Elk, Parish Church, Cecil County
Built in 1742

Littleton Dennis Teackle, buried in an unmarked grave under a great maple tree near the fence.

M. E. Waters, b. Dec 15, 1837; d. Sept. 4, 1847.

John Woolford, M. D., b. Oct 27, 1761; d. Nov 15, 1836.

Anna Irving Woolford, wife of John Woolford, M. D., b. Feb 5, 1777; d. Oct 11, 1839.

Thomas Williams, late merchant, son of John Williams of Dorchester Co., d. Sept 1, 1807, aged 29 years.

On tombs of a later date than 1850 are to be found the names of Atkinson, Bowland, Bratton, Dennis, Dixon, Gale, Handy, King, Polk, Stone, Whittington and others. Many of the Eastern Shore worthies of an early period bore these names, but no lasting memorial of any of them was found here.

It may prove interesting, as an illustration of the geographical changes effected in a tide-water country, to quote from a letter written about ten years ago, by the late Levin Waters of Princess Anne.

"In 1705," he writes, "Arnold Elzey and wife conveyed to Queen Anne of England, for church purposes, one acre of land, on the Manokin River, on which, there then stood a church. Not only the church, but the acre of land so conveyed has disappeared. It has been washed into the river and from tradition we learn, that certain red sandstone steps, which now mark the entrance to one of the old residences, on the Manokin River, are the last relicts of this old church. Certainly, if there was a burying ground attached to it, it has long ago disappeared with the "God's Acre" upon which the church stood, and the remains of the dead, if any were ever interred there, have gone into the river with the land which held them."

It was usually near the spot where the pioneers of the church exercised their functions, that the first parishes sprang into official being, and the earliest church in Somerset was undoubtedly the above. The parish church was destroyed by fire some years ago, and so St. Andrews is the lineal descendant of its predecessor on the banks of the Manokin. Rev. John Hewitt, the first church of England divine accredited to Somerset county, arrived here in 1685. To him is attributed the building of the early church.

Of Monie church, originally erected in 1712, Mr. Waters writes: "The old building was blown down, about twenty years ago, and reconstructed almost immediately afterwards, through the energetic efforts of the Rev. Dr. Barton, then rector of Somerset parish. But until recently, there was never any enclosed graveyard, and but few graves, about the old church, and these were of the nameless dead. Through the efforts of some of its present members, there is now a very neat enclosure about the church, and the ground enclosed is being used for the sepulture of the dead of the neighborhood. In this enclosure is found the stone—a large marble slab—which covered the remains of Squire William Stoughton, the donor to Somerset parish, of the beautiful, unique and very valuable silver communion service, which is now used in the churches of the parish, and cherished by the parish as a very precious memento of the colonial times. This Squire Stoughton was the grandfather of Mrs. Governor Winder. He was buried in the old family burying ground of the Elzey's, at 'Almodington,' the original residence of that distinguished family, on the Manokin river. This property, like nearly all others in Maryland, having gone out of the family to which it was patented, and the graveyard being absolutely neglected and unprotected, the slab, which was put there to commemorate his virtues, together with such of his remains as could be found, were removed, a few years ago, to the churchyard at Monie, where it is now to be found. This stone bears the following inscription:

Here lyeth the Body of Wm Stoughton Esq. Born in the year 1692 and departed this life the 12th day of December 1759 aged 67 years.

"Of the last resting places of John Elzey, the original settler of the 'Manoakin' plantations, and who appears so conspicuously in the colonial records, as early as 1663, and of his descendants of that name, there is now no trace. The same may be said of Randal Revel and Anne Toft, to whom large bodies of land were granted by the colonial government, on the opposite side of the 'Manoakin' river, as early as 1665."

Somerset county claims to have been and undoubtedly was, the cradle of the Presbyterian church in America, and certainly Rev. Francis Mackemie, the first pastor of "Old Rehoboth," was the father of the sect on these shores. The only tablet erected to the memory of this eminent divine is in the church. On the banks of Holden creek, across the Pocomoke river, and ten miles below the scene of his ministrations, is his grave. He was sent to this country in 1683, and before 1690 had organized congregations at Rehoboth, Snow Hill, Rockawaukin, Salisbury and Manokin. Would that we might explore these spots! And yet it is well to console ourselves with the reflection that the Presbyterian churchyards have probably shared the same fate as many of those of the Episcopal church. The tombstones around the Manokin church, Princess Anne, without exception, all date from the nineteenth century. They follow here:

Rev. Henry Blatchford, A. M., eldest son of Rev. Samuel Blatchford, D. D., of Lansinburgh, N. Y., d. Sept. 7, 1822, in the 34th year of his age.

He was pastor of the Manokin and Rehoboth churches, and the tomb was placed in the cemetery by both congregations, as a joint memorial tribute.

Ellen R., consort of John W. Crisfield, d. March 8, 1835, aged 24 years and 3 months.

Mrs. Julia Ethelwide Crisfield, wife of J. W. Crisfield, d. June 28, 1841.

We will note here that J. M. Crisfield was an eminent lawyer, a member of Congress, president and builder of the Eastern Shore railroad. He was born November 6, 1808, and died January 12, 1897. "Strong of will, to strive, to seek, to find and not to yield."

Martin L. Haynie, M. D., d. in New Orleans, La., Feb. 1815.

Henrietta B. Haynie, daughter of Ezekiel and Betty Haynie, b. Aug 1, 1789; d. Jan 15, 1850.

Elizabeth Hargis, b. Oct 11, 1767; d. March 1811.

Sally Handy, wife of George Handy, and daughter of Denwood and Margaret Wilson, b. Oct 11, 1786; d. May 3, 1845.

Henrietta H. Jones, wife of Alfred H. Jones, d. Feb 13, 1845.

Elizabeth Stewart, b. June 1776; d. 1811.

Mary S. Wilson, d. Oct 17, 1837, aged 56 years.

At Rehoboth there is also an Episcopal church, said to have been erected in 1735, with churchyard and graves about it, but none of these date from colonial times.

A mile below the ancient church, on the Jenkins plantation facing the Pocomoke, was discovered about ten years ago, a broken tombstone flat on the ground, thus inscribed:

Under this stone lyeth the body of Madam Mary Hampton, who departed this life the 19th of October 1744, aged 70 years, wanting three days.

Remains of other stones are here also, but they are all broken and illegible, and were it not for the fact that Madam Mary Hampton was a well-known character in her day and generation, the name would pass by without significance. Her maiden name was King and her father, Sir Robert, was an Irish baronet, who, according to Irving Spencer, was in official life in Maryland in 1690.

The lady was married three times, her first husband being Col. Francis Jenkins, one of the justices, a member of the Governor's Council and a man of large wealth. Upon his death in 1710, his widow married the Rev. John Henry, who succeeded Rev. Francis Mackemie as pastor of Rehoboth church. Among the graduates of the University of Edinburgh in 1703, appears the name of John Henry, and as the reverend gentleman first mentioned was a man of ability, who brought with him the sympathy of influential men in Scotland and Ireland, and stood high in his adopted country as a citizen and a divine, we may assume that he was the University graduate of 1703. Madam Hampton had no children except by this marriage. Her daughter, a talented and distinguished woman, died before her in 1722, but her two sons, Maj. Robert Jenkins Henry and Col. John Henry, lived to become prominent in public affairs; the first as judge of the Provincial Court in 1736, the second as member of the House of Delegates from Worcester county. John Henry, son of the colonel, was first a member of the Continental Congress, then United States Senator and finally Governor of the State.

What little we have to say about the private burying grounds of Somerset county can best be given in the words of the late Mr. Levin Waters, from whom we have quoted before, and the remainder of whose letter now follows:

"Among the few private burying grounds in Somerset, of which there remains any positive knowledge and in which marks are to be found, are the following. At 'Tusculum,' on Monie creek in Somerset county, which was formerly the estate and residence of the Gales, there are several stones and a brick vault, one of these stones marks the grave of Col. George Gale, who died in 1712, aged forty-one years, and bears the Gale coat-of-arms, which appears to be a shield bearing crosses above and below, and two griffins with an anchor in the center. The vault in this graveyard has fallen into decay and some years ago, when last seen by me, some of the bones of those within could be seen, on looking in through an aperture near the top.

"On the Pocomoke river, some fourteen miles below Princess Anne, is a stone marking the last resting place of William Stevens, one of the early settlers and among the first of his Majesty's, the King of England, Justiciaries in Somerset county. The inscription on this stone, which I here give verbatim, will give as much of the history of this once prominent man, as I have here space to write.

"Here lyeth the Body of William Stevens ESq, Who departed this life the 23rd, day of December 1687, Aged 57 years. He was 22 years Judge of this County Court, One of his Lordship's Council and one of the Deputy Lieutenants of this Province of Maryland. Vivit Post Funera Virtus."

"At 'Workington' on Back creek, which was formerly the residence of the Jacksons of Somerset county, are several stones bearing inscriptions dating back into the last century. At 'Westover' on the same creek, formerly the estate and residence of the Wilsons is a graveyard with stones marking the resting places of several members of that family, but none of these, as far as I recollect, bear dates earlier than the present century.

"At 'Cedar Grove,' on the Annamessix river, which formerly belonged to and was the residence of one of the branches of the Gale family of Maryland, is a graveyard with stones marking the resting places of members of that family. Among which, there is one over the remains of Gen. John Gale, a revolutionary soldier. This stone bears date 1813.

"The burial ground of the Winder family, in which rests the remains of the late Governor Levin Winder and Mrs. Winder, on little Monie creek, is now owned, and if I am correctly informed is occupied as a wood pile, by a man, who is a stranger to the family and without respect for the honored dead who lie there.

"Of lesser note, but still prominent in the history of the State, is the ancestry of the Bayleys, Whittinghams, Adams, Handys, Gunbys, Waters, Dashiells, Riders and others, whose graves are unmarked and except in some very few instances, their locations absolutely unknown. It is greatly to be regretted and a burning shame on the generations which have just preceded us, that so little was done toward preserving and noting the last resting places of our patriotic dead. Some few of these were prominent participants in the establishment of our government and in the events of the Revolution which secured to their descendants national independence and the sweets of civil liberty.

"Their names are written upon the pages of our State and national histories, but many others less prominent, but equally deserving, the pioneers and educators of their race, the heroes of the wilderness, who braved dangers and suffered much that their descendants might be free, are no less entitled to be held in remembrance by the living participants of the blessings, these dead heroes bequeathed.

"I am rejoiced to know the Colonial Dames are making an effort to rescue, some at least, of the resting places of these patriotic dead, from the utter oblivion into which in another generation, they in all probability would have fallen.

"I hope what I have thus briefly written, may be of some service in the work you have in hand.
"LEVIN L. WATERS."

Somerset county, when first laid out in 1666, extended from the Choptank river to the southernmost boundary of the Eastern Shore. From this section Dorchester was erected in 1669, Worcester in 1742 and Wicomico later. In the latter county, two churches have survived to add interest to the history of Stepney parish, one of the four originally apportioned to Somerset. These are St. Bartholomew's, or the Green Hill church, and Spring Hill or the Quantico church. The latter, built originally as a chapel of ease, was replaced by a church of good proportions just before the troublous days of the Revolution. It has suffered fluctuations of fortune ever since. Ancient Bartholomew's, constructed of brick, in 1733, as successor to a primitive wooden building, was abandoned a number of years ago on account of its ruined condition, but an interesting custom was established, which led eventually to its being restored. For years the descendants of former parishioners came here from far and near on St. Bartholomew's day, which falls in August, to join in out-of-door services under the trees. At one time the Wicomico river encroached upon the bluff where the church stands, making its safety a serious question, some of the old tombs having already fallen with the crumbling banks and been destroyed; but the catastrophe was averted, and it is said that many slabs and monuments remain bearing quaint and interesting epitaphs. Of these we have only been able to obtain one, thought to be the oldest. This specimen is placed over the grave of Captain Parker, a man of note in the latter part of the seventeenth century, who died the first year of the eighteenth. It has a special flavor of its own quite independent of the rules of poesy.

> This World is like a mighty city full of crooked streets
> And death is the market place, where all men meet.
> If life were merchandise that men could buy,
> The Rich would live always, but poor men die.

Another ancient parish belonging formerly to Somerset, but now to Worcester, is All Hallows', Snow Hill. The old church, completed in 1756, is still standing and is in an excellent state of preservation. Of the graves we have received different reports, but from them no epitaphs nor names of ancient date. The old Berlin churchyard, on the contrary, is said to be full of venerable tombs, but even a full list of these has been denied us. From the Presbyterian churchyard at Snow Hill, however, we have the following names:

Lieut. Col. Levin Handy, born Aug. 20th, 1754, died June 5th, 1799; Major James Handy, both of whom served in the Revolutionary army as members of Gen. Washington's staff; Mrs. Nancy Handy, widow of Lieut. Col. Levin Handy, born March 18th, 1769, died April 25th, 1817.

At "Beverly," the old Dennis place, on the Pocomoke

river, is a well-kept burying ground in which the following tombs are the oldest:

In Memory of Littleton Dennis Esq., who Departed this life the 6th Day of May, Anno Domini 1774, in the 46th year of his age.

In Memory of Susanna Dennis, Relict of the late Littleton Dennis. She was was born In the 8th Day of July 1733, And Died In the 17th Day of November 1784, In the 51st year Of her age.

In Memory of Littleton Dennis, Junior, who Dyed the 23rd day of September 1764.

In Memory of James Dennis Esq., who departed this life the 6th Day of November 1774, In the 20th year of his age.

In Memory of Henry Dennis, son of Littleton and Elizabeth Dennis, who was born May 29th. A. D. 1791, And departed this Life January 31, 1793.

When the graveyard was put in order some years ago, an old Englishman was employed to clean the stones. He remarked on the "Esq.," and said that none but the "gentry" could use it on their tombstones.

The original parishes of Dorchester, two in number, were Great Choptank and Dorchester. Christ Church, Cambridge, not an old building, but standing in the midst of an ancient churchyard, represents the first, and Old Trinity, on Church creek, a few miles from Cambridge, the second. The name of the creek is sufficient of itself to indicate the locality where there was a place of worship in early times, and the present Trinity, a venerable edifice of uncertain age, containing many valuable relicts, is to-day the historic church of the county. To the graveyard at Cambridge, however, we must turn for memorials of those who lived in the long ago. To be sure the oldest have crumbled away and mingled with the dust of the dead; some are illegible, others are partially buried under the earth; others again are broken and scattered, and the dates are lost, but a goodly number of names obtained from various sources are sufficiently distinct to be added to our list. Apart from the Latin inscription, given below, there are none that are not of a fragmentary kind.

Hic conduntur ossa Caroli Goldsborough, Armiger, Roberti Goldsborough & Elizabethæ, uxoris suis, Filius; Qui post hujus Vitæ Tædia Vigilias Laboresque Perquam assiduos Tandem Animam exhalavit, July Die decimo quarto, Annos Christi MDCCLXVII, Ætatis suæ LV.

Here is buried Henrietta, the young wife of Hon. Daniel M. Henry, formerly member of Congress for Cambridge district, and the daughter of Gov. Chas. Goldsborough. She was born in 1828, was married in 1845, and died as a bride of thirteen months. The disconsolate husband had the following lines engraved on her tomb:

>Thou art gone my wife, The dates upon thy tomb
>Will tell what cause I've had to weep;
>How soon death called thee from thy youthful bloom,
>And marred the Joys I hoped to reap.
>
>In wedded life we loved with truest love,
>And now 'tis sad to be alone.
>Heaven saw thy worth & needed thee above.
>Thou art gone! Oh God, Thy will be done!

The list continues thus:

Hon. Chas. Goldsborough, Governor of Maryland in 1818, born July 15, 1765; died December 13, 1834.

Wilhemina, first wife of Chas. Goldsborough of Horn's Point, died 1790.

William Murray, 1763. Sarah, wife of Wm. Murray, 1742.

Eleanor Warren Holliday, second wife of William Murray, 1750. "She was remarkable for her piety & for being a good stepmother."

Daniel Murray, 1781.

John Caile, 1772.

Susan Morton, 1809.

Henrietta Chaplain, 1808.

John Reid, 1813.

Peter Ferguson, 1812.

Henry Waggaman, 1809.
Hall Caile Waggaman, 1776.
Robert Harrison, 1802.
Milcah Harrison, 1780.
John Caile Harrison, 1780. (Slab much broken.)
John Hall Caile, 1783.
John Caile, 1767.
John Leeds Nesmith, 1810.
Hon. Josiah Bayley, 1846. (At one time Attorney General of Maryland.)
John Ryder Nevitt, drowned in the Choptank river in 1772.
Isaac Steele, 1806. (The slab over his grave was placed there by his brother.)
Henry Page, 1843. (A monument inclosed by an iron railing was erected to his memory "by his dearest friend.")

On the outskirts of Vienna, about eighteen miles from Cambridge, the county seat, once stood a brick chapel of ease of great Choptank parish. Built between the years 1727 and 1730, and known through its declining years as the "Old Brick Church," it remained until the middle of the last century, when being in ruins, it was pulled down and some of the brick was used in the foundations of St. Paul's church, in the town. The old churchyard was thus left to its fate, and though long disfigured by the encroachments of briars and undergrowth, the beauty of its wide spreading oaks saved it from being abandoned altogether. Something should be said, also, about the veneration and sentiment of a later generation, who revered its memories, had it cleared of rubbish, and reconsecrated it to the burial of the dead. Though now used as a cemetery, the ancient monuments, alas, suffered during the interim and we have been unable to obtain a satisfactory report about the worthies of the past buried there.

CHAPTER XII

THE District of Columbia, as it now stands, is a part of what was originally Maryland territory, and before the city of Washington was even dreamed of, Georgetown, on the other side of Rock Creek, was already a social center among the inhabitants of Prince George's county. It is not strange, therefore, that Georgetown should have added the attractions of a society "eminently polite," to such talent and culture as the Federal city, even in its infancy, allured to its borders. Here Gilbert Stuart had his studio, from 1803 to 1805, and many notabilities of the time were his patrons. Here Thomas Moore, the melodious "Bard of Erin," while on a tour in this country, tuned his lays, and here Francis Scott Key, "the pensive singer of piety and patriotism," gained a popularity, which became fame after the events that inspired him to write "The Star Spangled Banner." James Madison and his charming wife "Dolly," who to the day of her death was the society heroine of the Capital, lived at Georgetown while he was Secretary of State, and the ill-fated Aaron Burr made his headquarters there. On the Heights of Georgetown many diplomats also had their homes.

The most noted of these was "Kalorama," which with its old graveyard, alas, is now a thing of the past. Still it is pleasant to allow our interest to linger about just such spots. Our chief concern about the past is, after all, with the people who lived in the past, and "Kalorama" was eminently the center of life one hundred years ago. It was owing to the number of celebrities who were entertained there, that it

ENTRANCE TO AN OLD FAMILY BURYING-GROUND
Showing the English ivy planted over one hundred years ago

gained for itself the name of the "Holland House of America," and now we perpetuate its memory, because of the many distinguished men who were laid to rest in its graveyard.

    Joel Barlow, upon his return from France in 1805, established himself at "Kalorama," "on the Heights" and drew around him many interesting personages. Among these was Robert Fulton, who had lived with Barlow in Paris for seven years before his return. Fulton, whose invention of the steamboat has made his name a household word, was also an artist, though this is not so generally known. He started life as a miniature painter, and before leaving France he superintended the execution of the plates of Barlow's *Columbiad*. This work was published in Philadelphia in 1807. Being illustrated with engravings executed by the best artists in London, it was one of the most costly publications that had been attempted in America. We find him visiting his friend at "Kalorama" in 1810, when Jefferson, Madison and a number of members of Congress were invited to meet him, to witness the demonstration of his latest plans for applying steam navigation to submarine warfare. He did not live to perfect these plans, but died in 1815, when his efforts were about to be crowned with success.

    Barlow's death preceded that of his friend by three years. He had been sent on a mission to France by Monroe, who recognized his skill as a diplomatist; but on December 22, 1812, while hastening in the depths of a northern winter to a rendezvous with Napoleon, he succumbed to the exposure. A tombstone was erected to his memory in the graveyard at "Kalorama." Massachusetts avenue now skirts the once hallowed spot, while modern dwellings cover it, and Rock Creek, unmindful of the part it played in the furthering of steam navigation, flows on past Lyon's mill, which ere long will also have to give way before the march of progress.

    In course of time the widow of Stephen Decatur became

the presiding genius of "Kalorama," counting among her intimate friends such men as Robert Goodloe Harper, Sir Stratford Canning and Charles Carroll of Carrollton. It was doubtless owing to her association with the latter that she became a Roman Catholic, as it was to the influence of Mr. Harper that she declined the honor and risk of becoming sister-in-law to Napoleon, thereby escaping the fate of the beautiful Betsy Patterson of Baltimore. For thirty-five years she lived faithful to the memory of her dead hero, and died in the convent at Georgetown, in 1855.

Commodore Stephen Decatur was one of those historical personages whom romance writers delight to honor. One might say that the conflagration in the harbor of Tripoli, caused by firing the recaptured ship *Philadelphia*, had thrown a glow over his deeds that has not faded after the lapse of a century. In the fatal duel fought with Commodore James Barron at Bladensburg, he has been looked upon as a martyr to the revengeful spirit of his opponent. Decatur was born at Sinnepuxent, Md., January 5, 1779, and though for many years his home was on the high seas, he died on Maryland shores. This occurred March 22, 1820. He was buried at "Kalorama," and later his remains were transferred to Philadelphia.

Among the other bodies that have been removed from "Kalorama" are the following:

Abraham Baldwin, a Senator in Congress from Georgia, who died March 4, 1807, aged 52 years. "His devotion to his country his greatest fame; her constitution his greatest work." Abraham Baldwin was a member of the convention to draft the Constitution of the United States. After his death, the original manuscript of the Constitution was found among his papers.

Henry Baldwin, Judge of the Supreme Court, died April 21, 1844.

Ruth Baldwin, his wife, died May 29, 1848, aged 62 years.

George Bomford, Colonel U. S. A., died May 25, 1848, aged 66 years. While at the head of the Bureau of Ordinance, Colonel Bomford lived at "Kalorama."

Clara Bomford, wife of Colonel Bomford, died December 10, 1855, aged 74 years.

"Oak Hill Cemetery," located on the Heights of Georgetown and bordering on Rock Creek, was, previous to its occupancy as a cemetery, known as "Parrott's Woods." The hills, covered with lofty oaks, extended their shady bowers in every direction, and here the Sunday School children of the town used to assemble to celebrate the Fourth of July, "in prose and song." Many of our citizens, who as boys romped and played under these spreading oaks, little thought that they should find a final resting place beneath their shade.

This cemetery owes its origin to Mr. William Corcoran, a native and former resident of Georgetown, who conceived the idea of laying out a public burial place. Consequently, he purchased fifteen acres of land from Lewis Washington of Jefferson County, Va. When the charter of the Oak Hill Cemetery Company was granted by Congress on March 3, 1849, Mr. Corcoran generously conveyed this land to the company for the purpose of a cemetery. More land has since been added, until the number of acres in 1878 had increased to thirty-six.

The donor continued his beneficence from time to time in laying out and embellishing the grounds at his expense. The finest mausoleum in the cemetery is the Doric temple, in which is enshrined the dust of William W. Corcoran and that of his wife and children. Eight snow-white columns support the marble dome, plainly chiseled, but grand and solid. Except the word "Corcoran," there is not a line to designate who lies below the vaulted floor. The temple stands alone on an elevation.

The Van Ness mausoleum is also here. It was modeled after the temple of Vesta by George Hatfield, probably the same architect, who, with James Hoban, was employed to finish the north wing of the Capitol for occupation in 1800. The mausoleum, erected by Gen. John Peter Van Ness, formerly stood on H. Street, Washington city, in the grounds of the orphan asylum, of which Mrs. Van Ness was founder. In it were placed the remains of the members of the Burnes family, also of Mrs. Ann Elbertina Middleton, the lamented daughter and only child of General and Mrs. Van Ness, and wife of Arthur Middleton, Esq., of South Carolina. Near them now repose the bodies of the General and his wife. John P. Van Ness was born at Ghent, N. Y., in 1770, and died at Washington, D. C., March 7, 1847. His wife, whom he married in 1802, was Marcia, daughter and heiress of David Burnes, one of the proprietors of the land on which the Federal city was built. She was born in 1782 and died in 1832. Her husband's position and her own wealth gave her a conspicuous place in Washington society, and her numerous charities gained for her the distinction, unusual for a woman, of being buried with public honors.

The remains of Philip Barton Key, uncle of Francis Scott Key, rest now in this cemetery. Mr. Key was captain in the British Army in the Revolution, but after peace was restored, he settled down under the new order of things, was made Attorney-General, became Member of Congress and held other offices. His home, "Woodley," was one of the most noted in the vicinity of Georgetown; he died and was interred there in 1817. In 1869 his remains were removed to Oak Hill.

Just in the rear of the chapel is a monument to the memory of Maj. George Peter, who died June 22, 1861. He commanded a company of artillery from Georgetown at the battle of Bladensburg, on August 24, 1814. He was married three times, his first wife was Ann Plater, his second, Agnes Buchanan Freeland, and his third, Sarah Norfleet Freeland.

Among those who were buried elsewhere and subsequently removed to this spot was Commodore Beverly Kennon, United States Navy, who met with a tragic end, being killed by the explosion of a cannon on board of the United States steam warship *Princeton*, February 28, 1844. He was interred first at the Congressional Cemetery, and on April 18, 1874, was removed to Oak Hill.

In a prominent position in front of the mortuary chapel is the tomb of John Howard Paine, the author of "Home Sweet Home." He died April 1, 1852, at the United States consulate in Tunis, Africa, and his ashes were doomed for many years to lie in a strange land. On June 8, 1893, the one hundreth anniversary of his birth, they were deposited in this tomb with fitting honors.

The Honorable Samuel Sprigg, nineteenth governor of the State of Maryland, originally buried in St. Barnabas churchyard, about five miles from Upper Marlborough, is another of those whose remains have been transferred to Oak Hill.

Among the local families who constituted society in those days were the Custises, the Lingans, the Peters, the Forrests, the Keys and the Platers, most of whom were related by marriage and had their homes on the heights of Georgetown. Among these homes were "Rosedale," "Woodley" and "Greenwood," where Col. Uriah Forrest, Phillip Barton Key and Col. Thomas Plater, respectively, dispensed hospitality. Mrs. Forrest and Mrs. Key were daughters of Hon. George Plater, sixth Governor of Maryland, and sisters of Col. Thomas Plater of Greenwood. On the latter place, a little more than a stone's throw from the quaint brick dwelling, is all that remains of the family burying ground. Besides the stone coping which indicates the existence of a subterranean vault, there are scattered bits of marble, a foot stone marked "W. H. R.," and one tombstone with a legible inscription, which tells the pathetic story of one who, with everything to live for, was cut off in the flower of her youth. This was Mrs. Ann Peter, the first wife of George Peter, celebrated in her day as one of the lovely daughters of Colonel Plater and his wife, Martha, and known in the Capital society as the "beauty." She died in 1814, in the twenty-third year of her age, leaving no children. Maj. George Peter survived her nearly fifty years, and contracted successively two other marriages, as has been already mentioned, so that the name of Peter is in no immediate danger of becoming extinct.

Colonel Plater's wife, Martha, also a very beautiful woman, was the sister of Gen. James Maccubbin Lingan, a veteran of the Revolutionary war, who met his death at the hands of the Baltimore mob, in 1812. The General held a part interest in the *Federal Republican*, a newspaper edited by Alexander Contee Hanson and others and published in Baltimore, where the Democratic party was strongly in the majority. The opposition of this paper to the Madison war-policy of 1812 drew upon the editors and owners the fury of the mob, who first destroyed the building where the paper was printed, and about a month afterward, when General Lingan and his partners had succeeded in circulating another issue, attacked the house where they were prepared to defend their property. To escape the excesses of the mob, they surrendered to the civil authorities, who offered them the protection of the jail for the night. The building was carelessly guarded, the mob broke in, and the scenes that followed were as horrible in their brutality and cruelty as any depicted on the gruesome pages of the French Revolution.

Though many of his friends were left for dead upon the floor of the jail, General Lingan alone was killed outright.

His body was buried secretly,—the condition exacted by the ringleaders before surrendering it,—and it was not until some time afterwards that his relatives had it removed to Georgetown and quietly buried in a grave on his own farm "Harlem." Here, many years later, his wife was laid by his side and still later, an infant grandson. During the civil war the whole field was used as a camping ground and all signs of an inclosure disappeared, but in 1874 or 1875, the grandchildren of General Lingan had an iron fence placed around the graves. These are now to be found at the back of a laborer's cottage on the Foxhall Road and are to be identified by the name "Lingan" on the iron gate of the inclosure.

In spite of the secrecy which attended the disposal of his body, General Lingan's memory was honored by a stately funeral. On September 1, a little more than a month after his death—during which the wounds and bruises of his friends and colleagues had time to heal—an immense concourse of people, too large for any church to hold, moved in procession to Parrott's Woods, now known as Oak Hill Cemetery, in the following order:

Marshals on horseback; four clergymen of different denominations; Committee of Arrangements; Mr. Custis of Arlington, orator of the day; Music; Captain Stull's Rifle Corps, commanded by Lieutenant Kurtz; eight venerable pall-bearers with white scarfs; hearse with the horses clad in mourning; Mr. George Lingan, the General's son, chief mourner; the General's horse in mourning, led by a groom; family and relatives of the deceased in coaches; the wounded veteran, Major Musgrove, who survived the midnight massacre in which his brother soldier fell, bearing the General's sword, and supported by two heroes of the Revolution; Mr. Hanson, and other survivors of the band who defended the liberty of the press; veteran band of the Revolution; strangers of distinction; citizens from the counties of Montgomery, Baltimore, Frederick, Charles, Prince George's and St. Mary's, and from the cities of Georgetown, Washington and Alexandria; marshals on horseback; Captain Peter's troop of horse commanded by Lieut. John S. Williams.

The orator of the day, spoken of above, was George Washington Custis, grandson of Mrs. Martha Washington. He was born at Mount Airy, Prince George's county, Md., the seat of his grandfather Benedict Calvert, on April 30, 1781, and died in 1857. His grave and that of his wife, Mary Lee Custis, who was a Miss Fitzhugh of Virginia, lie at Arlington under a tree, near a woodland path, apart from the soldiers' graves. According to the inscription on her tombstone she was born April 22, 1782, and died April 23, 1853. He was the seventh child of John Park Custis and Eleanor (Calvert) his wife, being only a few months old when his father died from camp fever, contracted while acting as General Washington's aid-de-camp at the siege of Yorktown. He was adopted by the latter and lived at Mount Vernon until his grandmother Washington's death, in 1802, when he built Arlington House. His daughter, Mary Randolph, was the wife of the Confederate hero, Gen. Robert E. Lee, and they lived at Arlington, which has since become the National Cemetery.

It is said that this estate passed into the hands of the government through confiscation at the time of the civil war. As a matter of fact, it was appropriated for taxes, but when Robert E. Lee's son was old enough to claim his Custis inheritance, the accident of his being the son of a "rebel" could not be made to interfere with his right as a citizen, and it was decreed that he should receive a compensation for his land over and above the amount of the taxes for which it had been taken. Uncle Sam's version of the case stands on record in the entrance hall of the old mansion, where two bronze tablets supplement the history of the tract.

Back of St. Alban's church in the Cathedral Close, on the heights above Georgetown, are two old-time tombstones mounted on brick foundations and inclosed by an iron railing. These stones, which were brought here in 1898 from the old burying ground at Croom, cover the remains of the

Rt. Rev. Thomas John Claggett and his wife, Mary. A more fitting spot for the last resting place of the first bishop consecrated in America, could not have been chosen, and the fact that Francis Scott Key was the author of his epitaph, adds an additional halo to his surroundings. The epitaph, written in Latin, states that Thomas John Claggett, the first bishop of Maryland, was born in the year 1743; ordained deacon and priest in London in 1767; consecrated bishop in 1792, and died in the peace of Christ in 1816. It ends with a tribute to his good qualities as man and servant of the church. The bishop was born in Prince George's county, at Croom, an ancestral estate of about 500 acres. Here he lived in his later years, while engaged upon the combined duties of bishop of the diocese and parish priest. St. Thomas church, where he officiated, is about a mile distant from his home. This church is not only interesting on account of its associations with him, but also because of its venerable age. Among the early worshipers here were the Calverts of Mount Airy, a daughter of whose house was the heroine of a runaway marriage, the groom of twenty-one, being no less a person than John Custis, stepson of George Washington, and father of G. W. Custis of Arlington, who has been referred to on a previous page. No very ancient graves have been preserved in St. Thomas' churchyard, for in Prince George's county the custom obtained of burying the dead in private burying grounds. In that at Croom, whence the remains of the bishop and his wife were removed, the graves of some of his children are still to be seen, but the old home has long since been destroyed by fire.

John Thomas Claggett was consecrated on November 17, 1792, in Trinity church, New York, and the four American bishops—Seabury, Provoost, White and Madison, who had received consecration in England—united in the ceremony, the first of its kind to take place in America.

In a hollow of the college grounds at Georgetown is a little spot laid off in symmetrical mounds, ten in a row, where the presidents and professors of this well-known institution sleep, and here lies also the body of the Rt. Rev. John Carroll, the first Roman Catholic archbishop, under whose direction as head of the incorporated Catholic clergy of Maryland the college was founded in 1789. The first step toward its establishment was taken in 1786, when the necessity for an institution of the kind was urged before the general chapter at Whitemarsh. Another important matter occupying the minds of the Catholic clergy at this time, was the establishment of a See in this country. The manner in which the appointment of the Rev. John Carroll took place can best be described by quoting the words of Pope Pius VI in the official document given "under the Fisherman's Ring the 6th day of November 1789."

"And whereas by special grant and for the first time only, we have allowed the priests exercising the cure of souls in the United States of America to elect a person to be appointed bishop by us, and almost all their votes have been given to our beloved son John Carroll, Priest, we . . . . declare, create, appoint and constitute the said John Carroll Bishop and Pastor of said church in Baltimore . . . . and we commission said Bishop elect to erect a church in the said City of Baltimore in the form of a Cathedral Church."

The consecration of the new bishop was performed on August 15, 1790, in the chapel of Lulworth Castle, England, the seat of Thomas Weld, Esq.

About five miles from the city of Washington, on what is called the Sligo branch of the Anacostia river, otherwise the eastern branch of the Potomac river, lies an old estate which formerly bore the name of Green Hill, but now is known as the Riggs' Farm. The original dwelling has disappeared and few of the old landmarks remain, but in a sheltered corner of what was probably the old garden, is a slight mound covered with periwinkle and surmounted by a simple cedar cross. In this spot lie the remains of Charles L'Enfant, the brave and talented Frenchman who fought in our Revolutionary war and to whom we are indebted for the plan of our national capital. Appleton's Cyclopedia of American Biography accords him a brief mention as a military officer, architect and engineer, but a better knowledge of his life in its essentially human aspect is to be drawn from a variety of sources, including his own papers, the only fortune he left behind him, the letters of General Washington, contained in volumes IX, X, XII of Spark's Life of Washington, and traditions handed down by those with whom he passed his latter years.

Born in the year 1755, he was still young when the war ended. Possessed of good taste and ability, both of which were early recognized by Washington, he had every prospect of a successful career before him, but owing to a proud spirit, trained to military obedience alone, and to his being one of those unfortunate characters, who so often stand in the way of their own success, he seldom realized any profit from his professional services. To quote from a recent writer: even "The task that . . . . won for his name enduring fame, brought him personally nothing but disgrace, neglect and poverty prolonged through more than a quarter of a century." Under the custody of the War Department is still to be seen L'Enfant's map, the title of which appears in one corner as follows: "Plan of the City intended for the permanent Seat of the Government of the United States, projected agreeable to the direction of the President of the United States in Pursuance of the act of Congress passed the 16th day of July, 1790 establishing the Permanent Seat on the bank of the Potommac."

In March, 1791, Major L'Enfant began the congenial

task of laying out the city, and on July 20, following, Washington writes to David Humphries: "You have been informed of the spot fixed for the seat of government on the Potomac; and I am now happy to add that all matters between the proprietors of the soil and the public are settled to the mutual satisfaction of both parties and that the business of laying out the city, the grounds for public buildings, walks &c, is advancing under the inspection of Major L'Enfant with pleasing prospects." Under these promising conditions a public sale of lots was advertised to take place on October 17, of the same year; but unfortunately L'Enfant failed to recognize the authority of the commissioners in the matter and withheld the plat of the city from the inspection of the commonalty, lest they should "leap at once" as he expressed it, "upon my best squares and vistas and raise huddles of shanties which will permanently embarrass the city." That his prophecy was only in part fulfilled was due to Washington and Jefferson who approved of his plan and protected it from perversion so long as they were in office, thereby fixing the main features of the original scheme beyond possibility of loss. The "huddles of shanties," conjured up by L'Enfant's fears materalized as he foresaw they would, but they failed to become a permanent embarrassment to the city owing to the heroic measures adopted in the cause of good taste, about three-quarters of a century later; since when L'Enfant's conception of a beautiful city laid out on an extensive scale has become more and more possible of realization.

L'Enfant's attitude to the commissioners made it impossible to employ him "about the Federal city in that degree of subordination which was lawful and proper," and so, in March, 1792, he was dismissed by Jefferson after having for one year thrown himself heart and soul into his work. In compensation for his services, $2,500 or $3,000 were considered ample, but he would not accept less than $50,000, and to quote again from the same article: "until the day of his death, in 1825, the tall erect figure of the courtly Frenchman trod the corridors of the Capitol as he vainly pleaded with Congress for the reward he believed his due."

In 1812 L'Enfant again appears as the planner of Fort Washington—his last work—for again he became restive under certain restraints and was mustered out of the service.

For seven years he lived at "Warburton Manor," the seat of Thomas Digges, within sight of the fort he had built. Here he found consolation in the companionship of a generous and sympathizing friend. Thomas Digges died in 1821 and L'Enfant's troubles began anew; but William Digges, the nephew of his former friend and benefactor, received him into his home at Green Hill, and here shortly afterwards, at the age of seventy, he died and was buried. His fame is his only monument.

The oldest places of burial in Washington, owing to the growth of the city, are now extinct. Old St. John's, belonging to the Episcopal Church, which was begun about the year 1796 on land given by Col. Wm. Deakins, was the first to be disturbed. This occurred just before the civil war, and immediately after peace was restored St. Matthew's Roman Catholic cemetery and the Methodist burying ground, known as the "Foundry," were made to follow; but a graveyard older than either of these was "Holmead's," bounded by 19th and 20th streets, N. W., and S. and Boundary streets, where interments were permitted as late as 1874. It is estimated that they reached the number of 10,000. The history of this last habitation of the dead is worth preserving with others of its kind.

Tradition says that Anthony Holmead, whose farm lay in the western section, set apart a plot of ground 120 feet by 100 for a graveyard; as a matter of fact a paper preserved among the records of the commissioners shows that a graveyard existed or was contemplated by Holmead as early as 1791. In 1796 a conveyance was made to the commissioners by which Holmead was to be allowed to retain his buildings and graveyard, should the arrangement of the city lots and streets not interfere. For this privilege he was to pay to the President at the rate of £12. 0 s. 10 d. per acre; on the other hand, if the city lay through the property to the interference of his buildings and graveyard, the commissioners were to pay him damages.

And so the matter rested till between the years 1810 and 1816, when the Corporation of Washington allotted squares numbered 109 and 1026 respectively, as places of burial. These were considered to be at a proper distance from the populous parts of the city to accommodate the inhabitants at either end. A sexton was appointed to take care of each of them, to dig the graves and to keep a register of persons interred. Square 109, located between 19th and 20th streets, S. street and Florida avenue, at that time the boundary, embraced Holmead's reservation and became the public burying ground of the northwestern section, or, as it is stated among the general acts of the Corporation, was one of the squares "assigned . . . . to the public as burial grounds for the interment of all people." The act provides also for the fencing in of these squares with good and sufficient locust or cedar posts and chestnut rails under the direction and supervision of three commissioners for each burial ground, to be appointed by the Mayor. The latter was also to cause the necessary gates and stiles to be made and fixed thereto. Provisions were made both for white people and for "people of color" and slaves. A thorn fence was to mark the line of separation between the two. The later history of the graveyard shows that a distinction between the colors was preserved up to the end of its existence.

Among the other provisions of this act, was one that allowed persons whose dead were already buried there, to have a first choice of lots, and they were not to be charged more that $3.00 nor less than $2.50 for any one site. The funds thus raised were to be used to keep the grounds in order and to build a house for the sexton. The latter was not only to keep a regular and exact account of all interments made and the numbers of the graves and sites, but also the names of the persons interred, and every three months he was to make a return of the same to the register of the city, whose duty it was to file and keep them for future reference. It is doubtless owing to this fact that so many names have been preserved.

The first interment on record is that of Robert Smith of Boston, who was buried there on May 30, 1794, and the list includes the names of many well-known families. Among the oddities there laid to rest was Lorenzo Dow, the eccentric minister, who with his wife, Peggy, preached in the market houses and handled crowds just as the leaders of the Salvation Army began to do some fifty years later. Nominated President by Crow, Lorenzo Dow was elected by his followers and proceeded to the White House to take his seat. Arrest instead of inauguration very naturally followed. William Seaton, the journalist, James Hoban, the architect, Andrew Way, the well-known printer, and others, who in their day and generation played a part in civic or national life, were also buried at Holmead's.

About the year 1884 the commissioners sold the ground for building lots, and with $4,000, a part of the proceeds, they had most of the bodies and tombstones removed to other places of burial. Six hundred bodies were said to have been provided for elsewhere by relatives and friends. The rest of the funds thus raised, amounting to $48,000, were devoted to the use of the public schools.

The body of Joseph Meigs, the father of General Meigs, buried at first at Holmead's, now reposes in the Oak Hill cemetery; that of George Moore, who died in 1810, lies at Mt. Olivet, but most of the bodies were reinterred in the Rock Creek Cemetery.

A partial list has been obtained of some of the persons buried at Holmead's: Andrew McLean, Joseph McIntosh, 1809; George Morland or Morlin, Samuel Douglas, 1815; Alexander Smoot, Robert Breckingridge, John Sessford, Nicholas King, Thomas H. Gillis, Alex. Cochran, 1812; John Lenthall, 1808; Walter Lennox, Robt. Underwood, John McClelland, Cornelius McLean, Ezekiel King, Major Stone, 1826; Peter Lenox, 1832; Mrs. Shieffly, 1839; Mrs. A. J. Larned, James Larned, 1847; Wm. O'Neil, 1837; aged 86; Alex. McIntire, 1843; Chas. Polkinhorn, 1844. Interspersed through the list we find the names of Stanley, Hines, Somers, McIntosh and Handley.

Square 1026, set aside for the inhabitants of the eastern section of the city of Washington was abandoned, as being too low. The National, now the Congressional, cemetery, on 17th street and Georgia avenue, existed already in 1830, when it is described by a writer of the day as "South East of the Capitol and sloping towards the margin of the Eastern Branch." Either this cemetery or the Washington Parish burial ground adjoining it and now included in it, may have served the original purpose of the commissioners.

The Congressional burying ground is easy to find and well worth a visit, and so we shall mention only a few names of the dignitaries buried there: George Clinton, a friend and contemporary of Washington who was born July 26, 1739, and died in Washington, April 20, 1811; Elbridge Gerry, Vice President of the United States, who died there in 1814, and the Hon. Wm. Pinkney, senator for Maryland, who died

February 25, 1822, aged 58, besides many "Honourables" from other states of the Union.

Pushinataha, "the Eagle of the Choctaws," who served with Jackson through all the perils of the Pensacola war, and died from diphtheria while on a mission to Washington, was buried there with funeral honors. His monument, which his tribe were allowed to choose to mark the resting place of their chief, is of sandstone now dark with age. It is a rectangular block resting on a pedestal and surmounted by a pyramid; on one of its sides are inscribed the following words taken from a eulogy pronounced by John Randolph of Roanoke:

"Pushinataha was a warrior of great distinction. He was wise in council, eloquent in an excellent degree, and on all occasions, under all circumstances, the white man's friend."

Old St. Paul's, around which are now to be found the graves of Rock Creek Cemetery, was described by a writer in 1816 as being "in the bosom of the woods." It is on the Brightwell road, about three miles from the Capitol, though since the introduction of the trolley, it might be said to lie at its doors. Near it, in the early part of the nineteenth century, stood the home of Samuel Harrison Smith. The name of this place, "Turkey Thicket," carries us back to a time when the neighborhood was still more or less of a wilderness.

As editor of the *National Intelligencer*, the first newspaper published in Washington, Samuel Smith deserves mention in passing. He was the son of Jonathan Smith, a wealthy Philadelphia merchant, and patriot in the Revolution. He associated himself from the first with the vital interests of the infant Capital. The *Intelligencer* was started by him during the Adams administration on October 31, 1800, and he remained the editor until 1818, when he handed over the control to his young assistant, Joseph Gales, and became a manager of the Washington branch of the United States Bank. He died in 1845.

Another newspaper, which is not to be confused with the *National Intelligencer*, is the *National Journal*, a daily, founded by Peter Force, who, as the patient collector of "Force's Tracts" is the literary "old mortality" to whom the modern antiquarian turns. It is said that he is buried in the Rock Creek cemetery. John T. Agg, the gifted Englishman who edited the *National Journal*, certainly lies there, if we are to believe the testimony of the stone erected by the parish as a grateful tribute to his memory. He died April 19, 1855, aged 75 years, having outlived his journal twenty-five years.

To him were attributed the following lines that appeared in the *National Journal*, January, 1824:

> Wend ye with the world to-night?
> Brown and fair and wise and witty;
> Eyes that float in seas of light;
> Laughing mouths and dimples pretty;
> Belles and matrons, maids and madams
> All are gone to Mrs. Adams.

In the Rock Creek cemetery lie also the remains of Mrs. Carolina Virginia Marylanda Frye. Her two husbands, Gen. Andrew Buchanan and Nathaniel Frye, are buried beside her. She was the daughter of Joshua Johnson, brother of Thomas Johnson, first governor of Maryland after her independence as a state, and the sister of Catherine, Mrs. John Quincy Adams, whose ball given in honor of Andrew Jackson on January 8, 1824, furnished the motive for John T. Agg's graceful lines, quoted above.

The old inscriptions in this churchyard are few in number because of its neglected condition during the disturbed period of the Revolution and the years immediately following it.

Washington

They appear as follows:

In Remembrance of J. White who died March 8, 1801 Aged 86 years.

Eleanor White Wife of J. M. White departed this life Aug. 12th 1795 the 90th year of her age and 60th of her marriage.

Here lies the body of Abram Mason born the 14th day of January 1798 and died on the 22nd. day of July 1801. The oldest child and only son of John T. Mason and Elizabeth His wife of Georgetown.

In memory of David Steuger late of the City of Philadelphia who departed this life on the 8th day of Nov. 1802. Aged 21 years and 4 months.

> When I lie buried deep in dust
> My flesh shall be thy care
> These withering limbs with thee I trust
> O raise them strong and fair.

In Memory of Susanna Borrows wife of John Borrows who departed this life July 31, 1803 Aged 71 years.

Nathaniel Frye Aged 77 years.

Caroline V. M. Frye Born October 5th, 1777 Died May 14th 1862.

In Memory of Elizabeth Gramphin wife of Thomas Gramphin who departed this life . . . of March . . . 1775.

In Memory of Robert Gramphin Son of Thomas and Elizabeth Gramphin who departed this life April 1775 Aged 19 years.

In Memory of Thomas Gramphin who departed this life 29th of July 1783, aged 68 years.

In Memory of Mary wife of Wm. Tunnicliff also Robert Tunnicliff who died Nov. 1798. This slab is broken into six pieces and cannot be further deciphered.

In Memory of Mrs. Amelia Lovering wife of Wm. M. Lovering, Architect of the City of Washington who departed this life the 14th day of January 1791 Aged 30 years.

> This humble grave though no proud structures grace,
> Yet truth and goodness sanctify the place.
> O from life I am safe on that calm shore
> Where sin and pain and suffering are no more.
> What never wealth could buy nor power decree
> Regard and pity wait secure on Thee.

John Agg of Eversham England Died 19 April 1855 Aged 75 years.

John Agg A communicant, long the Senior member of the Vestry, a faithful and generous friend of the Church. Erected by the Parish as a grateful tribute to his Memory.

In Memory of Charles Shremaker of Philadelphia Deceased April 14th, 1807 In the 54th year of his Age.

On the outer wall of St. Paul's church, the venerable structure that stands in their midst, are inscribed these words:

Erected 1719.   Rebuilt 1775.   Remodelled 1868.

These dates represent the decisions of the vestry rather than the ultimate accomplishment of their plans concerning the erection and rebuilding of the church.

As early as 1710 the Rev. John Frazier, rector of St. John's Piscataway parish, preached to the inhabitants in the eastern branch of the Potomac and Rock Creek Hundred, and it is to be inferred, from what is already known of the customs of those days, that the services were held sometimes at the house or in an outbuilding of one landowner, sometimes in that of another.

On September 18, 1719, the rector of Piscataway parish called a meeting of the inhabitants of Prince George's county to consider ways and means for the erection of a chapel in the location where his nine years of ministry had drawn together a congregation sufficiently large to need a meeting place of its own. It was in response to his appeal that John Bradford, a vestryman of the parent church of St. John, contributed 1,000 pounds of tobacco, the staple of that period, and 100 acres of land. The latter constitutes what is known to-day as the glebe of Rock Creek parish. About one-half of this land has been laid off into a cemetery, composing perhaps the largest churchyard in existence, the usual number of acres allowed to a church being one, known simply as "God's acre." Here the walls of the present church have stood since the beginning of the Revolution, the completion of the structure having been interrupted at that time. In the first quarter of the next century it was roofed in and became a place of worship, and later still it took the form in which it now appears.

All the old parish records that have been rescued from

oblivión or probable destruction are now kept at the diocesan library in Baltimore, and to make their ultimate preservation doubly sure the Maryland Historical Society has procured copies of them. From these records and from other sources, principally the researches of the Rev. James A. Buck, a late rector, who served here for thirty-five years, an outline of the church's history may be gathered. The principal events connected with it are its creation as a parish church in 1726 under the name of Prince George's parish, and its ultimate adoption in 1856 of the popular name of Rock Creek parish, when by a further subdivision its metes and bounds were again defined. This is a case like others in Maryland, notably that of St. John's Piscataway parish, better known as the "Broad Creek" church, where the proximity of some river or creek provided it from the beginning with a name to preserve its identity.

The first object that meets the eye upon entering the cemetery is a large iron cross bearing the name of John Bradford. This surname, though well known in the history of a sister colony, has had but few representatives in Maryland, and the little that can be obtained concerning the beneficent donor of land to the church is to be found in the rent roll of Calvert and Prince George's counties and in the church records of St. John.

As early as 1704 we find him owning a portion of "Twiver," a tract of 440 acres in Mattapony Hundred, and also a tract of 300 acres called "Essex Lodge," west side of Patuxent, 150 of which he had purchased from the Widow Bagby. In 1714 and in 1715 he takes up land with others in Mount Calvert Hundred. These tracts were called respectively "Good Luck," "Butterwick" and "Haddock Hills." The latter consisted of 500 acres, 100 of which were in possession of John Deakins, whose surname is one of those associated later with the history of Georgetown. The ownership of

"Butterwick" was confirmed to John Bradford by patent on May 11, 1715, and that of "Bradford's Rest" on June 3d of the same year, and here he is designated by the name of "Captain." Ere this time he had become one of the leading men of Prince George's county, appearing on St. John's church records as vestryman in 1712, where the baptism of his son William is recorded in 1713. He is next alluded to as Maj. John Bradford, and finally as Col. John Bradford, late of Prince George's county, deceased, June 23, 1726. His wife Joyce, and his son John are named as executors in his will, and Henry Darnall and Daniel Carroll of the same county went on their bond to the amount of $8,000.

Unless some descendant of John Bradford should stand forward to tell us more about him, we shall have to remain contented with this scant outline of one, known to the present generation by his gift alone.

Piscataway parish, to which Rock Creek owed its origin, was one of the first four laid out in Charles county in 1692. By the creation of Prince George's county in 1695, it fell within the boundaries of the new county, extending from the Mattawoman Creek, an estuary of the Potomac, to the Pennsylvania border; all the parishes, therefore, since erected in the northwestern section of Maryland are direct descendants of the Piscataway parish, and St. John's, the quaint old brick church which stands on Broad Creek within easy access of Washington, is its most venerable monument. The few crumbling stones remaining in St. John's graveyard, however, furnish no record of the men who contributed to its erection or support. A headstone to James Jones, who died in 1760, is the only stone of any antiquity that has resisted the vicissitudes of time, weather and neglect, though there is another inscription that has been partly deciphered as "Boston D———tts, died 1743."

We cannot, therefore, seek in this spot for enlightenment

about the past. Fortunately the church records are not silent on this point. The inhabitants of Piscataway Hundred, empowered by the Act of 1692, met at the house of Col. John Addison, to elect the first vestry. Colonel Addison was chosen foreman, the other members being William Hatton, John Smith, William Hutchinson, William Tannehill and John Smallwell. John Addison and William Hutchinson were appointed to direct the building of the church, and specifications of what was required show that the first vestry of St. John's was composed of men who had brought with them to the wilderness a just appreciation of the fitness of things, in all that appertained to an abode for Christian worship. The church was ready for the use of the congregation in 1697. They were ministered to by lay readers until the year 1709, when the Rev. John Frazier took charge.

Much of the local tradition of the past is linked with the name of Addison and with the old family estates of Barnaby, Oxen Hill and Gisborough.

At Oxen Hill is the family vault and graveyard where the dead of several generations repose. Col. John Addison died in England in 1706, and probably the first to be laid in the vault was Thomas, his only son and heir, with the latter's wives, Elizabeth Tasker and Eleanor Smith. The third generation is represented by John, Thomas and Anthony, all of whom were born to Thomas by his second marriage; also, possibly, John's wife, Susannah Wilkinson; then comes John's son Thomas, who married Rebecca Dulany, and some of their children and grandchildren. This brings us down to the Rev. Walter Dulany Addison, who was born at Annapolis, January 1, 1769, and died January 31, 1848. He is buried in the adjoining graveyard by the side of his first wife, Elizabeth Dulany Hesselius. She died July 31, 1808, at the age of 33. His brother John of Colebrook, who preceded him in 1835, lies near by. The gravestones are few in number and none of very ancient date.

An interesting tribute to the memory of the Rev. W. Dulany Addison appeared in 1895 in book form under the title of *One Hundred Years Ago*. In it his life and times were depicted from the year 1769 to 1848. His great-uncle, the Rev. Henry Addison, who lived at Barnaby, was the first of the name in this country to carry on the ecclesiastical traditions held by the family in England. In both lives we see an incessant display of a true missionary spirit employed to sustain and promote the influence of the church throughout that portion of the country, where their ancestor, Col. John Addison, vestryman of St. John's, had been among the first to establish its outward forms. Col. John Addison and his brother, the Rev. Launcelot Addison, the father of the renowned Joseph Addison of *Spectator* fame, were sons of a clergyman. They had a brother Anthony, also in orders, and the distinguished Joseph had himself been destined to the Church, only the Government was at that time on the alert to bind just such men to the service of the State, and so he was induced to join the secular body to his own glory and to the great satisfaction of generations to come.

To return to his uncle, Col. John Addison, we first find him settled in St. George's Hundred, St. Mary's county, in 1667. He married Barbara, the widow of Thomas Dent, and daughter of the Rev. Wm. Wilkinson, the pioneer clergyman of the Church of England on the western shore, who preached here in 1650. The old Poplar Hill church marks the scene of his early ministrations.

We find Gisborough mentioned among the tracts of land left by Thomas Dent in his will with other land in Charles county, and this may account for Colonel Addison having established himself in a portion of the province where he could look after his wife's and stepchildren's property.

There is every indication that the house at Barnaby is of an earlier period of architecture than that at Oxen Hill, which was destroyed by fire, and it was doubtless at the older Addison home that the first meeting of the vestry of Piscataway parish was held. The house is described as having offices in front of it and, unconnected with it, a lovely grass plot between. One of these smaller buildings was used as a library, and the other may have served the purpose of sleeping apartments for masculine guests, as was so often the custom in olden times, when the main dwelling was full. A sundial in front of the buildings is inscribed thus:

The beginning of Barnaby Manor as resurveyed for the Rev. Mr. Henry Addison the 24th day of December, 1767 by John F. A. Priggs, Surveyor.
Ah subtle fugitive how swift thye flight
But I will seize the moral of thy shade.
G. Adams No. 60 Fleet street London, England.

The Rev. Henry Addison was born in 1717, and died at Barnaby, in 1789. He married Rachel, widow of William Knight, and daughter of Daniel Dulany, Sr. He was rector at Broad Creek church for thirty-three years, and was very much beloved.

Barnaby was left to his son Anthony, and by him to the son of his sister Eleanor, who had married Garland Callis, with the request that he should take the family name and bear the family arms. This Henry Addison Callis did not do; but after the death of his children, he left the place to his fourth cousin, Anthony Addison, whose heirs still own it, together with some interesting family relics. An old graveyard is there, but no stones. It is said that from this estate Mr. Callis gave the land on which St. Barnabas church now stands.

INDEX

INDEX

A

Abell, Philip	34
Acquasco	76
Adams	71
Adams, Mrs. John Quincy	262
Addison family	71, 267, 268
Addison, Col. John	268
Addison, Joseph	55, 268
Addison, Robert	55
Addison, Thomas	267
Agg, John	262, 263
Airey, Louisa	219
Airey, Rev. Thomas	219
Alexander, John McK.	230
Alexander, Walter	229
Alleghany County	169, 170
Allen	71
Allen family	98
Allen, Margaret	220
Allen, Rev. Bennett	220
Allnutt, Francis	61
Allnutt, Gideon	61
Allnutt Sarah	61
All Faith church	31
All Hallows	20
All Saints parish	159
Alter, A. Horace	88
Altvater	111
Amblers, The	17
Amos	106
Amos, Catherine	153
Amos, David	153
Amos, James	153
Anderson	71
Anderson, Dr. Asa	24
Anderson, Isaac	150
Anderson, Rachel	123
Anderson, Capt. Richard	176
Aneslie	152
Anne Arundel County	1-26
Archer, Geo. W.	101
Armacost, Julia	142
Armacost, Ann	142
Armacost, Thomas	14
Armour, David	152
Armour, Mary	152
Armstrong	71
Arnold, Alicia	13
Arrants, Herman	229
Arrants, Jacob	229
Artis, Elizabeth	44
Artis, Jane R.	43
Artis, Jeremiah	44
Artis, Joseph	44
Artis, Mary	44
Ashcom, George	45
Ashcom, John	45
Ashbey, Father	35
Ashman, Constance	141
Atwood, Peter	35
Austin, Rev. Charles	119
Austin, Francis B.	172

B

Back River Neck	112
Bailey, Arietta J.	137
Bailey, Harriet Ward	137
Bailey, James P.	137
Baden	80
Baillie	71
Baker, Rev. Charles	141
Baker, Catherine	68
Baker, Elizabeth	141
Baker, Francis	197
Baker, Mary T.	197
Baker, Roger	52
Baker, Thos. of Battle, Esq.	50
Bald Eagles	83
Bald Friar Ferry	105
Baldwin, Abraham	246

Index

Baldwin, Francis	25	Beaty, Frances	96
Baldwin, Henry	246	Beaty, Jane	99
Baldwin, Col. John	227	Beaty, Dr. William	99
Baldwin, Ruth	247	Beavin, Patsy	67
Baldwin, Sarah	25	Beck, James	197
Baldwin Memorial Churchyard	24	Beck, Mary T.	197
Baldwin-Milligan-McLane		Becket, Betty H.	62
graveyard	227	Becket, Capt. John	62
Baltimore County	92–152	Becket, John	62
Banning, Anthony	199	Becket, Mary H.	62
Banning, Catherine	199	Becket, Richard	62
Banning, Henry	211	Beggar's Neck	35
Banning, James	211	Bell	71, 111
Banning, Capt. Jeremiah	211	Bellefield	10
Banning, Susanna	211	Belleville	210
Barber, John T.	3	Belmont	145, 156
Barker	71	Belt, Addison	173
Barlow, Joel	245	Belt, Alfred	181
Barnes	71	Belt, Charlotte T.	181
Barnes, Abraham	30	Belt, Ann	44
Barnes, Elizabeth	30, 96	Belvoir Mansion	12
Baron, Father Walter	35	Bennett family	43
Barron, Com. James	246	Bennett, Elizabeth	186
Barry, Jemima	135	Bennett, Harriet	220
Barton, James H.	204	Bennett, John	220
Barton, Rev. Dr.	234	Bennett, Joseph	43
Bastin	71	Bennett, Rachel	220
Batte, Rev. Mr.	215	Bennett, Richard	7, 44, 186
Battle Creek	50	Bennett, Susanna	43
Batson, James	129	Bennett, Thomas	220
Bausman, Mrs. Mary	59	Bennett, William	43
Bausman, Rev. John	59	Benson	71
Bay Farm	33	Berry, Samuel	67
Bay Hundred district	212	Berry, Teresa	67
Bayley, Hon. Josiah	243	Bertram, Rev. Paul	54
Bayleys, John B.	110	Bethel Church	103
Baysman, Joseph	123	Betty's Cove	223
Baysman, Rachel	123	Beverly	240
Beadnall, James	35	Biddle, Raymond	200
Beale	71	Biggs, Hon. Seth	23
Beall, Jane	173	Billingsly, James	11
Beall, Upton	173	Billingsly, Susan	11
Bean, Samuel	43	Billop, Rev. Thos.	75
Bean, Thos. N.	34	Birkhead, Abraham	23
Beanes, Mary	76	Birkhead, Christopher	23
Beanes, Sarah H.	76	Birkhead's Meadows	23
Beanes, William	76	Birmingham graveyard	89
Beard, Capt. Alex.	57	Biscoe family	42, 43, 44
Beard, Capt. Lewis	124	Black, James, M. D.	202
Beard, Rachel	4	Black, Jennet	202
Beaty (or Beatty), Archibald	99, 100	Blackiston, James	200

Index 275

Blackiston, Mary M.	200	Borrows, John	263
Blackiston, Thos. M.	200	Borrows, Susanna	263
Bladen, William	5, 107	Bosley, Elizabeth	108
Blair	111	Boswells	106
Blake, Charles	185	Boswell, Elizabeth	66
Blake, Mary	62	Boswell, John	67
Blakiston, Elizabeth	197	Bourne's Island	56
Blakiston, John	197	Bourne, Thos. H. Benton	56
Blakiston, Thos. P.	197	Bourne, Jas. J.	56
Blatchford, Rev. Henry	235	Bourne, Dr.	56
Blatchford, Rev. Samuel	235	Bourne, Sarah J.	56
Blay, Mm. Ann	202	Bowham, Matakiah	161
Blay, Catherine	203	Bowre-Brawner	71
Blay, Edward	203	Bowie family	173, 177
Blay, Col. Edward	199, 202	Bowie, Mary W.	78
Blay, Isabella	203	Bowie, Robert	78
Blay, Rachel	203	Bowles, Hon. James	29
Blay, William	202	Bowles, Rebecca Addison	29
Blenheim	94	Bowling, Aloysius	66
Bloomsbury	31	Bowling, John H.	66
Bloxton	71	Bowling, Margaret	66
Boarman, Alexius	69	Bowling, Mary	66, 69
Boarman, Ann	68	Bowling, Mary A.	66, 68
Boarman, Anne	69	Bowling, Marsham	66
Boarman, Francis	68	Bowling, Polly	68
Boarman, George	68	Bowling, Richard	69
Boarman, Mary	65	Bowling, Thomas	66
Boarman, Matilda	68	Bozman, John Leeds	211
Boarman, James	68	Brady, Benj.	151
Boarman, Raphael	65	Brady, Samuel	151
Boarman, Sally	68	Braddock, William	173
Bogart, Chas. E.	88	Bradford, John	264, 266
Bogart, Mary	88	Bradford, Joyce	266
Bogart, Peter	88	Bradford, William	266
Bolingly	187	Bradshaw	71
Bolton, John	35	Brawner, Catherine	41
Bomford, Clara	247	Brawner, Edward	165
Bomford, George	247	Brawner, Henry	41
Bond, Basil Duke	59	Breckingridge, Robert	260
Bond, Elizabeth	124	Brent family	173, 174, 175
Bond, Mary W.	59	Brent, Henry	63
Bond, Mrs. Sarah H.	42	Brent, Jane	63
Booker, Emily	190	Brenton, Rear Admiral	22
Booker, Lambert	190, 208	Brenton, Louisa	22
Boone Julia	67	Bretton, Wm.	35
Bordley, Elizabeth	1, 4	Brewer family	3
Bordley, John	197	Brice House	1
Bordley, John Beale	4	Brice, John, Chief Justice	2
Bordley, Matthias	4	Brice, Tilghman	16
Bordley, Rev. Stephen	3	Briscoe, James	200
Bordley, Thomas	3, 4	Briscoe, John	38

Index

Briscoe, Philip	38	Bullitt, Thomas	207
Briscoe's wharf	29	Bullitt, Thos. J.	207
Brittingham, James	232	Bullman	71
Brittingham, Lydia	232	Burch, Augustine	66
Brome (or Broome), James M.	45	Burch, Catherine	38
Brome, Margaret	45	Burch, Henry Dade	38
Brome, Sarah H.	34	Burch, Hilary	68
Brooke	14, 71	Burch, Susanna	66
Brooke, Anne	50	Burchell	71
Brooke, Baker	39	Burgess family	11, 21
Brooke, Basil	50	Burnham, Edward	123
Brooke, Ellinor	63	Burnham, Elizabeth	123
Brooke, John	59	Burnham, Samuel S.	122
Brooke, Col. John	58	Burns (or Burnes), David	248
Brooke, Mrs. Juliet	59	Burr, Aaron	244
Brooke, Mrs. Mary A.	164	Burris	71
Brooke, Richard	51	Burroughs, Aquilla	37
Brooke, Robert	39, 50, 51, 63	Burroughs, Susan E.	37
Brooke, Susan	51	Bush	71
Brooke, Thomas	51, 52	Bush River meeting	106
Brooke, Col. Thomas	50, 79	Bushwood	32
Brooke, Maj. Thomas	78	Butler, Francis	208
Brooke Court Manor	83	Butterwick	266
Brookefield	78		
Brown, Frances F.	64	**C**	
Brown, Dr. Gustavus	63, 64		
Brown, Jacob	96	Cadwalader, Gen. John	203
Brown, James	193	Cady, Wm. Spelton	172
Brown, Josiah	151	Caile, John	242, 243
Brown, Margaret	64	Calvert County	49–62
Brown, Mary Ann	193	Calvert, Benedict	91
Brown, Peregrine	203	Calvert, Charles	2, 91
Brown, Rachel	203	Calvert, Chas. B.	90
Brown, Robert	176	Calvert, Eleanor	252
Brown, Samuel	157	Calvert, George	90, 91
Brown, Sarah	151	Calvert, Father James	35
Browsley	19	Calvert, Col. Leonard	42, 184
Bryan, Daniel	201	Calvert, Rosalie E.	90, 91
Bryantown	84	Cameron, Anthony	200
Buchanan, Andrew	127, 262	Cameron, Joseph	200
Buchanan, Charles	152	Campbell, Ann	47
Buchanan, Dr. George	126	Campbell, George	47
Buchanan, James M.	152	Canning, Sir Stratford	246
Buchanan, William	152	Capron, Horace	89
Buck, Rev. Mr.	48	Capron, Louisa V.	89
Buckler, Eliza	149	Carbery, Rev. Joseph	27, 29
Bucknell, Mary	131	Carmichael, William	195
Bucknell, Benj.	131	Carnan, Cecil	118
Bullen, Marion E.	220	Carnan, Christopher	118
Bullen, William	220	Carnan, John	118
Bullitt, Mary	207	Carpenter, John	37

Index

Carpenter, Susannah	37	Charles County	62-73
Carpenter's Point	14	Charlotte Hall	40, 86, 87
Carricoe, Abel	68	Chauncey, Ann	100
Carricoe, Joseph	67	Chauncey, Eliza	100
Carricoe, Louisa	68	Chauncey, Elizabeth	96
Carricoe, Mary	66	Chauncey, Miranda	100
Carroll, Charles	5, 186	Chesley's Hill	41
Carroll, Charles, of Carrollton	158, 246	Chesley, John	41
		Chestnut Ridge	134
Carroll, Daniel	174, 175	Cheston, Mrs. James	18
Carroll, Dorothy	185	Chichester, Mary B.	177
Carroll, Eleanor	175	Chichester, Washington	177
Carroll, Father James	35	Chilton	71
Carroll, John	119	Christison, Wenlock	223
Carroll, Geo. R.	176	Christ Church	53, 156, 216
Carroll, Rt. Rev. (John)	254	Christie, Catherine	227
Carroll, Margaret	5	Christie, Gabriel	97
Carroll, Mollie	33	Christie, James	227
Carroll, Nicholas	119	Christie, Thomas	227
Carroll, Thomas H.	119	Church bridge	93
Carroll County	156-158	Churchville	102
Carter, Sarah Weems	146	Cissell, George	34
Carter, Richard	211	City cemetery	4
Carter, Thomas	211, 220	Claiborne, Col. William	184
Cathell, Sarah	17	Clagett, Susan	76
Cathell, William	17	Clagett, Thos.	76
Caviller, Charles	197	Claggett, Elizabeth	77
Cay, Rev. Jonathan	54	Claggett, Mary	253
Cay, Robert	54	Claggett, Samuel	77
Cecil County	225-232	Claggett, Rt. Rev. Thos. J.	77, 83, 156, 253
Cedar Park	18		
Cedar Point	33	Clarke	71
Chamberlaine, Henrietta M.	210	Clarke, Dr. Wm. Jones	198
Chamberlaine, James Lloyd	210	Clator, Elizabeth	19
Chamberlaine, John	217	Clator, John	19
Chamberlaine, Robins	210	Clean Drinking	183
Chamberlaine, Samuel	210	Clinkscales	71
Chamberlaine, Susannah	210	Clinton, George	260
Chamberlaine, Col. Thomas	210	Cobey	71
Chambers, Gen. Benj.	197	Cochran, Alex.	260
Chambers, Cary C.	197	Cockeys	106
Chambers, E. F.	197	Cockey family	133, 134, 140, 141
Chambers, Elizabeth C.	197	Cockey, Chas. T.	126
Chandlee, Benj.	99	Cockey, Capt. John	121
Chandler	14	Cockey's old tavern	140
Chandler, Col. Wm.	62	Coffer	71
Channing	71	Coleman, Parson	104
Chaplain, Henrietta	242	Coley, David	195
Chapel Point	63	Collier, William H.	232
Chapman, Ann	197	Collings, Henry C.	142
Chaptico church	35	Collings, Mary Ann	142

Index

Collins, Elizabeth G.	204	Crane, George	43
Collins, Wm. H.	204	Crane, Susan	43
Combs, Father Ignatius	35	Cranford Place	79
Compton, Mrs. John	84	Craufurd, David	77, 79, 80
Conn, Elizabeth	115	Craufurd, Sarah	77, 80
Conn, Rev. Hugh	115	Crawford	71
Connelly, Bridget	176	Craycrofts	84
Constable family	196, 197	Cremona	39
Contee, Alexander	78	Crisfield, John W.	235
Contee, John	77	Crisfield, Julia	235
Contee, Margaret	77	Cromwell family	212, 227, 228
Contee, Richard	77	Croom burying ground	252
Contee, Col. Thomas	78	Crosdale, Rev. Henry	232
Cook, Ann	123	Crosdale, Mary	232
Cook, Eleanor A.	154	Cross, John	171
Cook, George	154	Cross, Mary	171
Cook, Rev. Geo.	55	Crouch, Elizabeth Ann	17
Cook, Greenberry	123	Crouch, Thos. M.	17
Cook, James	37	Crossly farm	194
Cook, John	55	Croxall, Rebecca	126
Cook, Mary	37, 154	Croxall, Richard	126
Cooke, John	93	Cryer, Mary	58
Cooke, Nathan	179	Curzon, Elizabeth	120
Cooke, Rebecca	37	Curzon, Richard	120
Cooke, William	38, 67	Custis, Eleanor	252
Cooke, Zadoc M.	179	Custis, Mary	252
Cooks, The	17	Custis, Geo. W.	251, 253
Copley, Sir Lionel	45	Custis, John P.	252, 253
Corcoran, William	247	Cuthbert's Wharf	27
Cornfield Harbor	42		
Corrie, John	201	**D**	
Coster, Wm.	56		
Cottman, Esther	231	Dade, Col. Robert	172
Cottman, William	231	Dade, Rev. Townsend	171
Coudon, Rev. Richard	226	Daffin, Joseph	28
Courts (or Courtes), John	183	Daffin, Mary	28
Covington, Leonard	76	Dallam, Richard	94
Covington's Fields	76	Dallam, Maj. Wm.	94
Cox, Susan	220	Daniel, John	202
Cox, Whittington	220	Daniel, Joseph	202
Cowpens	153	Dare, Elizabeth	50, 56
Crabb, Anthony	85	Dare, Eliza	62
Crabb, Chas. H.	174	Dare, E. Snowden	61
Crabb, Elizabeth R. G.	177	Dare, Dr. George	61
Crabb, Gen. Jeremiah	177	Dare, John	58
Crabb, Mrs. Mary L.	174	Dare, Dr. John	50
Crabb, Sarah G.	177	Dare, Maria Hodgkin	56
Cradock family	116, 117	Dare, Marietta H.	56
Craige, Capt. James	198	Dare, Priscilla	61
Craik	71	Dare, Richard	61, 62
Cranberry	94	Dare, Sally S.	61

Index

Dare, Sarah	61	Dick, Margaret	21
Dare, Thos. C.	61	Dick, Thomas	21
Darnall, Eleanor H.	63	Dickerson, Margaret	181
Darnall, Maj. Henry	63	Dickerson, Nathan	181
Dashiell, George	232	Dickon, James	35
Dashiell, Sarah Bishop	232	Digges	84
Daugherty, Addison	87	Digges, Catherine	175
Davis	71	Digges, Edward	63
Davis family	178, 179	Digges, Mrs. F.	68
Davis, Allen Bowie	155	Digges, George	175
Davis, Solomon	174	Digges, Nora	176
Dawkins, Alexander	56	Digges, Thomas	34, 257
Dawson, Elizabeth,	172, 220	Digges, William	257
Dawson, Robert D.	172	Digges, Wm. W.	175, 176
Dawson, Thos.	172	Dillon, James E.	190
Dawson, T. H.	220	Dilworth	111
Dawson, Thos. S.	220	Dinian, Thos.	33
Day, Edward	110	Dipple	64
Day, Eliza	110	Dobbins, James Alex., S. J.	29
Day, Elizabeth	218	Dobson, Henry	229
Day, John	219	Dodd, Hannah	150
Deakins, John	266	Dodon	19
Deakins, Col. Wm.	257	Dooley, Capt. James	16, 17
Deale, James	16	Dorchester County	239–243
Deale, Henry	16	Dorsey family	19, 154, 155, 156
Deale, Mary	16	Dorsey, Ann	20
Deaver, Aquilla	105	Dorsey, Catherine	19, 20
De Butts, Dr.	125	Dorsey, Edwin M.	79
De Butts, Miss	125	Dorsey, Eli	161
Decatur, Com. Stephen	240, 245	Dorsey, Emma E.	20
Deer Creek congregation	103	Dorsey, Frances	228
De la Brooke Manor	39	Dorsey, Harry W.	179
Delahay	33	Dorsey, Henrietta	177
Delmore-end	212	Dorsey, James M.	20
Denmead, Adam	128	Dorsey, Joshua	177
Denmead, John	128	Dorsey, Lloyd	20
Dennis family	241	Dorsey, Noah E.	20
Dent	71	Dorsey, Owen	19
Dent, Anna M.	41	Dorsey, Rachel	179
Dent, Katherine	41	Dorsey, Sarah	20, 161
Dent, Judith P.	40	Dorsey graveyard	19
Dent, Rev. Hatch	40	Doughoregon Manor	158
Dent, Thomas	268	Douglas, Samuel	260
Dent, Wm. Hatch	41	Douglass, John	179
Dent Memorial	40	Dow, Lorenzo	259
Dent Memorial Chapel	87	Downs, Mary E.	189
Denton, Mrs. Ann	2	Doyal	71
De Kalb	170	Druid Hill Park	126
Derose, Rev. G.	33	Drum Point	33, 57
Deye, Capt. Thos. C.	133	Drumquhasel tract	152
Dick, James	21	Duckett, Mrs. Bowie	19

Duckett, Thos.	3	Edelen, Mrs. George	67
Dudderrar, Barbara	161	Edelen, Father Leonard	35
Dudderrar, George	161	Edelen, Philip	67
Duhammel, Charles	165	Edelen, Walter	67
Duke family	58	Edge, James	217
Duke, Alexander	59	Edge, Thomas	217
Duke, Ann M.	58	Edmondson, Anne Harvey	212
Duke, Ann R.	59	Edmondson, John	212, 223
Duke, Basil	59	Eichelberger, Martin	149
Duke, Carrie O.	58	Elder, George	124
Duke, Eliza H.	58	Elder, Ruth	124
Duke, James	58	Ellenborough	46
Duke, Dr. James J.	58	Ellicott, Andrew	153
Duke, Mary B.	59	Ellicott, Elizabeth	154
Duke, Moses P.	59	Ellicott, Esther	153
Duke, Rebecca	58	Ellicott, John	153
Duke's Adventure	50	Elsroad, Michael	143
Dulaney's valley	139	Elsroad, Susan	143
Dulany, Mrs. Ann	5	Elzey, Arnold	233
Dulany, Daniel	5	Elzey, John	235
Dulany, Rebecca	5	Emory, John M. G.	220
Dunbar, Joseph	37	Episcopal graveyard	167
Dunkenson, Ann	28	Ergood, Jacob	97
Dunkenson, Robert	28	Evans	71
Dunnington	71	Evans, A. W.	228, 231
Durham church	70	Eversfield, Mary A.	77
Dutton	111	Evergreen	127
Duvall, Mrs. Mary	167	Ewen, John	11
Duvall, Rebecca	77	Ewen, Maj. Richard	11
Duvall, Wm. W.	77	Ewen, Mrs. Sophia	11
Dyer, Dorothy	73	Ewing, James	204
Dyer, Eliza	68	Ewing, Robert	204
Dyer, George	68, 73		
Dyer, Horatio	68	**F**	
Dyer, Jeremiah	68		
Dyer, Mary Rose	68	Faherty, Father Mark	35
Dyer, Oswald	68	Fairfax	71
Dyer, Sally G.	67	Falls	111
Dyer, Theodore	68	Farnandis graveyard	104
Dyer, Thos. M.	73	Faulkner family	220
		Fawn Grove	106
E		Feddeman family	191, 192
		Fenwick	34
Eager, John	114	Fenwick family	27, 73, 175
Earle, Hon. Richard	190	Fenwick, James	68
Earle family	190, 191, 195	Fenwick, John	176
Eastburn, Dr. Edward	159	Fenwick, Mary	68
Ecker, Elizabeth	161	Fenwick, Philip	176
Ecker, John	161	Fenwick's Manor	29
Eden, Gov.	24	Ferguson	71
Edelen, Frank	67	Ferguson family	140

Index

Ferguson, Colin	200	Frye, Nathaniel	262
Ferguson, Elizabeth Ann	190	Frye, Mrs. C. V. M.	262
Ferguson, Peter	242	Fulford, Catherine	99
Ferril	71	Fulford, Mary	99
Filbert	71	Fulford, William	99
Fishpaw, Mary	142	Fulford farm	104
Fitzherbert, Rev. Mr.	27	Fulks, Elizabeth	3
Fitzhugh, Mary Lee	252	Fulton, Robert	245
Flanagan	71	Furniss, Eli H.	220
Flant, Father Nicol, S. J.	29		
Fleming	71		
Flowry	71	**G**	
Foard, Hezekiah	229	Gaither family	162, 167, 182, 183
Forbes, John	42	Gaither, Ephraim	183
Force, Peter	262	Gaither, Thomas	9
Ford, Hopewell	190	Gale, George	16
Ford, Thos. H.	190	Gale, Gen. John	238
Forman, Ezekiel	193	Gale, Lloyd	17
Forman, Thos. M.	193	Gale, Martha	17
Forrest, Richard	80	Gales, Joseph	262
Forrest, Sarah	80	Galloway, Mary	18
Forrest, Col. Uriah	249	Galloway, Richard	16
Forrester, Catherine R.	202	Galloway, Samuel	18
Forrester, Rev. Geo. Wm.	202	Galt, Sarah	208
Foundry	258	Gambrill, Augustine	25
Fountain Rock cemetery	168	Gambrill, Maria	25
Four Mile Run church	30	Gardener, Ann	67
Fowke	71	Gardiner family	66, 68, 69
Fowke, Gerard	64	Gardner	71
Fowler	71	Garner	71
Fox, George	23, 54	Garrett, Amos	4, 5
Francis, Major Thos.	18	Garrett, James	5
Franklin	71	Garrett, Sarah	5
Franklin, Eliza	16	Garrettson, Mary	96
Franklin, Jacob	16	Gartrell, Bushrod	182
Franklin, Father John	35	Gaskin	71
Franklin, Mary	16	Gassaway, Nicholas	4
Franklin, Ruth	107	Gassaway, Col. Nicholas	22
Franklin, Thomas	16	Gassaway, Thomas	22
Franklin, Col. Thos.	107	Gassaway, Susanna	22
Frazier, Rev. John	264	Gates, James	68
Frederick County	159-166	Gaunt (or Gannt) family	59
Freeland, Agnes	249	Georgetown	244-254
Freeland, Sarah	249	German Reformed cemetery	164
Freeman	111	German Reformed churchyard	166
Freeman, Edward	201	Gerry, Elbridge	261
Fresh Pond Neck	42	Gibbons, John H.	73
Frietchie, Barbara	164	Gilbert	71
Frietchie, John C.	164	Giles, Edward	99
Frisby, Widow	4	Giles, Jacob	101
Frisby, William	193	Giles, Martha	101

Index

Gill, Edward, Sr.	146	Greenfield, Ann	40
Gill, Mary	146	Green Hill	254
Gillis, Ezekiel	2	Green Hill church	239
Gillis, Thomas	260	Green Spring valley	140
Gist, Gen. Mordecai	118	Greenwood	178, 249
Gittings family	111	Grey, Mary	68
Gittings, Thomas	126	Grice family	121, 122
Godsgrace, Rebecca	98	Griffin	71
Godsgrace, William	98	Griffin, Greenberry	216
God's Graces	53	Griffin, Mary	216
Golden	71	Griffith family	95, 96, 97, 180, 181
Goldsborough family	179, 206, 207, 209, 212, 221, 242	Griffith, John	204
		Griffith, Orlando	56
Goldsmith's Hall	114	Griffith, Prudence	173
Goodfellow, Henry	176	Griffith, Sarah	177
Goodwin, Milcah	155	Grimes, Mary A.	173
Goodwin, Rebecca	155	Groome, Eliza	221
Goodwin, William	155	Groome, Peregrine	221
Goose, Adam	125	Groome, Samuel	220
Gore, Michael	125	Grosses	212
Gorsuch	111	Grover	111
Gorsuch, John of T.	132	Groves	71
Gorsuch, Sarah	132	Gruber, John G.	198
Gosnell, Mistress	113	Grupy family	110
Gough, Elizabeth	31	Gumaer, Sarah	172
Gough, John R.	31	Gunnison, Almon	200
Gough, Stephen	31	Gwynn family	108
Gough, William	199		
Goul, Eleanor	28	**H**	
Govane, James J.	153		
Graham, Alex.	221	Haddaway, Oakley	190
Graham, Charles	21	Hager, Capt. Jonathan	166
Graham, Eliza C.	221	Hager, Capt. Jonathan, Jr.	166
Graham, Miss	63	Hagon, Martha	67
Grammar family	3	Haislip	71
Gramphin, Elizabeth	263	Hall	71
Gramphin, Robert	263	Hall family,	95, 96
Gramphin, Thomas	263	Hall, Major Elihu	229
Gravelly	93	Hall, Hannah	105
Gray	71	Hall, Rev. Henry	23
Green	71	Hall, Mrs. Martha	187
Green, Rachel R.	115	Hall, Philip Moore	100
Green, Maj. Richard	176	Hall, Rice J.	105
Green, Sarah	176	Hall, William	99
Green, Vincent	115	Hallowing Point	42
Green, William	115	Hambleton, Elizabeth	221
Greenberry, Ann	6	Hambleton, Samuel	221
Greenberry, Charles	6, 8	Hamilton	71
Greenberry, Col. Nicholas	6	Hamilton, Josiah	68
Greenberry tombs	5	Hamilton, Mary	190
Greenfield family	40, 73, 82	Hammond family	25

Index 283

Hammond, Charles	156	Harry, David	167
Hammond, Elizabeth	166	Harryman family	132
Hammond, John, son of Chas.	156	Harryman, Clarissa	131
Hammond, Maj. Gen. John	4	Harryman, George	131
Hammond, Dr. Lloyd T.	157	Hart, Gov. John	2
Hammond, Mary	166	Hartford Baptist Church	106
Hammond, Dr. Nicholas	221	Harwood family	3
Hammond, Thomas	166	Haskins, Barclay	210
Hammond, Vachel	166	Haskins, Elizabeth	210
Hammond graveyard	25	Haslup (or Hauslap)	22, 88
Hammond's Creek	4	Haslup, Albert S.	88
Hammondtree, Dorcas	172	Haslup, Capt. Henry	22
Hampden	218	Hatcher	71
Hampton	147	Hatfield, George	248
Hampton, Madam Mary	236	Hatton, William	267
Hance, Molly	119	Haubert, Elizabeth	124
Handley	260	Hawkins family	97
Hands family	196	Hayden, Peregrine	38
Handy family,	240	Haynie, Betty	236
Handy, George	236	Haynie, Ezekiel	236
Handy, Sally	236	Haynie, Henrietta B.	236
Hannah, James	125	Haynie, Martin L.	236
Hanson	71, 197	Hayward family	71, 210
Hanson family	65	Hazlett, James	212
Hanson, Alex. Contee	250, 251	Heahead, Miss Priscilla	70
Hanson, Ann	76	Heath, Rev. Mr.	68
Hanson, Chas. W.	148	Heatherland, Elizabeth	34
Hanson, Mr.	139	Hebb family	45, 46
Hanson, Rebecca D.	148	Heister, Gen. Daniel	166
Hanson, Samuel	76	Heister, Rosana	166
Harbin, Adeline	68	Hempstone family	181
Harbin, Catherine	67	Hemsley family	195
Harbin, John	67	Henderson, George	99
Harbin, Mary	68	Henderson, Rev. Jacob	75
Harbin, R.	68	Henry family	236, 237
Harden, John	173	Henry, Hon. Daniel	242
Hardy, John	66	Henry, Father John	35
Hardy, John H.	68	Hepburn, Elizabeth	127
Hardy, Theodore	68	Herbert family	99, 100
Hargis, Elizabeth	236	Herman, Augustine	226, 229, 231, 232
Harlem	251		
Harlen, Louis	228	Herman, Gasper	225
Harper, Robt. G.	246	Herring Creek church	22
Harris family	46, 47	Hesselins, Elizabeth	267
Harris, Alexander	60	Hesselins, Gustavus	4
Harris, Mary B.	232	Hesselins, John	10
Harris, Susan	60	Hewitt, Rev. John	234
Harris, Capt. Thomas	102	Hickory	103
Harris, William	198	Higbee, Rev. Edward Y.	101
Harrison family	193, 194, 243	Higbee, Mary	101
Harrison, Mrs. Charles C.	206	Higbee, Mary Sophia Thomas	101

Index

Higgenbottom, Rev. Ralph	9
Hillary, Widow	76
Hilleary, Mary	172
Hilleary, McHenry	173
Hillen family	152
Hillen Road	151
Hines, Isaac	198
Hitchcock	106
Hitchcock, Jemima	109
Hitchcock, Col. William	108
Hoban, James	248, 259, 260
Hobart, Rev. Basil	63
Holdsworth house	59
Holdsworth, John	55
Holland House of America	245
Holliday, Eleanor W.	242
Hollingsworth family	119, 158
Hollingsworth, Col. Henry	230
Hollyday family	169, 192
Hollyday, E. S.	78
Hollyday, Col. Leonard	78
Hollyday Miss	53
Holmead's	258
Holt, Arthur	195
Holt, Mrs. Margaret	195
Holt, Mary E. Seth	204
Holton, William	34
Homeland	152
Homewood, Capt. Thomas	10
Hood family	147
Hope	211
Hopkins, Ann	111
Hopkins, Charles	111
Hopkins, Capt. David	120
Horsey, Thomas Sim Lee	165
Howard County	152–156
Howard family	110, 124
Howard, Rev. Charles	148
Howard, James Govane	153
Howard, John	156
Howard, John Eager	114, 148
Howard, Joshua	176
Howard, Julianna	148
Howard, Matthew	117
Howard, Sarah	117
Hoxtons	84
Hudson	71
Hughes, Maj. Thomas	230
Hughlett, Mary	221
Hughlett, William	221
Hull	106
Hulse, Mrs. Elizabeth	119
Humphreys, Rev.	37
Humphries, David	256
Hunt family	123
Hunter family	152
Hunter, Father William	63, 124
Hutchins, Col. Nicholas	109
Hutchins, Zarey	109
Hutchinson, William	267
Hyland, Col. Stephen	230
Hynson, Harriet	188

I

Impey, Thomas	212
Ingle, Rev. Osborne	160
Ireland, Capt. Gilbert	35, 36
Ireland, James J.	57
Ireland, John	57
Ireland, John D.	61
Ireland, John Thomas	61
Ireland, Joseph	57
Ireland, Mary	57
Ireland, Sarah	60
Isthmus	211

J

Jackson	71
Jackson, Andrew	262
Jacobs, Rev. Chas. W.	221, 222
Jacobs, Sarah R.	199
Jacobs, William	199
James, Rev. Richard	184
Jameson family	67, 68
Jamison, Henry	164
Jamison, Leonard	164
Jarboe family	34
Java	18
Jefferson, Thomas	256
Jenifer	71
Jenkins	71
Jenkins family	111
Jenkins, Eliz.	68
Jenkins, Col. Francis	236
Jenkins, Joseph	27, 28
Jenkins, Ned	68
Jenkins, Sarah	69
Jennings, Thomas	53
Jessop family	135 *et seq.*
Jesuit Fathers	29

Index

Jewett	106	Keene, John	193
Johns, Ann R.	147	Keibeard	71
Johns, John	146	Kemp, Bishop	36
Johns, Kensey	146	Kennard family	221
Johns, Kinsey	146	Kennedy	71
Johns, Richard	145, 146, 147	Kennedys	47
Johns, Sarah	147, 173	Kent County	195–204
Johns, Susan	145, 146	Kent Island	184
Johns, Thomas	173	Kerr family	211
Johnson, Alex.	66	Key family	36
Johnson, Ann	67, 124, 147	Key, Mrs. Ann Arnold	12, 14
Johnson, Caecilius	124	Key, Edmund	82
Johnson, Dorcas	52	Key, Francis	12
Johnson, Elizabeth	119	Key, Francis Scott	12, 244, 248, 253
Johnson, Elisha S.	146	Key, Judge	84
Johnson, Heith H.	146	Key, Margaretta	82
Johnson, Hickman	146	Key, Philip	37
Johnson, John	67	Key, Philip Barton	258
Johnson, Joshua	262	Kilty, John	3
Johnson, Margaret	159	Kilty, William	3
Johnson, Samuel	119	King	233
Johnson, Thomas	52, 124	King, Nicholas	260
Johnson, Thomas, M. D.	124	King, Sir Robert	236
Johnson, Gov. Thomas	52, 160, 262	King, Samuel	157
Johnson, William Fell	119, 124	King, V.	17
Johnston, Elizabeth	232	Kingsville	109
Johnston, George	232	Kirby family	221
Johnston, Rosina	232	Kirk family	87
Johnston, William W.	232	Kirk, Hannah	100
Joice, George, Sr.	142	Kirk, John	99
Jones	71, 106	Kirkpatrick, Abraham	231
Jones family	42, 43, 114	Knipe, Rev. Thomas	13
Jones, Col. Arnold E.	232		
Jones, Edward	226		
Jones, Elizabeth Augusta	199	**L**	
Jones, Rev. Hugh	226		
Jones, James	266		
Jones, Mary H.	232	Lafayette	105
Jones, Dr. Matthias	232	Lanakin	71
Jones, Milcah Gale	232	Lancaster, John	73
Jones, Samuel W.	232	Landelle, Fr. de la	3
Jones, Walter C.	183	Landsdale, Wm. Moylan	100
Joppa	109	Langley, Alex.	68
Jordan, Richard	35	Langley, Nic	68
Jowles, Col. Henry P.	42	Langley, Pres.	67
Joy	81	Langley, Tom	67
		Larned family	260
K		Lasonby, Madam Margaret	2
		Latemer, David	192
Kalorama	244	Latham, Elizabeth	201
Kane, James	85	Laveille family	59

Index

Laveille place	59	**M**	
Laytonsville	180		
Lazenby, Daniel L.	17		
Lazenby, Selina H.	17	Mace, Margaret	154
Lazenby, William Lingon	17	Macgill family	167
League	111	Macgill, Rev. James	157, 167
Leakin, Rev. G. A.	79	Macgill, Mary	167
Lee, Gov. Thos. Sim	75	Mackall, Benj.	53
Leftwitch	71	Mackall, John	45
Leigh, Walter	28	Mackall, Margaret Gough	45
Lemmon, Hannah	131	Mackalls	53
Lennox, Walter	260	Mackensie, Rev. Francis	236
Lenox, John	192	Mackey, Martha A.	222
Lenthall, John	260	Mackubin family	3
Leonardtown	31, 46	Mackubin, Hester Ann	26
Lindsay, Edward	162	Macpherson, Mr.	83
Lindsay, John L.	161	Macubin family	9 *et seq.*
Lingan, Gen. James Maccubbin	250	Macubin, John	9
		Maddox	71
Linganore cemetery	161	Maddox family	37
Lingans, The	249	Madison, Bishop	253
Little Falls Meeting	106	Madison, James	244
Livers, Henry	166	Magruder family	178
Lloyd family	212 *et seq.*	Magruder, Deborah	182
Lloyd, Anna Maria	195	Magruder, Elizabeth	180
Lloyd, Francis	35	Magruder, Otho	180
Lloyd, John	44	Mahoney, Cornelius	35
Lloyds	211	Malambre	159
Locust Grove	210	Manly, Mrs. Mary	172
Lomax	71	Mannon, James	125
Long Green	111	Manoakin plantations	235
Long Neck	42	Marbury, Mrs. Fendall	78
Loockerman family	221	Margetty family	164
Lookinbeal, Elizabeth	162	Marriott, Adelia	166
Lovering, Amelia	263	Marsh family	137, 193
Lowe, Charles	13	Marsh, Ann Alethea	200
Lowe, Henry	29	Marsh burying ground	137
Lowe, Maria Susannah	29	Marsh, Joshua	137
Lowe, Vincent	13	Marshall, Amanda C.	137
Lower Cross Roads	102	Marshall, Mary A.	221
Lowndes, Andrew	131	Marshall, Mrs. Charles	90
Luckett	71	Marshall Hall	73
Lugenbeel, Peter	161	Martin family	218 *et seq.*
Lux, Darby	134	Martin	2, 71
Lux, Mary Nicholson	134	Martin, Anna Mary	100
Lux, Wm. and Co.	21	Martin, Ann Elizabeth	100
Lynch, Jas. A.	165	Martin, John	100
Lyles, Cecelia Brown	38	Maslin, Wm. J.	199
Lyon, Joseph	119	Mason	71
Lyon, Major Robert	119	Mason, Abram	263
Lyon, William	21	Masons, The	17

Index

Mason, Thomas Wm. Thompson	154	Merryman, Clara A.	136
Mather, Elizabeth	108	Merryman, Jos. R.	136
Mather, John	108	Merryman, Notty	122
Mattapani	33	Michael, Ethan	101
Mattapony Hundred	265	Michael, Martha	101
Mattapony Street	47	Middleton	71
Mattawoman	70	Middleton family	248
Matthews family	87	Middleton, Ann	68
Matthews, Amos	137	Middleton, Mrs. Ann Elbertina	248
Matthews, Clara W.	138	Middleton, Dr. Donatus	68
Matthews, Ignatius	35	Middleton, Nancy	67
Matthews, James	35	Middleton, Polly	67
Maulsby	159	Middleton, Rosella	68
Maxey, Mary	18	Miles, Augustine	69
Maxey, Virgil	18	Miles, Capt. Aquilla	109
May	71	Miles, Austin	66
Maynadier family	3	Miles, Capt. D. D.	109
Maynadier, Rev. Daniel	206	Miles, Mrs.	68
Maynadier, Elizabeth	14	Mill Mount	57
Mayo family	3	Miller, Mrs. Mary	3
McBayne	71	Millersville	25
McCallamont, Matilda	222	Milligan family	227
McConkie	71	Milstead	71
McCoy, David C.	106	Mitchell	71
McDaniel	56	Moale family	120
McDaniel Place	57	Moale, Mrs. Ellen North	120
McDonnel, Ann	17	Moale, Richard	120
McDonnel, Samuel	17	Monocacy cemetery	171
McDowell, Leanna J.	17	Monk, John Clarke	100
McIntire, Alex.	260	Monks, Mary	96
McIntosh	260	Montgomery County	171–183
McIntosh, Joseph	260	Montgomery, Ally	68
McKenny, Wm.	194	Montgomery, Henry	69
McKenzie, Rebecca	52	Montgomery, Jas.	67
McKinney, Mary	102	Montgomery, Mrs. Jos.	67
McLane, Catherine	227	Montgomery, Josh.	68
McLaughlin, Anne	99	Montgomery, Mary Emily	68
McLemon	71	Montmorence	145
McMurdie, Henry S.	165	Montpelier	90
McPherson	160	Montrose	133
McPherson	160	Moore, Mordecai	11
McPherson, Ann	37	Moore, Thomas	244
McPike, Sarah	159	Moore, Ursula	11
Medford, McCall	201	More	106
Meek	71	Morice, Joseph	67
Meigs, Joseph	260	Morice, Martha	67
Merrick, Robert	73	Morland, George	260
Merritt, Arthur M.	199	Morn, Tedro	165
Merryman family	131 *et seq.*	Morris, Peter	35
		Morris, Randolph	85
Merryman, Charles	136	Morris, Robert	205

Index

Morton farm	60	Nelson, Garrett V.	97
Mosher, Theodore	176	Nelson, Roger	164
Mountain View cemetery	168	Nelson, Gen. Roger	159
Mt. Olivet cemetery	162	Nesmith, John Leeds	243
Mt. Pleasant	211	Nevill, Elizabeth	189
Mt. Stewart	21	Nevitt, John Ryder	243
Mudd, Benj. N.	67	Newman family	222
Mudd, Julia	67	Newman, Roger	6
Mudd, Leonard	68	Newnam family	193 *et seq.*
Mudd, Mrs. Leond.	67	Newport mission	63
Mudd, Margaret	67	Newton church	35
Mudd, Sally	68	Nichols	211
Mudd, Walter	68	Nichols family	208
Mulgare, Patrick	89	Nicols, Rev. Henry	216
Mulliken, Mr.	208	Nicholson family	3
Muncaster	71	Nicholson, Anna Eliza	87
Munroe family	3	Nicholson, Rev. James D.	86
Murdock	71	Nicholson, Mr.	85
Murphy, Capt. James	217	Nisbet family	133
Murphy, Michael	35	Nolan, Edward	25
Murphy, Semelia A.	100	Norris, Basil	162
Murray	111	Norris, Sarah	118
Murray family	3	North family	119 *et seq.*
Murray, Daniel	242	North, Capt. Robert	119
Murray, Mrs. H. M.	18	Nottingham	78
Murray, Kezea	147	Nourse, Marion	181
Murray, Susan	68	Nowland, Peregrine	97
Murray, Susannah	222	Numbers, Hannah M.	204
Murray William	242		
Murrays	17	**O**	
Muschett	71		
My Lady's Manor	107	Oak Hill	248
		Oak Hill cemetery	247
N		Oberinger, Leonard	165
		O'Brien, James	67
Nally	71	O'Brien, John	165
Nanjemoy	64	O'Connor, Martin	175
Neale	185	Ogle family	77
Neale, Bennett	35	Ogle, Gov.	75
Neale, Rev. Bennett	103	Ogle, Sam'l	9
Neale, Boswell	63	Old Brick church	243
Neale, Edward	187	Old Chester parish	205
Neale, Jeremias	67	Old Christ Church	72
Neale, Priscilla	175	Oldfields' Chapel	65, 85
Neale, Susanna	67	Oldham, Edward	230
Neales	62	Old Orchard	50
Needham, Jonathan	56	Old Place	50
Neill	167	Old Rehoboth	235
Nelson	71	Old St. Barnabas church	74
Nelson, Acquilla	97	Old St. John's cemetery	257
Nelson, Frances	98	Old St. Paul's church	261

Index

Oler	122	Pattison, John		58
O'Neil, Thomas	165	Peach Blossom		209
O'Neil, Wm.	260	Pearce		109
Onion, Elizabeth Russell	110	Pearce, Eliza		201
Onion, Stephen	110	Pearce, Martha J.		199
Orem's Delight	210	Peel, Robert		22
Orrick, Eleanor C.	147	Peel, Samuel		22
Osborne, William	93	Peerce family		139
Osbourn, Henry	67	Pennington, Francis		35
Owen, Eliza Sophia	202	Perry		71
Owens, Eleanor L.	107	Perryman family		100
Owens, Richard	141	Perryman, Chas. W.		97
Owings, John	154	Perryman, Isaac		96
Ownings, Samuel	120	Peters, Anderton B.		189
Oxen Hill	267	Peter, Mrs. Ann		250
Ozman, John	222	Peter, Maj. George	248,	250
Ozment, Lucy	222	Peyton, Mary J.		57
		Philpot, Brian		119
P		Philips, James	92, 93,	94
		Philips, Martha		93
Paca, Elizabeth	107	Philips, The		94
Paca, John	94	Picken		71
Pacas, The	94	Piggot, Rev. Dr.		158
Paca, William	216	Pigman		159
Padian, Mr.	134	Pile, John H.		62
Page, Henry	243	Pinkney, Hon. Wm.		261
Paine, John Howard	249	Piscataway parish		264
Painter, Nicholas	11	Plaindealing		210
Painter, Wm. P.	71	Plat, Ann		132
Palmer, Elizabeth J.	189	Plater, Ann		249
Pamonky	73	Plater, Hon. George		29
Pardoe place	59	Plater, Jane		172
Parker, Captain	240	Pleasant Valley		211
Parker, Henry	68	Pleasants, Caroline		202
Parks	106	Plessier, Jos.		165
Parks family	134 et seq.	Plinhimmon		208
Parks, Harriet	142	Plowden, Edmund	32,	33
Parran family	55 et seq.	Plummer, Mary Eliza		222
Parran, Elizabeth	59	Polk		233
Parran, Francis	46	Polkinhorn, Chas.		260
Parran, Samuel	59	Pollard, Capt. George		149
Parrans, The	53	Pomona		125
Parrish graves	125	Pool, Benj.		172
Parrott's Woods	247	Poplar Hill		81
Pascault, Maria Josephine	222	Poplar Hill church		268
Patapsco Neck	114	Port Tobacco Creek		62
Patterson, Avarilla	99	Posey		71
Patterson, Bertha	99	Poston		71
Patterson, George	99	Poteet, Georgiana		130
Patterson, John	99	Potter, Gen. Wm.		204
Pattison, Elizabeth	58	Poulton, Henry		35

Index

Poynton Manor	64	Reigle, Eliza	24
Pratt, Mrs. C. Augusta	187	Reigle, John A.	24
Preston Place	58	Reisterstown	125
Preston, Walter W.	104	Rennons family	121
Price	71	Rennons, Susanna	121
Price, Edward	107	Retler	71
Priest Neale's Mass House	103	Reyner, Ebenezer	201
Priest's Ford	103	Reynolds, John	87
Priest's Point	27	Rice	71
Prince George's County	74–91	Rich, Hon. Peter	3
Prout, Rev. Robert	71	Rich Neck	217
Provoost, Bishop	253	Richard, Polly	68
Puddington, George	11	Richards' graves	125
Purviance	150	Richardson family	178
Pushinataha	261	Richardson, A. L.	220
Pye	14	Richardson, Mrs. Isabella	198
Pyne Hill	33	Richardson, Joseph	204
		Richardson, Thomas	208
Q		Riddell, Robert	125
		Riders	238
Quaker burying ground	16	Ridgely	118
Quantico church	239	Ridgely family 5, 130, 147 *et seq.*	
Queen, Ann	69	Ridgely, Chas. C.	176
Queen, Clemintina	68	Ridgely, Henry	4, 156
Queen, Dr.	69	Ridgely, Henry II	16
Queen, Elizabeth	67	Ridgely, James H.	130
Queen Anne County	187–194	Ridgely, Osborne	3
		Ridgely, Sophia	31
R		Ridgely, Wm. S.	31
		Ridgely Worthington Estate	15
Rackliffe, Rider Henry	232	Ridout, John	9
Ralph, Rev. George	125	Ridout, Mary	9
Ramsay, Nathaniel	230	Riggs, Rev. Elisha	216
Ramsey, Col. W. W.	100	Riggs, Henry	225
Randall family	3	Riggs' Farm	255
Randolph, Mary	252	Ringgold	111
Ranelagh	76	Ringgold family	168 *et seq.*
Ratliff	71	Ringgold, Catherine	196
Raven, Gould Smith D.	113	Risen	71
Raven, Capt. Isaac D.	113	Risteau family	153
Read, Mary	142	Risteau, John	120
Reason, Sarah A.	96	Risteau, Joseph	120
Reaves, Thos. C.	68	Risteau, Mrs. Susanna	97
Redbourne	191	Riversdale	90
Reeder family	46	Riverview cemetery	168
Reeder home	46	Roberts, Jane	98
Reely, William	19	Roberts, Owen	98
Reeves, Elizabeth	69	Robertson	71
Reeves, Monica	68	Robertson, Wm.	181
Reeves, Thomas C.	72	Robins, George	210
Reid, John	242	Rochester, Bishop of	13

Index

Rock Creek parish	264	St. Joseph's Catholic church	31
Rockland	124	St. Luke's church	216
Rockland house	169	St. Margaret's	24
Rockwell, Lancelot	115	St. Margaret's Parish Register	9
Rodgers, Mrs. Delia	96	St. Mary's Catholic church	85
Rogers family	127	St. Mary's City	44
Rogers, Elizabeth	126	St. Mary's County	27–49
Rogers' burial ground	126	St. Mary's Manor	47
Rosecroft	47	St. Michael's Manor	42
Rosedale	249	St. Michael's parish	205
Rose Hill	63	St. Nicholas' church	32
Ross, Alicia	13	St. Nicholas' churchyard	33
Ross, Mrs. Ann Graham	160	St. Paul's church	81, 195, 243
Ross, John	12	St. Peter's cemetery	72
Round Top	194	St. Peter's church	196
Rousby	30, 185	St. Thomas' church	253
Rousby, Christopher	33	St. Thomas' graveyard	63
Rousby, John	33, 59	St. Thomas' Manor	62
Rowlenson, Mrs. Caroline	222	Sanders, Ann	67
Royston family	137 et seq.	Sanders, Elizabeth	47
Royston, Wesley	137	Sanders, John	47
Rozer	185	Sanderson, Rev. Ambrose	54
Rozer, Thomas Whetenhall	187	Sandy Bottom	30
Rozier	14	Sarah, Duchess of Marlborough	94
Rudolph, John	230	Sater family	121
Rudolph, Michael	230	Sater's Meetinghouse	106, 121
Rumsey Mansion	110	Satterfield, Mary	222
Rusk, Elizabeth	52	Sauner, Elizabeth	34
Russel, Rebecca	120	Sawyer, John	207
Russell	71	Scarbrouch, Dan	105
Rye	71	Scarff	111
		Scharf, Hannah	149
S		Scharf, William	149
		Schell, Mrs.	68
St. Andrew's church	30, 234	Scott	71
St. Anne's church	1 et seq.	Scott, Upton	14
St. Barnabas' church	74, 270	Scrimeger, John	172
St. Bartholomew's church	239	Seabury, Bishop	41, 253
St. Clement's Manor	32	Seaton, William	260
St. Francis' church	32	Sedgwick, Dorcas	52
St. Francis Xavier church	35	Sedwick	56
St. Ignatius cemetery	103	Sellman family	172
St. Inigoes churchyard	27	Semmes, Elizabeth	67
St. James' Episcopal church	107	Semmes, Thomas	67
St. John's Catholic church	174	Seney, Joshua	192
St. John's church	32	Sennet	71
St. John's churchyard	143	Sessford, John	260
St. John's Protestant Episcopal church	109	Sewall	14
		Sewall family	33
St. John's Roman Catholic church	111	Sewell, Rev. Richard	226
		Seymour, His Excellency John	2

Shanks, Elizabeth	159	Smith, Margaret	44
Sharpe, Governor	2	Smith, Martha	98
Sharpe, Peter	223	Smith, Rachel	107
Shaw family	3, 115	Smith, Richard	53
Shaw, Thomas	114	Smith, Capt. Richard	54
Shaw, Capt. Wm. G.	113	Smith, Robert	259
Shepherd	72	Smith, Robt. W.	143
Sheppard, Moses	105	Smith, Samuel	261
Sherwood, Mrs. Sarah	222	Smith, Samuel Griffith	98
Shieffly, Mrs.	260	Smith, Samuel Harrison	261
Shields	72	Smith, Thomas	44
Shipley, Robert	156	Smith, Walter	124
Shremaker, Charles	264	Smith, Col. Walter	55
Shreve family	182	Smith, William	94
Shrewsbury church	199	Smith, Winston	97
Silver, Jeremiah	105	Smithson, William	104
Simkins, Maria North	119	Smithson, William, Sr.	104
Simmons	72	Smithson graveyard	104
Simms, Eliz.	67	Smoot	72
Simpers, Jacob H.	190	Smoot, Alexander	260
Simpson, Cath.	68	Snowden family	89 et seq.
Simpson, Elizabeth	67	Sollers family	56
Singleton family	222	Soloman's Island	56
Skinner	72	Somers	260
Skinner, Ann	60	Somerset County	232–239
Skinner, Mrs.	82	Somersville	56
Skinner, Robert	60	Somervell family	60 et seq.
Skipper, Nimrod	142	Somervell, Col. Alex.	53
Slade	106	Soper, James	158
Slye, Capt. Gerard	32	Sothoron, Colonel	42
Slye, George	32	Sotheron, Henry Greenfield	42
Slye, Robert	32	Sotheron, Mary	42
Smallwell, John	267	Sotterly	29
Smallwood	72	Sourton, Francis	48
Smallwood family	69 et seq.	Southerland	72
Smallwood's Retreat	70	Southgate, Rev. Edwin M.	67
Smith	72	South River church	20
Smith family	164	South River Neck	2
Smith, Alex.	68	Sparks, Absolom	198
Smith, Ann	43	Sparrows Point	114
Smith, Cassandra	97	Spaulding, Susan	67
Smith, Eleanor	53, 267	Speake	72
Smith, Eliz.	67	Spedden, Elizabeth	222
Smith, Henry	143	Spencer family	200, 202, 203, 218
Smith, Jas.	68	Spencer Hall	218
Smith, Mrs. J.	67	Spencer, Harriet Malvina	198
Smith, Jonathan	261	Spesutia church	93
Smith, John	267	Sprat, Helen Wolseley	13
Smith, Mrs. L.	68	Sprigg, Hon. Samuel	249
Smith, Larkin	140	Spring Hill church	239
Smith, Larkin H.	107	Stacey, Wm.	118

Index

Stanley	260	Talbott, Joshua	127
Stansbury	106	Talbott, Elizabeth	108
Stansbury family	150 et seq.	Tallmarsh	72
Stansbury, Catherine	150	Taney, Mary	53
Stansbury, Maj. Dixon	109	Taney, Michael	53
Stansbury, Luke	150	Taney, Mrs. Monica	163
Stansberry, Th.	68	Taney, Roger Brooke	163
Steele family	3	Tannehill, William	267
Steele, Isaac	243	Tasker, Benj. Jr.	5
Stepney parish	239	Tasker, Elizabeth	267
Steuger, David	263	Taylor	72
Stevens, William	237	Taylor family	149
Stevenson, Wm. R.	232	Taylor's Meetinghouse	149
Stewart	72	Teackle family	212
Stewart family	3, 19	Teackle, Littleton Dennis	233
Stewart, Anthony	11, 20	Terry, Sarah Ann	3
Stewart, Edward	67	The Eastern Shore	184–186
Stewart, General	11	Thomas	72
Stewart, Wm.	68	Thomas family	47, 101
Stier, Sieur Henry J.	90	Thomas, Ann	17
Stockett, Dr. R. G.	157	Thomas, Children of	17
Stoddart	72	Thomas, Miss Eliza	40
Stokes, Eleanor Rodgers	96	Thomas, Elizabeth M.	17
Stokes, Hannah	105	Thomas, James W.	44
Stone	34, 72, 233	Thomas, John	17
Stone, William	64	Thomas, John Hanson	161
Stonestreet, Mrs.	68	Thomas, Dr. Philip	159
Stormatt	72	Thompson	72, 111
Story, Thomas	16	Thompson family	46
Stoughton, Squire William	234	Thompson, Capt. Alex.	168
Strange	72	Thompson, Elizabeth	46, 193
Stuart, Gilbert	244	Thompson, John	225
Sudbrook	124	Thompson, Col. John	193
Sudler, Charlotte	10	Thompson, Nancy	68
Sudler, Wm. M.	10	Thompson, Richard W.	207
Sullivan, Arrementa	122	Three Notch road	83
Summers, John L.	174	Three Notched road	39, 42
Suter, Jacob	97	Tilden, Catherine and John	203
Sutor, J. Nicholas	100	Tilden, Mary E.	194
Sutor, Mary	100	Tilden, Dr. Wm. Blay	199
Sutton, Jonathan	100	Tilghman	185
Sweaney, Sarah	175	Tilghman family	169, 187, 209, 217 et seq.
Sweeney, McHugh	163		
Sykesville churchyard	158	Tilghman, Elizabeth	195
		Tilghman, Col. Frisby	169
T		Tilghman, Henrietta Maria	212
		Tilghman, James	196
Talbot County	205–224	Tilghmans	211
Talbott family	128 et seq.	Tillotson family	204
Talbot, George	33, 229	Todd	114
Talbot, Henry W.	172	Todd family	115

Index

Tolley, Elizabeth	57	Veazey, Mary	96
Tolley, John B.	57	Veazey, Gov. Thos. W.	228
Tolly, Mary	144	Veazey, William	230
Tongue family	56	Vein	72
Towson	150	Vergnes, Rev. Mr.	68
Towson, Ann	121	Vernon	159
Towsons	106		
Trappe church	104	**W**	
Tred Avon	106		
Trent Hall	39, 41	Waggaman family	243
Trifett, Nathan	204	Wainright, Thomas	156
Trinity parish	87	Waldorf	72
Trundle family	181 et seq.	Walker family	123
Truman family	40, 60	Walker, Charles	117
Truman, James	60	Walker, Elizabeth	208
Tuchton, Elizabeth	101	Walker, George	80
Tucker	34	Walker, Mrs. Martha	80
Tulip Hill	18	Walker, Dr. Thomas C.	117
Tunnicliff, Mary	263	Walkers	106
Turkey Thicket	261	Wallace family	200
Turnbull, Elizabeth	133	Wallace, George	230
Turner	20, 37	Wallace, Mary E.	151
Turner, Jesse	204	Wallace, Michael	230
Turner, Rev. Mr.	75	Wallace, Solomon C.	151
Turton, Eleanor	24	Walton, Rev. James	28
Turton, William H.	24	Waple	72
Tusculum	237	Ward	72
Twiver	265	Ward, Mrs. Margaret	217
Tyler family	79	Ward, William	225
Tyler, Dr.	159	Ware, Amy Amanda	199
Tyler Place	79	Warfield, Capt. Benj.	157
Tyson	106, 111	Warfield, Dr. Chas.	157
		Warfield, Gov. Edwin	157
U		Warfield, Geo. Frazer	158
		Warfield, Susannah	158
Underhill, Clarina	187	Waring family	78
Union Hall	150	Waring farm	78
Upper Marlborough	75	Warner, John	161
Utie, Col. Nathaniel	94	Washington	255–270
		Washington, George	256
V		Washington, Mrs. Martha	252
		Washington County	166–168
Vale	169	Washington parish cemetery	260
Vanderhuyden, Matthias	226	Waters	238
Van Ness	248	Waters, Levin	233
Van Ness family	248	Waters, M. E.	233
Van Sickkle, Henry	98	Watkins	158
Van Sickle, Elizabeth	98	Way, Andrew	260
Vaughan, Rev. Maurice	48	Wayside	72
Vauxhall	135	Webster, Chas. H.	96
Veazey, Edward	230	Webster, George	96

Index

Websters, The	94	Williams, Elizabeth	24
Welch, Hannah	150	Williams, Gen. Osborne	24
Weld, Thomas	254	Williams, Gen. O. H.	167
Wells family	58	Williams, Mary	28
Wells, Janet	152	Williams, Thomas	233
West, Joseph	118	Williams, Thomas Watt	50
West, Violetta	118	William's Fortune	42
Western Run parish	143	Williamson, Rev. Alex.	183
Westover	238	Willis, George Ivory	128
West River	18, 106	Willoughby, John	57
Wethered, Eliza Y.	202	Willoughby, Rebecca	57
Wethered, Samuel	201	Willow Tree graveyard	174
Wethered, Thomas H.	201	Wilmer, Simon	199
Wharton	14	Wilson	56
Wheeler, Mary	59	Wilson, Abraham	130
Whelan, Julian	176	Wilson, Anne Maria	174
Whelan, Mary	176	Wilson, Lydia	152
Whettenhall	14	Wilson, Robert	172
Whisler	111	Wilson, R. T.	68
Whisler, Abraham	110	Wilsons	238
White family	263	Winder family	238
White, Bishop	125, 253	Winder, Mrs. Governor	234
White, John Campbell	149	Wolfenden, John	160
White, Mary	172	Wolseley family	13
White, Sarah	119	Wolstenholme, Daniel	47
White, Col. Thomas	94, 98	Woodley	248, 249
White, Walter F.	185	Woodward	72, 150
Whites, The	94	Woodward family	24 et seq.
Whitechurch	51	Woodyard	81
Whitefield	103	Woodyard, The	63
Whitehall	9	Woolford, John	233
Whitehouse farm	199	Worden	72
Whitemarsh parish	205	Workington	238
White's Landing	83	Worrell, Elizabeth G.	199
Whitney, Elizabeth	204	Worrell, Thomas	199
Whitson, Mary Ann	99	Worthing, Mrs.	67
Whittingham, Bishop	36	Worthington	154
Whittinghams	238	Worthington family 16, 25, 143 et seq.	
Whittington	233	Worthington, Beale M.	16
Wildman, Ellen	73	Worthington, Capt. John	117
Wilkinson, Rev. Christopher	216	Worthington, John	117
Wilkinson, Mark T.	34	Wright	72
Wilkinson, Mrs.	82	Wright, Ann	68
Wilkinson, Mrs.	78	Wrightson, Elizabeth	210
Wilkinson, Rev. Stephen	94	Wye	212
Wilkinson, Rev. Wm.	268	Wye Mills	216
Willes, Rev. Mr.	82	Wynne, Lewis B.	172
Willes, Rev. Frank	77		
Willet, R.	68	**X**	
Williams	72		
Williams, Capt. Benj.	28	Xanpi, H. X.	165

Y

Yeates, Mrs. Mary	201
Yeo, Rev. John	111
Young	73
Young family	162
Young, Andrew	164
Young, Elizabeth Laura	77
Young, Prof. Henry	168
Young, Henry H.	173
Young, Josias	31
Young, Rebecca M.	173
Young, Robt.	68

Z

Zouch, Elizabeth	13
Zouch, Sir John	13

www.ingramcontent.com/pod-product-compliance
Lightning Source LLC
Chambersburg PA
CBHW071314150426
43191CB00007B/618